Th

HIDDEN

C000002389

of the

HEART OF ENGLAND

STAFFORDSHIRE, W. MIDLANDS , WARWICKSHIRE, NORTHANTS, LEICESTERSHIRE, & RUTLAND

Front Cover Picture by
Graham Lewis

Acknowledgements

*The Publishers would like to thank the following for their
assistance in the production of this book:*
*Elaine, Deborah, Administration. Graham, Joanne,Production.
Bob, Research. Gerald, Joanna, Jennie, Writing.
Simon at Scorpio for the maps.*

OTHER TITLES IN THE HIDDEN PLACES SERIES
(ORDER FORM AT BACK OF BOOK)

Ireland
Scotland
North Wales
South Wales
The Welsh Borders
Northumberland &Durham
Lake District
Yorkshire
Lancashire, Cheshire, I.O.M
East Anglia
Somerset, Avon, Glos, Wilts.
Dorset, Hants, I.O.W.
Thames & Chilterns
The South East
Devon & Cornwall

Printed & Bound By Guernsey Press C.Islands.
©Copyright M & M Publishing Ltd. 118 Ashley Rd .Cheshire. U.K. WA14 2UN

All information is included by the publishers in good faith and is believed to be
correct at the time of going to press. No responsibility can be accepted for error.
This book is sold subject to the condition that it shall not by way of trade or otherwise
be lent ,re-sold, hired out, or otherwise be circulated without the publishers prior
consent in any form of binding or cover other than that in which it is published and
without similar condition including this condition being imposed on the subsequent
purchaser.

THE
HIDDEN PLACES
OF THE

HEART OF
ENGLAND

CHAPTER ONE

North Staffordshire

Cheddleton Flint Mill

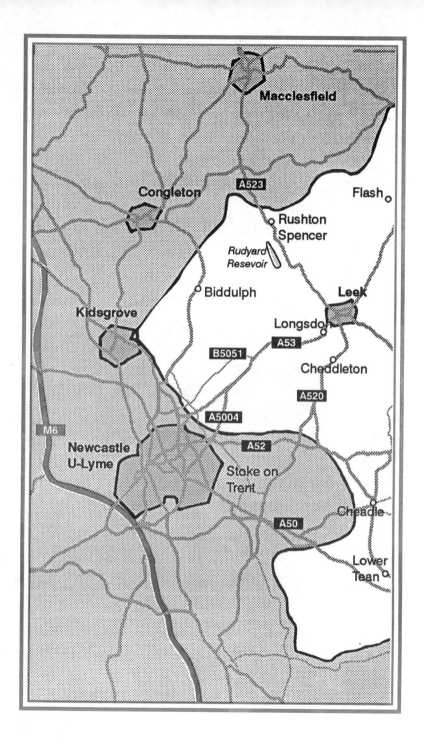

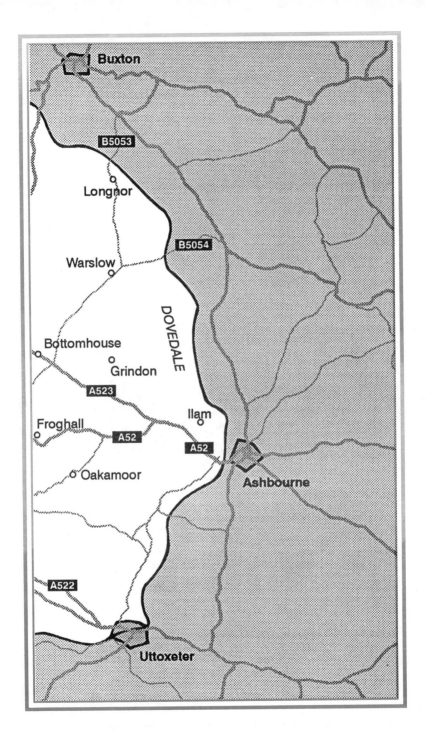

Cheddleton Flint Mill by the River Churnet.

CHAPTER ONE

North Staffordshire.

We hope that our journey through this part of England will help arouse your curiosity and interest in the landscape and architecture of the Staffordshire dales, as attractive in our eyes as many other more renowned beauty spots. **Lichfield,** *for instance has a most beautiful cathedral which can hold its head amongst its peers. The villages are many and there are few without interesting tales to tell. We discovered that the county has a wealth of history which is enriched by the many famous people who were born here. Samuel Johnson, Anna Sewell and David Garrick all came from Lichfield and then there were writers such as George Eliot, Izaak Walton and Arnold Bennett whose novels of the ' Five Towns ' have their own niche within English literature. There is more which surprises, delights and is of interest in our first area within the Heart of England, North Staffordshire.*

Starting our journey in the north east of the county in **Leek,** known as the 'Capital of the Moorlands' a deserving title for this attractive textile centre. French Huguenots settled in Leek after escaping from religious oppression and helped establish the silk industry here. It was the areas abundance of soft water off the millstone grit on the moorland that made it such an ideal place for silk manufacturing. Until the 19th century it was a domestic industry, the workshops being located in the top storey of the houses. Many examples of these 'top shops' survive today. Leek was the home of James Brindley, the 18th century engineer who built much of the early canal network. A water-powered corn mill built by him in Mill Street has been restored and now houses the **Brindley Water Museum** devoted to his life and work.

Every road coming into Leek seems to converge on the old Market Place with its cobblestones and old, slightly blackened buildings. The road west from the Market Place will take you to the parish church which seems to be largely 17th century although the original church was burnt down in 1297 and rebuilt some twenty years later. The timber roof of the nave is the church's pride and joy. It is boasted that each cross beam was hewn from a separate oak tree. In the west part of the nave, an enormous 18th century gallery rises, tier by tier, giving the impression of standing in the dress circle of a theatre rather than a parish church.

The church is very much the focal point of the town and a one time vicar, the Rev. P.D.S. Blake, wrote a guidebook about the church, in which he managed to express with biblical comparisons the approaches to Leek . *'Coming down over Ladderedge, the sight of Leek on its hill in its valley, reminds one of coming over the Mount of Olives and seeing Jerusalem standing on Mount Zion'.*

There was a lot of alteration in the church in 1865 when G.E. Street rebuilt the chancel, the reredos, sanctuary, pulpit and stalls. There is a profusion of Victorian glass including Morris glass in the Lady Chapel. Much of the embroidery work on the frontals was done by the famous Leek School of Embroidery founded by Lady Wardle in the 1870's. You can see and learn much more about this intricate and wonderful work in Leek Art Gallery.

Leeks central location makes it a good starting point for trips to the many attractions in the surrounding area. Places such as, **Alton Towers** and **Chatsworth** are nearby or you can visit pottery centres to view a wide variety of china. Close by, in the foothills of the Pennines and at the edge of the Peak National Park, lie the **Roaches**, an outcrop of rocks thought to be one of the best examples of masses of millstone in the country.

Close by Leek in **Longsdon**, you'll find comfortable accommodation and a friendly welcome at Mrs. Barbara Whites, **Micklea Farm**. Set within five acres of land, with wonderful views down the valley to Cheddleton, this charming farmhouse was built during the 17th century and still retains much of its original character. There are four lovely guest rooms and Mrs. White goes out of her way to make you feel at home during your stay. Visitors here will find themselves well fed, with a substantial breakfast setting you up for a day's exploring and on your return, by prior arrangement, a wholesome evening meal. As a touring base from which to explore the many local places of interest,

Micklea Farm is ideal. Out of consideration to others, please no smoking.

Micklea Farm, Longsdon. Tel: 01538 385006 Fax: 01538 382882

Out of Leek in a north easterly direction you will find the **B5053** which runs through the village of **Longnor**. The village has some fascinating narrow flagged passages which seem to go nowhere but suddenly you emerge into the most beautiful scenery. The Longnor Market square is one of the oldest in England, dating back to medieval times and it is here in the old Market Hall that you will find the wonderful treasure trove that is **Longnor Craft Centre**. Run by the Fox family since 1991, they specialise in beautiful English hardwood furniture, with various designs of tables, chairs, dressers and other items. You can even have a piece custom made for you. In addition to the large range of quality furniture, there is also a display of locally produced arts and crafts, ranging from beautiful paintings to intricate, handmade jewellery. With a lovely tearoom to relax in after making your purchases, complete with freshly brewed tea and coffee and homemade cakes, Longnor Craft Centre is a real gem.

Longnor Craft Centre, The Market Hall, Longnor. Tel: 01298 83587

Opposite the village square and craft centre in Longnor, stands **The Crewe & Harpur Arms Hotel,** a rather grand looking brick-built establishment which gets its name from the Crewe-Harpur estate to which it once belonged. Pamela and Alan Naden are new proprietors, who came here in May 1993 having owned and run the pub opposite for over eight years. Despite its impressive exterior, when the Nadens moved in, the hotel required a considerable amount of refurbishment and through sheer hard work, Pamela and Alan have created a very special place. Ideally situated as a holiday or touring base, the hotel offers very comfortable accommodation in six well furnished guest rooms, three with en-suite facilities and Pamela's culinary talents make dining a pleasure with a varied menu to suit every taste.

The Crewe & Harpur Arms Hotel, Longnor. Tel: 01298 83205

For the curious the tomb stones in Longnor churchyard give an insight into the lifestyle of villagers in these remote areas in times gone by. One extraordinary epitaph tells of the life of William Billinge, who was born in 1679 and lived until 1791 which, according to our reckoning, made him one hundred and twelve years old! As a soldier he served under Rooke at Gibraltar, Marlborough at Ramilles and after being sent home wounded, he recovered to take part in defending the King in the rebellions of 1715 and 1745.

Only about three miles north of Longnor and through the picturesque hamlet of **Hollingsclough** is **Flash**. At fifteen hundred and eighteen feet above sea level, it is the highest village in England. Curious to know how it got its name, we were told that Flash being close to the borders of Cheshire, Derbyshire and Staffordshire became a haven to thieves and forgers. When pursued by the law they were able to make a dash for the next county thus avoiding arrest - be gone in a Flash!

Back on the **A523 Macclesfield** road lies **Rudyard Lake** from which Kipling got his unusual Christian name. His parents met here in 1863 and after their marriage they went to India where Kipling was born in 1865. Steeply wooded banks shelter this two mile long reservoir, built in 1831 to feed the **Trent and Mersey Canal**. The lake is a leisure centre in an attractive setting where there are facilities for picnicking, lakeside walks, fishing and sailing.

Four miles to the north of Leek on the A53 rise the dark-jagged grit stone outcrops of the **Roaches**, **Ramshaw Rocks** and **Hen Cloud**. If you like climbing and rambling this is paradise. Roaches is a corruption of the French word 'roches' or rocks, reputedly given by Napoleonic prisoners. 'Cloud' is a local word used for high hills. Just below the Roaches there is another delightful stretch of water, **Tittesworth Reservoir**, which is extremely popular with trout fishermen. It has some super trails, a visitors centre and a pretty picnic place.

About three miles south west of Leek off the A53 is **Deep Hayes Country Park** which lies in a secluded valley by the **Caldon Canal** and **Staffordshire Way**. If you walk up to the ridge here the views are breathtaking but if you do not feel that energetic, there is a very pleasant walk around two pools which has many offshoots into lovely countryside.

Rushton Spencer is a pleasant, small village, nestling under The Cloud. Its church was once known as the **'Chapel in the Wilderness'** and is worth a visit. It was originally built of wood in the 14th century which has since been replaced with a fine stone building, inside though, you can still see the original timber framing.

Situated in a pretty valley in the Moorlands to the east of Leek is a village called **Onecote**, an ideal place to start exploring **The Manifold Valley**. From **Hulme End** to **Ilam** the River Manifold runs southwards through a deep twisting limestone cleft, between steep, wooded sides. For much of this dramatic course, the river disappears underground in dry weather, through swallow holes. At mid distance its tributary the Hamp joins it, having flowed northwards along a similar course from **Waterhouses.**

You'll also find in the area, **Blackbrook World of Birds** in **Winkhill**, a super wildlife haven owned by the same family that owns Hillside Ornamental Fowl in Mobberley, Cheshire. This place can be found by taking the A523 from Leek and turning right after the Little Chef, following the signs for Alton Towers, and Blackbrook is the first entrance on the right. As well as a varied collection of swans, geese and ducks, there are some rare breeds of Cranes and Storks plus their longlegged counterparts, Ibis and Waders. The aviaries house a growing collection of pheasants and in the spring, you can see various chicks and ducklings taking their first wobbly steps in the bird rearing area. With various farm animals and a children's pet area and shop, you are assured of an enjoyable family day out.

Blackbrook World of Birds. Winkhill near Leek. ST13 7QR. Tel:-
01538 308293 / 01565 873282

Four miles from Leek on the A523 Ashbourne road you will find the delightfully named **Bottomhouse** and here on the top of the Staffordshire moorlands stands **The Green Man**, a family business where children as well as mum and dad are always made welcome. Your hosts, Dennis and Elaine have earned a reputation for quality and value for money with traditional ales and a wide choice of food including a big steak menu and wonderful ice creams. With an adjoining C.C. site, five caravans with electric hook ups and twenty tents can be accommodated. The pub is ideally situated for visiting Alton Towers and lies less than half a mile outside the Peak District National Park. If you're in the area pay a visit, you won't be disappointed.

The Green Man, Bottomhouse, Near Leek, Staffs. ST13 7QT 01538
304360.

Chinese Garden, Biddulph Grange Gardens.

Between Hulme End and Waterhouses, the **Leek and Manifold Valley Light Railway,** a picturesque narrow gauge line, used to follow the valleys of the Manifold and the Hamps, crisscrossing the latter on little bridges. Sadly trains no longer run, but its track bed has been made into the Hamps-Manifold Track, a marvellous walk which is ideal for small children and people in wheelchairs, since its surface is level and tarred throughout its eight miles. The Track can be reached from car parks at Hulme End, Waterhouses, **Weags Bridge,** near **Grindon** or **Wetton.**

At Hulme End the green railway sheds survive. Just over a mile downstream, the Track, and a public road, pass through a former railway tunnel, at **Swainsley;** look for the circular dovecote near here, now a fishing house. A copper spired folly is a reminder at **Ecton** of what was,during the 18th and 19th centuries, a great copper mine, with one shaft fourteen hundred feet deep and an underground canal network.

Wetton Mill has been sympathetically converted by the National Trust into a cafe, a very welcome sight after one's travels. There are toilets here, a car park and picnic tables for those who would rather cater for themselves. Much of the hillside either side of The Track also belongs to the National Trust and is a splendid place for walks.

Nearby in the ominous sounding **Thor's Cave** on **Thor's Crag** which can be reached by a steep path up from the Track or from Wetton village. The cave is a huge aperture, carved out by water long before the valley below was formed. The view from the inside of the cave, framed by the great natural stone arch is magnificent. Listen - for the acoustics, they are very strange. Sound picks up with great clarity and you can easily carry on a conversation with someone far below. At the bottom of the crag are openings known as **Radcliffe Stables** said to have been used by a Jacobite as a hiding place after Prince Charles Edward's retreat from **Derby**.

From **Beeston Tor**, National Trust land above Weags Bridge, there are more magnificent views. Below here there is no right of way along the valley of the Manifold itself, but the Track continues up the Hamps valley to Waterhouses, where it ends at a car park and picnic area. You can also hire cycles from here just across the A523.

Grindon is a unique moorland hill village which stands at over one thousand feet above sea level overlooking the beautiful Manifold Valley. You will find it in the **Domesday Book** where it is recorded as 'an ancient manor in the twentieth year of the reign of William the Conqueror' and it is reputed to have been visited by Bonnie Prince Charlie on his way to Derby.

The splendid isolation in which the villages like Grindon,

Onecote and Butterton have always stood is confirmed when you look around their respective churchyards. The names on the epitaphs and graves reflect the close knit nature of their communities. The Salt family for instance are to be seen everywhere, followed closely by the Stubbs, Cantrells, Hambletons and to a lesser extent, the Mycocks.

In Grindon church there is a memorial thatshows the visitor how bleak winter can be in these isolated spots. This particular memorial records the death of six R.A.F. men in 1947 who were killed when their Halifax aircraft crashed in a blizzard on Grindon Moor when trying to parachute food packages down to the villages who were totally cut off.

Fortunately the weather was much kinder during our visit to this beautiful area of Staffordshire. **Ilam,** being a model village of great charm was a place in the area where we were happy to linger. The village was bought by a wealthy manufacturer, Jesse Watts Russell in the early 19th century and he spent much of his wealth refurbishing the houses and building a fine mansion, Ilam Hall for himself. Seemingly very much in love with his wife he had this house built in a romantic Gothic battlemented style. In the centre of the village there is more evidence of his devotion to his wife; he had an 'Eleanor Cross' erected there in her memory. The church has a saddleback tower and is of ancient origins although it was largely rebuilt by Gilbert Scott in 1855. The visitor is not allowed to forget the village's benefactor here. There is an enormous Watts Russell mausoleum which dominates the north side. On the south side there is a little chapel which was rebuilt in 1618 and contains the shrine of that much loved Staffordshire saint, Bertelin. Otherwise it seems that if it is not some member of the Watts Russell family in evidence then it will be of the Meverell family of Throwley. Robert Meverell and his daughter who married the 4th Lord Cromwell are both buried there. Ilam Hall is no longer there but the park and woodland are in the hands of the National Trust and have been since 1934.

The River Dove runs nearby Ilam and on the Staffordshire side stands the Izaak Walton Hotel. Its correct postal address is Dovedale, Nr Ashbourne, Derbyshire DE6 2AY but we speak in truth when we say the hotel is on the Staffordshire side of the river. Before we tell you about the hotel it is probably a good moment to tell you something about this very different Englishman.

Eastgate Street, Stafford, - more of Stafford in the next chapter - is the birthplace of the famous author Izaak Walton, now renowned worldwide for his literary talent in the world of angling because of his book, ' The Compleat Angler ' which is considered to be the ideal handbook. Although little is recorded of his upbringing or education, we know that he was the son of an innkeeper named

Jervis Walton. By the time he was twenty, Izaak had gone to seek fame and fortune in the City of London, serving as an apprentice draper to his kinsman, Thomas Grinsell. It did not take Izaak long to become a well respected member of the community and he was invited to become a freeman of the Ironmakers Company. The year 1637 was to be a memorable year for Izaak when the distinguished regard in which he was held by the City Livery Company caused him to be elected warden of their yeomanry.

Then, as now, membership of a City Livery Company did not necessarily imply that members were actively engaged within that given trade. To become a member was a social distinction rather than having to qualify as an occupational employee of the trade. At this time Izaak was in fact engaged as a Mercer in Fleet Street. He retired from this business in about 1644. The business had now moved to Chancery Lane and he was fortunate enough to retire with a modest fortune.

Being a staunch Royalist, Izaak was later to return to his native home town of Stafford. It was considered to offer greater safety during the upheaval of the Civil War, which was then raging. Izaak was known to have performed a considerable service to the Crown when, in 1651, after the Royalist defeat at the Battle of Worcester, he retrieved one of Prince Charles' Garter Jewels and conveyed it safely to its custodian, a Royalist officer, then imprisoned in The Tower of London.

Later, he was appointed Steward to Doctor George Morley, the Bishop of Winchester, an appointment which recognised his loyalty to the Church and Crown. The Church figured greatly in the lives of the Waltons; his son, Izaac, became a canon of Salisbury Cathedral and his daughter, Anne, the wife of a prebendary of Winchester Cathedral. Izaak remained within the bishop's household until his death at the substantial age of ninety. Izaak's wife, Anne, had died some forty years earlier. He was buried in Winchester Cathedral where there is to be found to this day a superb memorial to this great man.

Although responsible for many biographies, his most famous book of all is considered to be 'The Compleat Angler', renowned as an anthology. The book was intended to serve the purpose of being humorous and digressive, a style well suited to the contemplative man's recreation. Izaak incorporated recipes, legends and poems into his text.

His love of angling often took him to Dovedale, situated between Leek and Ashbourne. It was whilst en route to Ashbourne that we discovered The Izaak Walton Hotel, a magnificent 17th century farmhouse where he regularly stayed, enabling him to indulge his

14

love of fishing in the nearby Dove. It was this area which inspired and encouraged him to collect his material for The Compleat Angler.

Just five miles away from this beauty spot and hardly a ' Hidden Place ' but all the same equally difficult to ignore is **Alton Towers,** the vast leisure park boasting the latest in gravity defying rides and other attractions, including attractive gardens surrounding a 19th century mansion which was partly built by Pugin. Though the nature of Alton is somewhat against the ethos of this book and ' Hidden Places ' should you be in the area and particularly with children it will be hard to avoid a day there. Not wanting to give the impression of being old 'stick in the muds' we have to admit to having paid a visit and quite enjoying it although some of the rides were not quite to our liking - being the type that don't enjoy hearts in mouths whilst upside down. The Rapids and Logs were more to our liking but there are over one hundred and twenty five rides to choose from for those with more daring tastes.

In contrast the village of Alton is one of great beauty. The remains of a castle perch high on sandstone rock above the river. It faces Alton Towers Flag Tower and as a result the place has been given the nickname of Staffordshire's Rhineland. The steep climb up to Toot Hill Rock is rewarded with magnificent views. The castle is now a school but substantial remains of the medieval castle have recently been found. The castle in its present form was mainly built by Pugin. Two miles south of Alton lies **Croxden Abbey,** founded by Cistercians around 1176, the attractive ruins are now overseen by the English Heritage Society

A short drive away situated on the **A522** at **Lower Tean, The Dog & Partridge** is an excellent freehouse pub and restaurant owned by Ron and Iris Chandler. Divided into a series of cosy little 'rooms',

The Dog & Partridge, Uttoxeter Road, Lower Tean, Stoke-on-Trent
ST10 4LN 01538 722468

seating between two and eighteen the main restaurant area has a warm, intimate ambience, while by contrast there is an airy conservatory restaurant, which enjoys lovely views. Here the tasteful decor and luxurious furnishings blend perfectly with the beautiful Masons Regency Staffordshire china upon which your meal is so attractively presented. The menu is both extensive and varied and in addition to a fine complementary wine list, there is a special selection of wines for the discerning palate. This a lovely place for a family meal out, with a play area to the rear for the children, but popularity makes weekend bookings advisable.

In the little market town of **Cheadle** which lies to the west of Alton the Roman Catholic church catches the eye, Pugin was responsible for its tall spire that dominates the town. In the High Street stand some pleasant 18th and 19th century houses and even one old three-gabled timbered Tudor house.

To the north east of Cheadle the **Hawksmoor Nature Reserve** overlooks the Churnet. The **Churnet Valley** has remained unchanged for hundreds of years and escaping development. The river runs freely, and the countryside around is beautiful. Much of the valley is inaccessible by car but **The Caldon Canal** runs through it and narrow boats ply their way on a route that has to be one of England's most scenic waterways. You can just gently follow the woodland trails stopping at the old-fashioned canal pubs and riverside restaurants or simply go picnicking. Not so many years ago this wonderful stretch of water from **Etruria**, near to Josiah Wedgwoods original factory, to **Froghall** was overgrown and unnavigable. Staffordshire County Council with the British Waterways Board have overseen the areas regeneration with great consideration.

From here we visited the pretty village of **Oakamoor** whose industrial links have now almost gone. It was once the home of the factory that produced some twenty thousand miles of copper wire for the first Atlantic Cable but industrial decline has seen the area cleared and transformed into an attractive picnic area astride the river. You get marvellous views of Alton Castle from here.

Awarded a Two Crowns Highly Commended grading by the English Tourist Board and 5Q Premier Select grading by the AA, **Bank House** is the charming home of Muriel and John Egerton Orme. A 'hidden' gem, it can be found tucked down Farley Lane in the village of Oakamoor about two and a half miles from Alton. Elegantly furnished throughout, this delightful house provides superior accommodation in three fully equipped en-suite guest rooms each with the added touch of a welcome tray for your arrival. The aroma of freshly baked bread entices you down to breakfast and you can enjoy the 'house party' atmosphere of an optional four course dinner each evening. The residential licence means you can complement Muriel's fine home cooking with a choice bottle of wine. There is ample private parking and the beautifully laid out garden provides the perfect setting for a pre-dinner drink on a balmy summer's evening.

Bank House, Farley Lane, Oakamoor, Staffs. ST10 3BD 01538 702810

At the **Star Crossroads** on the Oakamoor to **Cotton** road you will find a delightful pub, **Ye Olde Star Inn.** There has been an inn on this site for over 400 years and the present building, believed to be the oldest licensed house in Staffordshire, was at one time a courtroom and gaol. The attractive stone exterior with white shutters at the windows is matched by the beautiful interior where oak furniture is complemented with rich red carpeting, brass ornaments and stucco walls. Here in a warm, friendly atmosphere you can enjoy a delicious menu of bar food and a selection of fine ale, which on fine summer days can be taken into the lovely beer garden.

Ye Olde Star Inn, Star Bank, Cotton, Near Oakamoor, Staffs. ST10 3DW 01538 702489

Cheddleton seems to perch dangerously on the side of a hill which is why it has such spectacular views. You can look down on the Caldon Canal and the river in all its beauty. The church stands in open country and has some wonderful Morris windows and a lot of interesting Victorian decoration as the result of the restoration by George Gilbert Scott junior in the 1860's. The restored **Cheddleton Flint Mill**, houses a small Museum whose collection includes a rare 18th century 'haystack' boiler and a Robey steam engine. You can visit here at any time of the year. The water powered mill drove machinery which crushed flint. The material was brought in and taken away by narrow boat on the Caldon Canal to be used in hardening pottery at Stoke. You can also take trips along the canal on narrow boats.

The station is home to the **North Staffordshire Steam Railway Centre and Museum** which will give great delight to railway enthusiasts. There is a small collection of beautifully preserved locomotives and other railway mobilia bringing back many memories. It is open to the public at weekends in the summer with trains in steam summer Sundays and Bank Holidays.

We nearly missed **Consall Forge** which is a beautiful spot hidden in the deep valley downstream from Cheddleton. The little cottages keep in close company with the little bridges over the river and the canal. There is a boatman's pub, **The Black Lion** which is only accessible via **Consall** village or down the Devil's Staircase in Consall Nature Park.

Froghall is on the floor of the valley and here after passing through a short tunnel, the Caldon Canal ends its journey at Froghall Wharf. The old buildings and a fine battery of lime kilns around the wharf have been restored and an excellent picnic site has been created. You can walk if you wish some way along the remains of the gravity-operated incline, down which loaded tramway wagons brought the limestone from Caldon quarries, three miles away.

Situated on the **B5053** just outside the village of Froghall, you will find a lovely holiday base at **The Hermitage**, home of Wilma and Frank Barlow. Set in 73 acres of rolling farmland, this charming late 16th century farmhouse enjoys a lovely setting high above the Churnet Valley and is an ideal base for touring the many attractions in the area, such as Alton Towers, The Potteries and Dovedale. The farmhouse is beautifully furnished throughout and the splendid oak panelling, exposed beams and lovely spiral staircase all enhance its character and charm. The cosy bedrooms are all tastefully decorated and provide very comfortable accommodation, whilst outside, excellent self-catering accommodation is provided in The Hermitage Lodge which sleeps up to seven and has facilities for the disabled.

18

The Hermitage, Froghall, Staffs. ST10 2HR Tel: 01538 266515

At **Endon** we wandered slightly to the west and found that we had taken the **B5051** and turned left into **Hough Hill** heading north to **Lask Edge**. With such an intriguing name we felt we had to visit **Mow Cop** whilst in the area. As you drive you'll notice the land rising to Biddulph Moor from which the little village can be seen perched on the escarpment. The castle at the top of the hill, Mow Cop Castle, is in fact a folly. In 1807, the place gave birth to Primitive Methodism when Hugh Bourne, a Stoke-on-Trent man and William Clowes, a champion dancer from Burslem, called a meeting at the prehistoric camp which lasted almost fourteen hours. When Mow Cop Castle was given to the National Trust in 1937, ten thousand Methodists marked the occasion with a meeting on the hill. A small museum of Primitive Methodism can be viewed on Sunday only, from April to September in the afternoon between 2pm-4pm, in the school room of Englesea Brook Chapel just north of Balterley. The Chapel is one of the oldest Primitive Methodist Chapels to survive.

John Wesley was a frequent visitor to **Biddulph** which has a history that goes way back before it found itself becoming enveloped in the upsurge of Methodism. After the Norman Conquest the manor was granted by William to Robert the Forester, an overlord of what was then the extensively forested area of Lyme. Biddulph Grange belonged to the Cistercian monks of the Abbey Hulton until the dissolution. The Biddulphs, a staunchly Catholic family took control of the area. John Biddulph fought under the royal flag and was killed at the Battle of Hopton Heath. His son entrusted the defence of Biddulph Hall to Lord Brereton, who withstood a determined siege until 1644 when he was finally subjected to heavy artillery. The hall was then demolished to prevent its re-garrisoning.

You don't have to be a horticultural enthusiast to appreciate the sheer natural beauty of **Biddulph Grange Garden,** a superb example of traditional Victorian gardening. Situated on Grange Road in Biddulph, this is a National Trust owned property which has preserved all the gardening traditions of the Victorian era with plants brought from all over the world. Ranging from the exotic influence of a Chinese 'willow-pattern' to a damp Scottish glen. With such diversity of landscape there is something to inspire and appeal to everyone, from the weekend amateur to the professional gardener. Originally the creation of three people, James and Maria Bateman who owned Biddulph Grange, and their friend marine painter, Edward Cooke the garden was acquired by the National Trust in 1988 and has been carefully tended and preserved ever since as a natural monument for all to enjoy.

Biddulph Grange Garden, Grange Road, Biddulph, Staffordshire
ST8 7SD 01782 517999

It felt like a fitting visit to end our journey in this part of Staffordshire that had thus far given us many pleasant moments. It was only a matter of miles further along the road to our next area and its ' Hidden Places. ' The next chapter shall uncover our discoveries which we hope you'll share with us as we journey around the ' Potteries ' in this journey through the ' Heart of England'.

The Potteries

Izaak Walton's Cottage, Stafford

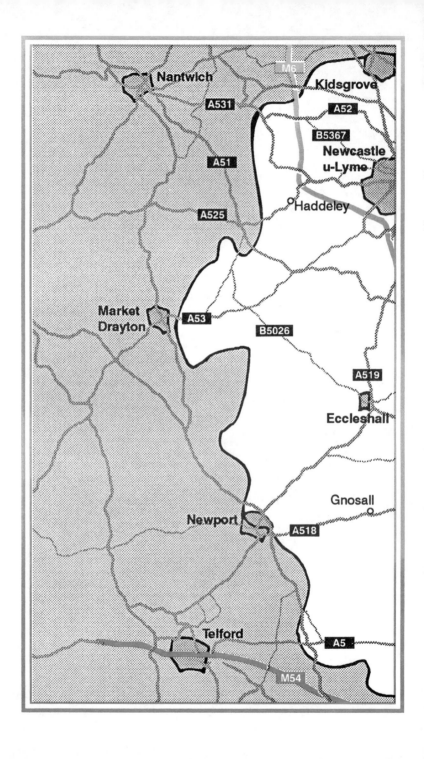

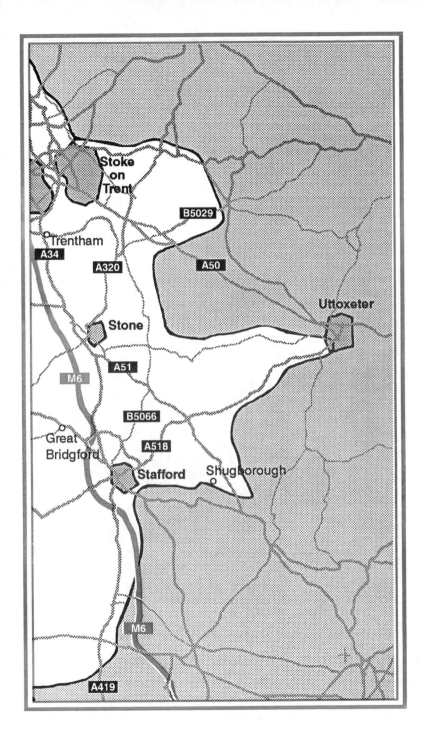

Harecastle Tunnel.

CHAPTER TWO

The Potteries

One of the main reasons to visit **Kidsgrove** is its connection with canals. The two **Harecastle Tunnels**, major engineering feats, carry the Trent and Mersey Canal from Cheshire into the Potteries. It might not be unfair to say that the canal created the town as Josiah Wedgwood dreamt of building a canal and became one of the pioneers of canal construction. He fought hard and long to get a Bill through Parliament for a canal linking the Potteries with the Trent and Mersey, undaunted by the fact that a tunnel nearly three thousand yards long would be needed to go through Harecastle Hill.

The Bill having been passed, many still scoffed at Wedgwoods conviction, but despite all, construction began and took eleven years to complete. Certainly some years later there was almost catastrophe when the hill started subsiding but fortunately Thomas Telford was on hand to design and build another alongside the first, thus averting disaster. The two tunnels which are still there today are an impressive sight and although Josiah's original tunnel is not in use, the Telford tunnel has been restored.

Moving on towards the ' Five Towns' of Arnold Bennett which, before they amalgamated to form **Stoke-on-Trent**, became six with the addition of Fenton. The Cities crest, of an ancient Egyptian potter at his wheel, in one quarter, sums up the fortune which has come to this area as **'The Potteries'**. The joint motto translated means 'Strength is stronger for unity ' and that has to be true when you consider all the marvellous things that have been created from the wealth of talent amassed here. Each one of the old towns is represented in the crest.

Basford, which has become part of Stoke-on-Trent was a rural location in the mid-nineteenth century between **Newcastle-under-Lyme** and **Etruria**. It consisted of Basford Hall and estate,the Queen's Inn and a farm with outlying cottages. It was during the years following 1861 that the Burslem and Tunstall Freehold Land

Society offered for sale plots of land, totalling nine acres, which subsequently were built upon to create the most northerly part of Basford as it is today. Basford immediately became a very desirable place of residence for the affluent pottery owners and the properties reflected this wealth.

The five pottery towns immortalised by Arnold Bennett are well known to be **Burslem, Hanley, Longton, Stoke** and **Tunstall. Fenton** should have been included but it was forgotten at the time . **The Potteries** is a Shopping Centre situated in the heart of Hanley and is every shopper's dream with a fantastic range of famous shops all brought together in a beautiful environment. Natural daylight filters through the Centre's many glazed roofs, and plants, trees and water features, create an outdoor feel.

There are sixty five shops spread over three spacious malls and linked by glass lifts, escalators and feature stairways. The Centre forms one side of the pedestrianised Market Square in the heart of the prime shopping area. Major department stores are fully integrated in the same way as one hundred and twenty market stalls, so it is full of life. Street theatre adds more colour to this busy area and should you need sustenance after you have looked round you'll find a five hundred seat food court with an amazing variety of foods and refreshments, from the rather elegant conservatory area to ten different food kiosks all providing a wide choice of meals and snacks to suit every taste. Car parking for twelve hundred cars is linked to the Centre by an enclosed walkway and there are bus stops just outside, as well as a special coach park for long distance visitors. The Centre provides a professionally staffed play-centre from 9.30am - 4pm for children from 2 - 5 years.

In contrast, **Trentham Gardens,** is just two minutes from junction 15 off the **M6**.The earliest reference to Trentham relates to a nunnery which was established by St Werburgh, daughter of the Anglo-Saxon king of Mercia in 680 AD, later by the daughter of Alfred the Great around 907. Ownership passed via Edward the Confessor and William the Conqueror to William Rufus. As a result of the Dissolution of the Monasteries by Henry VIII, the estate was bought by James Leveson, a wealthy wool merchant who founded the dynasty of the Dukes of Sutherland, owners of the estate for over three hundred years.

The gardens were landscaped by Capability Brown and given a more formal style by Sir Charles Barry, whose work can be observed in the lovely Italian gardens. Although the hall was sadly demolished in 1911, this style can still be recognised in such buildings as the orangery and sculpture gallery which remain today, to form a framework for the outstanding conference, exhibition and banqueting centre that is Trentham.

You can enjoy Trentham to the full in many ways. There is normally unrestricted access to eight hundred acres of woodland, lake and gardens, with opportunities for woodland walks, boating and jet skiing. There are first class facilities for trout and coarse fishing and clay pigeon shooting. Tuition in fishing and shooting is available for the individual or for parties.

The main complex houses a superb restaurant and bars, a ballroom, conference and exhibition centre, and is the frequent venue for fairs, banquets and special events that take place throughout the year. The vast grounds and lake create a huge natural amphitheatre in which many sporting and other outdoor events take place in idyllic setting under a backdrop which is breathtakingly beautiful in all seasons.

We'd also recommend anyone coming to Stoke-on-Trent to visit The Wedgwood Museum and Visitor Centre at **Barlaston.**(Tel :- 01782 204141/204218) It is like an Aladdin's Cave with all manner of wonderful exhibits showing the products of Josiah Wedgwood, the pottery manufacturers, from 1750 to the present day. You might remember our earlier references to the Caldon Canal and mention of Etruria where Josiah had his first factory. Here at Barlaston Wedgwood have re-created those 18th century workshops, complete with a reconstructed bottle kiln and an original engine turning lathe, which is still in use today.

The display vividly brings to mind the working conditions of those days and you are able to look at more than two centuries of the company's history. In rooms designed to recapture the style of specific periods there are hundreds of Wedgwood pieces from those eras. George Stubbs and Joshua Reynolds both painted portraits of the Wedgwood family and they are hanging in the art gallery. In the craft centre we were able to watch potters and decorators at work using traditional skills to create today's Wedgwood products. There is a cinema at the centre and a comfortable refreshment lounge. Never far away on these occasions is the souvenir shop where the temptation to spend money on acquiring some of the beautiful pieces is strong.

As one would expect there are a vast number of extremely good museums and galleries in Stoke-on-Trent. One of the finest and largest collection of pottery and ceramics in the world is to be found at **The Stoke-on-Trent City Museum and Art Gallery** (Tel :- 01782 202173). Apart from the sheer joy of seeing so much that is beautiful and priceless, the museum also tells the story of pots and potters in chronological sequence, showing the importance and expansion of the city.

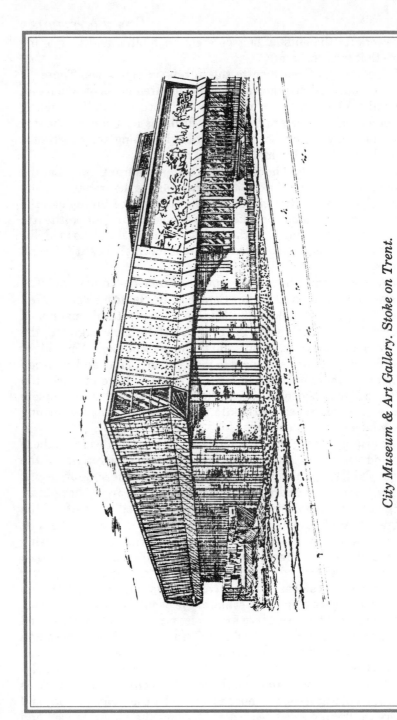

City Museum & Art Gallery. Stoke on Trent.

Housed in three separate galleries are constantly changing exhibitions. Two of them have been designed to be totally flexible and you would be amazed at the variations of art forms that you can see. Anything from the traditional to the avant-garde can greet you. The third gallery is also a surprise, for here is an unusual indoor Sculpture Court visible from all levels in the museum.

There is a Decorative Arts Gallery, a Natural History Gallery, a Social History Gallery and last, but by no means least, a fascinating Archaeology Gallery, in which there are displays of Staffordshire sites of all periods from the mesolithic to the 18th century and range from a cave shelter to a Cistercian abbey. The bias is towards the understanding of the origins and growth of the local ceramics industry but that is a blessing and makes it easier to get the best out of the many museums in Stoke devoted to that craft.

Apart from the wealth of talent which made and continues to make Stoke the centre of the ceramics industry, the local poulation has developed other skills . One place that demonstrates this is The Lowen Gallery, which displays a select range of crafts by leading national and local craftsmen and women, including innovative and exciting work by talented newcomers. The **Gladstone Pottery Museum** (Tel :- 01782 319232) in Uttoxeter Road, **Longton** also worth a visit. It is a working museum of British pottery. Housed in a Victorian pot bank, it tells the story of ceramics with a variety of pottery wares and demonstrations.

Still in the area is the **Chatterley Whitfield Mining Museum** in **Tunstall.** (Tel :- 01782 813337) Here, part of the tour includes an underground gallery where visitors can see local mining techniques old and new and all explained to us by knowledgeable former miners. This was not all, because on display are steam winding engines, locomotives and the delightful, courageous pit ponies.

From the Potteries one option is to take the **A525** which leads to **Madeley**. Sited on a packhorse route from Newcastle-under-Lyme, the name comes from the Anglo-Saxon 'maden lieg', which means 'clearing in the woods'. The centre of this enchanting place has been designated as a conservation area, the focal point of which is The Pool, which was formed by damming the river Lea to provide water power for the corn mill built at its northern end. Madeley's grandest building is **The Old Hall** an excellent example of a 15th century squire's timber framed residence. This beautifully preserved building, with its magnificent brick chimney, is now a two star listed building, standing in the centre of the village close to the pool.

Although it still possesses many of the original motifs, its most striking feature must be the inscription carved into the main beam on the west front facing the road; "*Walke knave what lookest at 47 I.S.B.*" The statement is thought to have been directed at local Roundheads so they would not suspect the owners of being sympathetic to the Royalist cause.

Newcastle-under-Lyme itself, received its first Charter from Henry 11 in 1173 and for several centuries it was the largest town in north Staffordshire. The town will give hours of enjoyment by wandering round the centre stopping to look at the many listed buildings. The town centre is designated a conservation area and many of the buildings carry an identification plaque.

The Borough Council have established two town trails which take in these buildings. Both of these walks begin in Nelson Place. The first follows Queen Street, visiting St George's church which was built in the early 19th century and Mayer House which was the former home of a famous veterinary family. There are two museums for you to see and in King Street are examples of fine Georgian houses. In Marsh Parade is a vast, imposing 19th century building which once housed the town's first silk mill. Holy Trinity Church for Roman Catholics was built of local stone in 1834 and finally on this walk is an old barracks which is now a centre for craft industries.

Borough Museum & Art Gallery, Brampton Park. 01782-619705
The second walk takes in the eye catching, Merrial Street from which there are marvellous views and then moves on to St Giles's church where the base of the tower dates from the 13th century. The medieval church was replaced by a brick church in 1720 but the prodigious talent of George Gilbert Scott shows in the second rebuilding in the 1870's. He managed to recapture all the beauty of the medieval times. High Street which has some fascinating buildings like the Pork Shop which was once the Golden Bell Inn, a timber framed building of about 1600. This wide street and market area indicate its medieval origins being surrounded by entrancing narrow lanes and alleys.

On this route you will see The Guildhall which was built in 1713 to replace an earlier timber building and beside it is the base of a medieval cross. From there to Cheapside which is very narrow and was once the Ironmarket, so called because of the flourishing local iron trade. Finally back to the starting point, Nelson Place, which was reclaimed from marshland in 1782 and laid out as a central open space with several short streets radiating from it.

The village of **Betley,** north west of Newcastle under Lyme receives mention in the Domesday Book and, as you might expect with such an ancient village, the influence of the centuries is etched in the variety of architecture. One particularly interesting building is **Betley Court** where the facade and elaborate wrought iron gateway carry the arms of John Craddock, an attorney at law, who built it in 1716. Originally a simple rectangular building, later additions have created a property of character with red and blue chequered brickwork and a slate hipped roof. The well laid out garden was designed by William Eames, an associate of Capability Brown and to the rear of the house there is a very attractive later 17th century dovecote.

Inside there is an ornately carved 18th century staircase and a drawing room which was remodelled by the celebrated John Nash in 1809. Adjacent to the house is the Gallery where you can see the '"Madeley Head", the oldest stone in the building. There is also an exact copy of the famous Betley Window (now in the Victoria and Albert Museum). There is much of interest here and history and art lovers will find a visit most rewarding.

Betley Court. Main Road, Betley, Newcastle -u- Lyme, Staffs. Tel :
01270 820652

Situated in North-West Staffordshire, close to the border with Cheshire and Shropshire, **Madeley Village,** originally a small agricultural community, has been extended to form a substantial

31

residential area. The centre of the village merits a visit, with its village street bordering the mill pool, and narrow lanes around the church retain much of the village's original character and charm. Madeley Pool is the essential feature which distinguishes Madeley from other villages , and is bordered by former turnpike properties.

At one end of the pool is the former mill,while at the other, you can glimpse All Saints Parish Church through the trees. The Church standing in a raised churchyard with yew trees, is cruciform in plan, extensively enlarged during the 15th Century and the Chapel was rebuilt in 1872. A handsome building, it has interesting window glass and a pulpit with ornamented panels, but more notable are the early 16th Century alabaster tombs of Ralph Egerton and his wife, and the Egerton family memorial brasses. Madeley village has many buildings of historical interest that make it well worth a visit.

Madeley Village & Church.   Nr. Newcastle -u- Lyme, Staffs.

For anyone visiting the area there is an interesting day out to be had just over the border in Cheshire, in **Nantwich** at **Stapeley Water Gardens**, the complete gardening experience that's a must. The world's largest water garden centre,Stapeley really is a whole day out for all.Set in 65 acres of green belt,with ample parking and easy access for the disabled to the whole site,there is a truly surprising variety of things to see and do.

For the gardener the main centre offers over two acres undercover where, in addition to a wide selection of shrubs,roses,trees,heather and border plants, every conceivable sundry item can be found, including gifts,furniture,houseplants and outdoor clothing. Stapeley are, naturally also well known for their extensive range of water gardening supplies and aquatic plants.

The Gardens also boast the most complete angling shop in the area as well as a large range of tropical,cold water and marine fish and equipment,and an extensive pet section ranging from birds and hamsters to chinchillas.

Stapeley also have a most reassuring policy on environmental issues. Glass, paper, metal and garden waste generated on site are recycled. Only captive bred pets are sold. Environmental education packs are available to school parties. And Stapeley sponsors conservation days,with the likes of wildlife painter David Shepherd,alongside its craft fairs,antique shows and falconry displays.

The Palms Tropical Oasis is a vast one and a third acre glass pavilion open all year round, housing exotic plants ranging from 30ft palm trees to giant Amazonian water lilies, displays from the National Rex Begonia Collection and National Water Lily Collection. Here you can see rare and protected species of birds and animals breeding,stingray lagoon,even piranhas,or have a try at the nature quiz, available to children during most school holidays.

Afterwards visitors can relax in the licensed Terrace Restaurant,with piano accompaniment at weekends or the Italian Garden Restaurant, both set amongst exotic flowering plants and pools, or alternatively rest in Palm court next to the Koi pool, with its avenue of palms and a beautiful sequencing display fountain at its head.

And that isn't all; the Yesteryear Museum is a fascinating display and includes a Churchill tank,toys, agricultural antiques and fashions. Inspired by over an acre of display gardens and water gardens? Why not buy a copy of the Stapeley Book of Water Gardens, from the garden centre and learn how to have a go yourself?

Stapeley Water Gardens. London Road. Stapeley. Nantwich.
01270 628628. The Palms 01270-623868

Keele, which is just two miles west of Newcastle is famous as the first of the post-war universities. It is now one of the largest and one of the most attractive of Britain's campuses. Some eighty five percent

Keele Hall

of students and staff actually live in residence which is extremely unusual but has made it so successful. The small village only has one shop, a post office, a parish church, village hall and a pub, The Sneyd Arms.

The A53 from Newcastle will lead you all the way to **Market Drayton** and on the way there is some beautiful countryside and pleasant villages. **Whitmore** is the first and it lies protected from the sight and sound of Newcastle and the Potteries by the plantations of **Old Swynnerton Park.** It is a neat place with a fine medieval church with timbered bell turret and west gable.

Situated in a pleasant rural setting only four miles from Newcastle -under- Lyme, **Whitmore Hall** is a splendid country mansion built in rich red brickwork with stone dressings and a stone balustrade at the top. It is not immediately obvious, but the Hall is actually of four stories, constructed around an older timber-framed house. Whitmore has been the home of the Mainwaring family since Norman times. As you stroll through the vast and ornately furnished rooms, you can trace the family history from paintings. Close by, to the west, there is a sandstone stable block, dating from the late 16th Century.

The Hall is set in an elegantly landscaped park, and the original drive forms an avenue taking you to the nearby medieval Church of St.Mary and All Saints. This Church, largely 12th Century, was extensively restored in the 1880's. It is worth a visit just to see its timber-framed clock tower which is the only example in North Staffordshire of this form of construction. The Hall is open Tuesdays and Wednesdays from 2.00pm - 5.30pm from May to August.

Whitmore Hall & Church. Whitmore. Necastle -u- Lyme. Staffs.
Tel: 01782 680235

The first turning on the right after you leave Whitmore will take you to **Willoughbridge,** a remote sort of place that laid claim to fame when Lady Gerard, of Gerard's Bromley, discovered warm springs here, and built a bath house. It almost became as fashionable as Tunbridge Wells but settled back into the quiet spot it is today.

The Borough of Newcastle -under- Lyme has many places of interest to discover, and one such place is the **Dorothy Clive Garden.** This beautiful garden extends over eight acres and was created by Colonel Harry Clive for his wife Dorothy. Today it is open to the public and you don't have to be a keen gardener to appreciate its sheer natural beauty. There are various walks through the garden and at every corner you are rewarded with a myriad of brightly coloured flowers, herbaceous borders and beautiful trees - some of the species being quite rare.

On the hillside, not far from the car park, is a lovely wisteria covered gazebo; whilst on the loose-gravelled scree, alpine plants and dwarf shrubs cling perilously, adding their own particular charm. The azaleas provide a lovely burst of colour and the pool with its water-based plants has a different appeal, and is home to a variety of insects. With eight acres to wander round, you will be amazed at how quickly time seems to pass, and you can easily spend a few hours at this beautiful oasis tucked away in the rolling countryside of North Staffordshire.

The Dorothy Clive Garden. Willoughbridge, nr. Market Drayton. Tel: 01630 647237.

Almost into Market Drayton and still on the A53 there is one delightful surprise to be experienced in **Ashley**, a stones throw from Loggerheads.in the form of the church which from the outside looks very ordinary and typical of the latter part of the 19th century but inside it is a feast for the eye.There is a very short nave with only two bays, a fairly long chancel protected by a beautiful rood screen, which allows you to catch a glimpse of the glory to come - the brilliant, lavish, gilded reredos screen. Other treasures to be seen are the marble floors, a marvellous organ gallery and some excellent furnishings. The church must also be blessed by an excellent and devoted team of cleaners whose labour of love includes cleaning the brass candelabra which are everywhere.

Meandering via **Loggerheads** the **5026** wanders in and out of the turnings to the many small villages, eventually arriving at Eccleshall. The very best way to see and enjoy **Eccleshall** is to take a guided tour with one of the professionally trained Village Guides. You meet your guide outside the Kings Arms Hotel and you will be taken all round this charming small town with its distinctive High Street and much that will remind you of its earlier days when it was on the busy coaching route between London and Chester and many of the buildings date from that period. The Parish church is impressive and stands at the end of the High Street beckoning you on towards the beauty of the miles of wooded countryside around, which we had already experienced as we drove along the road to this appealing town.

Just by the crossroads in the centre of Eccleshall stands **The Old Smithy** pub which houses a superb restaurant called **Fletchers Forge**. This is one of those rare 'hidden' gems which offers the connoisseur the finest cuisine imaginatively prepared and beautifully presented. Everything on the extensive and mouthwatering menu is homemade, from the bread to the delicious chocolates and petit fours which complete your meal. Granité is served between courses to refresh the palate and each main course comes with a choice of six different vegetables and two types of potato dishes. The small garden to the rear, complete with patio provides the perfect setting for an intimate dinner on those warm summer evenings and Julian Ankers is a welcoming host who goes out of his way to give his many customers complete satisfaction.

*Fletchers Forge at The Old Smithy, 8-12 Castle Street, Eccleshall
ST21 6DF 01785 851220*

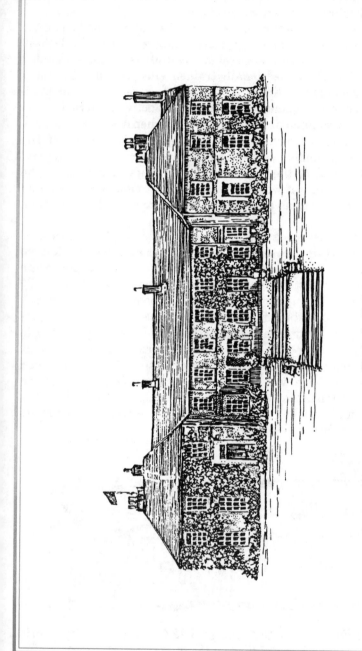

Eccleshall Castle.

For over a thousand years **Eccleshall Castle** was the palace of the Bishops of Lichfield but at the beginning of this century it became a family home when the Carter family moved from Yorkshire. The present simple sandstone house is typical of the best architecture of the William and Mary period, and incorporates part of the earlier 14th century castle. The interior of the house has been augmented by successive members of the family, one of whom added a magnificent Victorian staircase and dome.

Perhaps to remind them of the county from which they came, the Carters have collected a very interesting number of 19th century paintings by Yorkshire artists which give great pleasure. The Library is full of superb books, amongst them many first additions, including a complete set of the works of Charles Dickens. All over this very nice house you can find delightful pieces of porcelain, on display from all over the world, especially good are the Oriental displays and some fine 18th century European pieces.

There are also examples of craftsmanship with furniture ranging from the 17th century to Victorian times. Charles 1 visited Eccleshall in 1640 and you can almost imagine him sitting in one of the splendid chairs. Sir Walter Scott was another visitor here and would probably have found much to inspire him.

The gardens have been created around the ruins of the old Castle and have a great deal of romanticism. The old walls give wonderful support to the pear trees and all the busy climbing plants and shrubs. The rose garden stands serenely sheltered by the walls too. A thoroughly pleasant time can be had wandering along the moat which was drained in 1820 and looking at the magnificent trees. Because the grounds are so sheltered unusual birds are frequently to be seen and apparently kestrels nest every year in the old Castle tower. Eccleshall Castle is a place to be savoured and this you can do from Easter Sunday until the second Sunday in October. The open days are Mondays, Tuesdays and Sundays from 2pm -5.30pm.

Situated five miles south of Newcastle-under-Lyme and junction 15 of the M6 or three miles north of Eccleshall, **Mill Meece Pumping Station** provides a fascinating day out for the whole family. This is the home of the Gentle Giants, vast working steam engines which were once used to pump drinking water to Stoke-on-Trent. Today you can view the coal fired boilers which used to keep going all day, producing the steam necessary to power the steam pumping engines. There are various water processing displays and a selection of short videos, whilst outside children will particularly enjoy the hands-on exhibits and landscaped area for them to 'let off steam'. During the summer, additional events include steam weekends, Morris Dancing and craft fairs.

Mill Meece Pumping Station, Near Eccleshall Tel: 01785 813087

From Eccleshall we decided to move again along the A5026 but now in an eastwards direction towards **Stone,** where once thirty eight coaches a day pulled up at the bow-windowed Crown Hotel, the best building in the High Street. Today it is an attractive shopping and residential town. In the early days when Henry 11 granted the monks a market in 1251 it was a mecca for all the little hamlets around. The Augustinians founded a priory here in the 12th century but only one arch and some cloisters remain today. The present parish church dates from 1750 and contains several interesting monuments, including a bust of Admiral Earl St Vincent, the hero of the great naval victory off Cape St Vincent in 1797. It also contains the magnificent stained glass windows depicting the martyrs Wulfid and Rufin.

The Trent and Mersey Canal played a large part in the town's early economic development and even today it still brings work to Stone through the building of holiday canal cruisers and a growing tourist trade. Situated on the High Street in Stone, you will find **Country Lady,** a superb boutique which specialises in elegant wedding outfits and accessories for mother of the bride and guests. This high class boutique was established over fourteen years ago by the friendly and very professional proprietor Elizabeth Ball and the first Saturday of every month holds an in-store fashion show. Following major expansion just over two years ago, it now houses Stages Coffee Shop and Bistro. As with the boutique, everything within this delightful licensed bistro is of the highest quality, all the food freshly prepared and offering much more than standard café fare. With a choice of teas, coffees, homemade cakes and light lunches available, it is the perfect place to relax and consider your fashion purchases.

Country Lady / Stages Bistro. Stone, Staffs Tel: 01785 813214

Along the **B5027** from Stone is **Uttoxeter**, a town perhaps best known for racing. In the market place there is a little memorial to Dr. Samuel Johnson who when he was quite an old man, stood, bare-headed, on a pouring wet day, as a penance for having, in his youth, refused to help his father with his bookstall in the market. Wednesday is the busy day here when the traditional livestock and street market is held.   There are   several   nice   timbered buildings here but disastrous fires in 1596 and 1672 destroyed the majority of the town's architectural heritage.

From Uttoxeter along the **A518** and passing by **Amerton Working Farm**, visitors to the County Town of **Stafford**. A place well worth visiting during your stay in Stafford is The **Ancient High House,** a

The Ancient High House. Stafford Borough Council,
Riverside, Stafford. Tel: 01785 223181

beautiful Elizabethan house built in 1595 that is in fact the largest timber framed town house in England. Through painstaking efforts

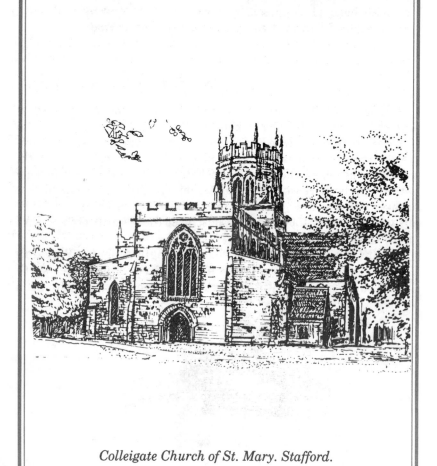

Colleigate Church of St. Mary. Stafford.

over several years, Stafford Borough Council have restored this amazing piece of architecture to its former glory and today the building houses the Museum of the Staffordshire Yeomanry and the Tourist Information Centre. You can follow The Ancient High House's varied history through the permanent displays in period room settings taking you through the 17th, 18th and 19th centuries and telling the life stories of people who came to know this house so intimately. Not surprisingly, the house has Royal connections, with both King Charles 1 and Prince Rupert having stayed here in 1642. The house also has a small heritage shop selling a variety of interesting and locally crafted gifts for those seeking a memento of their visit.

Close to the High House is the Collegiate Church of St. Mary. This is an unusual building which dates in part from late 11th century, but has received additions in the early English, Gothic and Victorian styles. The huge tower arches in the nave seem to divide the building into two, which is in fact exactly what they were intended to do, as St. Mary's is two churches under one roof. The nave was the parish church of Stafford with its own altar, whilst the chancel beyond was used by the Deans of the College of St. Mary, whose duty it was to pray for deceased members of the royal family. Although the 'college' was abolished in 1548, the screens which divided the church remained until 1841 and the church today is still referred to as the 'Collegiate'. It is easily spotted in the the town by its unusual octagonal tower dating from the Perpendicular period (14th - 15th century). Also worth noting is the splendid north transept and its beautiful doorway with carved leaf capitals, flowers and fleurons in the arch. St. Mary's looks across from its memorial gardens to the picturesque Church Lane, with its black and white cottages and l6th century coffee house.

Stafford Castle, Stafford Borough Council, Council Offices,
Riverside, Stafford. Tel: 01785 223181.

Situated high up above the town, one Stafford landmark that is

Church Lane. Stafford.

viewed by countless travellers along the M6 are the impressive earthworks of the **Norman Castle** which can be reached via the **A518** Newport Road, about a mile and a half from the town centre. Set within 20 acres, the remains of this splendid fortress are open to the public and visitors can follow an illustrated trail which leads from the outer bailey, and onto the site of a borough settlement. There is also a modern Visitor Centre where a video and detailed model reconstructions bring the past vividly to life. The Castle grounds are often used for historical re-enactments by such groups as the Napoleonic Society and are often the site for Sealed Knot battles as well as other outdoor entertainment which provide an added attraction if you happen to visit at the right time. A call to the local Tourist Information Centre should provide you with details of such events.

Shugborough Hall, Shugborough. Tel: 01889 881 388

South east from Stafford and probably one of the most impressive attractions within Staffordshire is **Shugborough,** the 17th century country seat of the Earls of Lichfield. This magnificent 900 acre estate includes Shugborough Park Farm, a Georgian farmstead built in 1805 for Thomas, Viscount Anson, where you can see rare breed animals and traditional farming methods, including hand milking, butter and cheese making and shire horses at work. In the former servants' quarters you find yourself taking a step back in time to the 19th century as you get a taste of life 'below stairs' wandering through the restored brewhouse, kitchens, laundry and coach houses. The mansion itself is a splendid piece of architecture, altered several times over 300 years, but always retaining its distinct grandeur. Passing through the vast rooms with their ornate plasterwork and cornicing, you can't help but be impressed and the collection of paintings, ceramics and silver plus a wealth of elegant French furniture is simply breathtaking. Outside as you explore the beautiful parkland you will spot an outstanding collection of neoclassical monuments dotted around and

St Mary the Virgin. Ingestre.

the Lady Walk leads you along the banks of the River Sow to the delightful terraced lawns and rose garden. Before leaving this splendid country estate, a visit to the walled kitchen garden provides you with the ideal opportunity to buy a living memento in the form of cottage garden plants.

Close to the main **A51** is the old village of **Great Haywood** which has the longest packhorse bridge in England. The 16th century Essex Bridge still has fourteen of its original forty arches spanning the River Trent. From here it is a good opportunity for a visit to the beautiful church of St Mary the Virgin at **Ingestre,** just two miles east of Stafford off the A51. It sits quite close to the Jacobean, Ingestre Hall and was probably built to Wren's design in 1676. One of the few churches that he designed outside London. Inside the church is totally elegant with a rich stucco nave ceiling and some of the earliest electrical installations in any church. In the chancel, which is barrel vaulted, there is a delightful garlanded reredos. There are many monuments to the Chetwynds and Talbots who were the Earls of Shrewsbury from 1856 and whose seat was Ingestre. The church is only open in daylight hours during the summer but we were told that in the winter months a key is available.

Izaak Walton Cottage, Stafford Borough Council. Riverside, Stafford. Tel: 01785 223181

Set in beautiful grounds in the tiny hamlet of **Shallowford**, near **Norton Bridge, Izaak Walton Cottage** is a pretty 17th century half timbered cottage which was once owned by Izaak Walton, famous biographer and author of 'The Compleat Angler'. Walton bequeathed the cottage to Stafford Borough Council and it was subsequently transformed into the museum you find today. Within the grounds there is an authentic 17th century herb garden, a lovely picnic area and orchard. Keen fishermen may also be able to fish the River Meece only yards from the cottage, where Walton himself fished for trout

47

some 350 years ago. The cottage is open daily Tues - Sun from 11.00am - 4.30pm and Bank Holiday Mondays from April to October.

Enjoying a lovely riverside location on the **A5013** Eccleshall Road, just outside Stafford, **The Mill at Worston** is a delightful stopping-off point in any journey. Originally built in 1814 by J. Milner, there are records of a mill on this site dating back as far as 1279, possibly before and there are records of a court battle of ownership of the present mill between Henry Le Whyte and Elena De Wynerston. Later, the mill came under the ownership of Ranton Abbey, after whose dissolution it passed through the hands of various local landed gentry until J. Milner bought and rebuilt it in 1814. Today, much of the machinery used during the mill's working life is retained and can be viewed by the many visitors here. In these characterful surroundings you can enjoy a pint of fine ale and a tasty bar meal, or alternatively choose from an extensive menu in the pleasant surroundings of the restaurant. There is a delightful nature trail to follow and on warm summer days, the beer garden and adventure playground provide the perfect setting for the whole family to enjoy a meal 'al fresco'. With a large function room seating up to 150, it is no surprise that this is a popular venue for wedding receptions and family celebrations.

The Mill at Worston. Great Bridgeford, Stafford. 01785 282710.

Back along the main **A518** in an easterly direction you come to **Gnosall.** There are some beautiful ash and sycamore trees here which form a delightful shaded arch over the road. It also has a ghost! On the night of January 21st 1879 a man was attacked at Gnosall canal bridge by an alarming black monster with enormous white eyes. The police were quite sure it was the ghost of a 'man-monkey' who had haunted the bridge for years after a man was drowned in the canal.

Wandering south from Gnosall we saw a sign for **Weston-under-Lizard** and discovered that it was uncertain whether it

48

belonged in Staffordshire or Shropshire. We took the opportunity to visit **Weston Park,** home of the Earls of Bradford for three hundred years. The house is situated on the site of the original medieval Manor House. This was successively the property of the de Westons and the Myttons. The last of the Myttons, Elizabeth married Sir Thomas Wilbraham who disliked the gabled building and pulled it down, replacing it with another of his own design.

The lack of male heirs in the 18th century meant two more changes in Westons ownership, both through the female line, first to the Newports, Earls of Bradford and then in 1762 to the Bridgemans, an old family whose origins went back to Devon. Disraeli was a frequent visitor here and at one time presented the house with a grotesque stuffed parrot. The parrot became famous when the present earl after leaving Cambridge published a book entitled 'My Private Parts and the Stuffed Parrot'. The stuffed parrot still enjoys the hospitality of Weston.

The present earl has achieved such great things here. Lord Bradford's mother undertook all sorts of improvements in the house and Lord Bradford was determined to revitalise Weston Park.

At one time Lord Bradford had a restaurant in London's Covent Garden, Porters, which was very successful and it is this knowledge of catering that has enabled him to radically and enthusiastically improve the standard of catering at Weston Park. Gourmet dinners are quite regularly held in the magnificent dining room as well as private banquets and wedding receptions.

The Park at Weston has matured over several hundred years into a masterpiece of unspoilt landscape. Many have left their mark, yet each successive generation has taken note of its predecessors. Disraeli loved the Park and in one of his letters to Selina, 3rd Countess of Bradford, refers to the 'stately woods of Weston' There are some wonderful architectural features in the park including the Roman Bridge and Temple of Diana, both designed and built by James Paine for Sir Henry Bridgeman in about 1760. There are Fallow deer and rare breeds of sheep roaming the vast parklands, you can follow an architectural trail or the many nature trails. We can list for you so many things to see and do, like the Miniature Railway, the Aquarium, the Butterfly farm, a Museum of Country Bygones and by no means least, the Adventure playground and pets corner.

As we meandered towards the next chapter in search of ' Hidden Places in East Staffordshire we made our final visit in this intriguing part of the county where rustic scenes were within easy reach of the urban centres. **Moseley Old Hall** once stood in a remote part of Staffordshire, surrounded by its own agricultural estate. Today that remoteness no longer exists for the outskirts of Wolverhampton reach

Weston Park.

to within a mile of the house and motorway access is clearly signposted from Junction 1 of the M54. We wanted to take a look at it because The Hall once sheltered King Charles II for two days after the Battle of Worcester in 1651. There have been innumerable accounts of the King's concealment there which have given the house its place in history. You would be forgiven for thinking the house belonged to the 19th century at first sight, but look more closely and you see the two groups of Elizabethan windows were replaced by casements. Much of the original panelling and timber framing inside the house are still visible. In 1962, by the generosity of the Wiggin family, who had acquired the house in 1940, the Hall and one acre of land were transferred to the National Trust. The house was virtually empty then and almost all the furniture and pictures now shown have been lent or given to the Trust. Although not of great architectural merit, the part played by Moseley Old Hall in the preservation of King Charles and thus in the restoration of the Monarchy make it a very interesting place to visit.

Moseley Old Hall.   *Telephone 01902 782808.*

Dorothy Clive Gardens, Willoughbridge

CHAPTER THREE

East Staffordshire

Fallow Deer

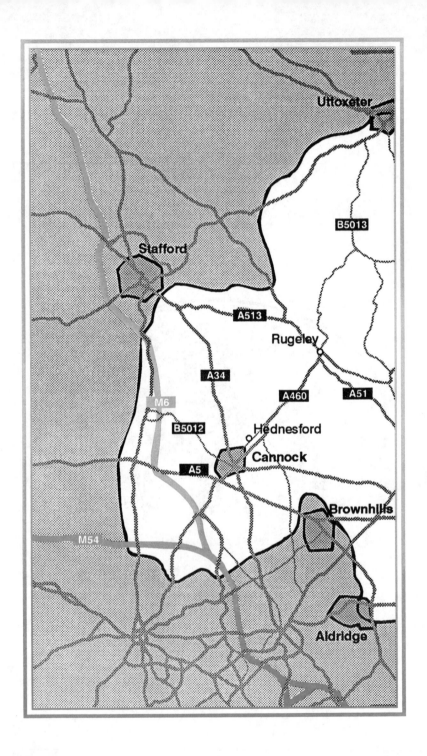

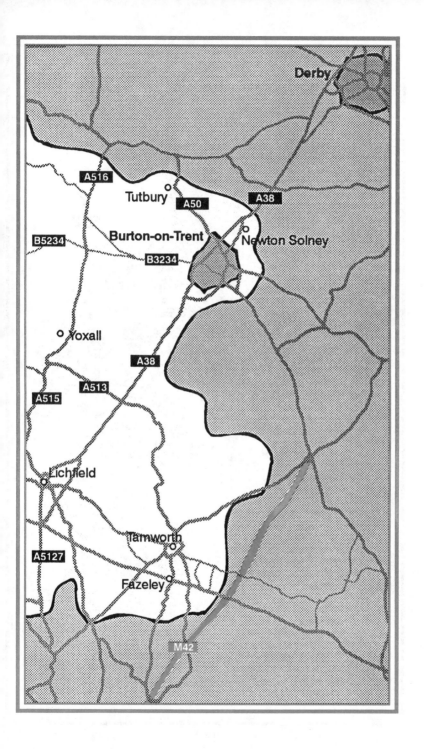

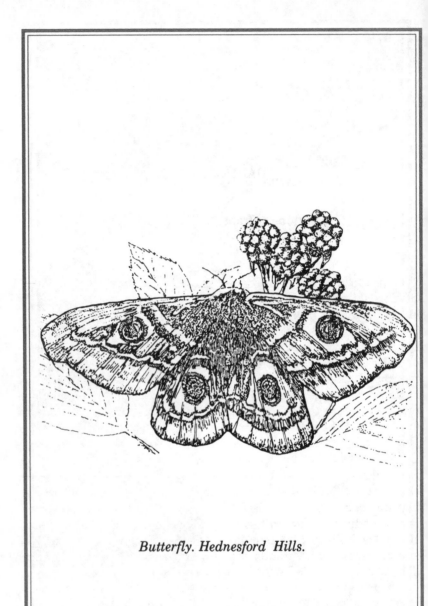

Butterfly. Hednesford Hills.

CHAPTER THREE

East Staffordshire.

Penkridge, the starting point for a journey through East Staffordshire has many delights for visitors. The whole of the centre of the village has been designated a conservation area,as it is so rich in character and history. From churches, cottages and houses to tombstones and even trees, nothing is allowed to be tampered with or altered in any way. A market can be traced to the granting of a market charter by King Henry 111 in 1244. Queen Elizabeth 1 is reported to have visited The White Hart Inn and other ancient features include the church of St Michael and All Angels, the stocks and gaol at the constables house, Cruck Cottage, Bellbrook - the Old Deanery Farm House and Church Cottage.

Without a doubt the most dominant feature in the centre of Penkridge is the parish church which was one of the six collegiate churches in Staffordshire before the Reformation. **Hednesford** lies by **Cannock Chase,** its oldest building is The Cross Keys Inn which is a splendid hostelry built somewhere around 1746. The Anglesey Hotel was built in 1831 by Edmund Peel of Fazeley as a form of summerhouse which stands proudly at the end of the main square, designed in a Tudor style with stepped gables.

Opened in May 1989, **The Valley Heritage Centre** is a new concept in the world of museums, arts and crafts. Once a former mining site, the Valley Heritage Centre took three years to convert and now is reporting far greater popularity and numbers than anticipated. Galleries provide different exhibitions, rooms are dedicated to The Natural History of the Hednesford Hills,the Shops Of Old Hednesford as they used to be and Castle Ring Hillfort, an exhibition which takes you back to the days before the Roman conquerors. Subjects covered in these galleries change every six months to deal with as many aspects of the area's history as possible.

The Valley Heritage Centre is only one of the many wonderful parts of Cannock Chase. The Council have encouraged visitors by helping in the conservation areas of beauty. **Brindley Heath** for example, is four hundred and twenty acres of beautiful mixed wood and heath and the nearest part to Hednesford. Its name reminds us that the Brindley family worked on the Chase for over three hundred years. **Brindley** village is of a much more recent origin. During the Great War a Military Hospital was built here, and later the Coal Board workers lived in the buildings.

We learnt that for thousands of men killed in France during World War 1, Cannock Chase was their last billet in England and so in some ways the surrounding beauty serves as a lasting memorial to them.

Hazel Slade Reserve very near to Hednesford which is just to the west, is a site where people are as important as nature, where it is possible to live next to nature and with care and effort conserve it for its own sake and for the interest and enjoyment it can give. People have always used this site. Thirty five years ago the old broadleaved wood that grew here was felled for timber. Hedges were planted and fields grazed. A small area of the wood managed to recover and grow from the stumps and seeds remaining in the ground. Thirty years ago the pool and marsh started to form as the land sunk through the mining subsidence and it became a popular fishing spot. More by luck than judgment, man's activities in the past have produced an old fashioned countryside of small fields, hedges, streams and pools, marshes and woods.

Rising over seven hundred feet above sea level, **Hednesford Hills** are a prominent local landmark, bringing the countryside of Cannock Chase into the heart of Hednesford. Originally covered in oak and birch these three hundred acres of heathland have been the scene of varied activities over the years. They have been quarried for sand and gravel, mined for coal and used for sport and military training. The land is now a registered common. It is wonderful; the Hills are a tract of wild landscape with a plethora of heathland plants, abundant wildlife and the opportunity for recreation for the people who live nearby.

The Hills have other sporting connections too. Cock fighting once took place at **Cockpit Hill,** but we didn't find the exact location of the old cock pit. In the last century prize fighters prepared themselves at the nearby Cross Keys Inn for boxing bouts on the Hills. Horse racing was another important part of life in those days. The area was well known for the stabling of horses in the 18th and 19th centuries. Meetings were held regularly until 1840 when the racetrack at **Etching Hill,** near **Rugeley** became more popular. Grand National winners were stabled and trained here. Jealousy won the race in 1861, Eremon in 1907 and Jenkinstown in 1910.

The Military also liked these hills for their mock battles. In 1873 there were extensive manoeuvres on Cannock Chase with one army based at Etching Hill and the other army at Hednesford Hills where the battle took place.

Cannock is still a colliery town but do not dismiss it because of this, there is much to see. It lies on the southern edge of Cannock Chase and goes back to the Conquest. In the Domesday book you will see it called 'Chenet'. It has an attractive market place with three busy market days, Tuesday, Friday and Saturday. The ancient bowling green has been there since time immemorial.

Overlooking the green is an imposing Georgian house that once housed the council and nearby is the former conduit head building of **Cannock Conduit Trust,** founded in 1736 to bring a water supply to the town. Known as the Tank House, it supplied water for the area until 1942.

There are some nice shops around the Market Place and in the attractive precinct on Market Hall Street. Henry 111 granted Cannock a market charter in 1259. On the far side of the Market Place is the parish church of St Luke. According to the records, the church had a chantry and a grammar school linked to it as early as 1143. The battlemented church tower dates from the 14th century and together with the west end of the nave are the oldest surviving parts of the building. The arms of Humphrey de Stafford who was killed at the Battle of Northampton in 1460 are on display.

During the 18th century **Lichfield** was a prominent city, but it failed to compete with other towns in extensive rebuilding programmes and consequently still retains a medieval grid pattern streets with elegant Georgian houses and mixed in amongst them, black and white Tudor cottages. Little alleyways, such as Tudor Row, invite shoppers to visit specialist boutiques and a 16th century cafe - so different from the usual high streets found in today's cities and towns.

The Lichfield Heritage Exhibition & Treasury is part of **St. Mary's Centre** in the Market Place at the very heart of the city. A church has stood on this site since the 12th century, with the present building being the third one, dating from 1868. Due to the declining population in the city centre over the last thirty years, drastic action was needed to save St. Mary's from redundancy, or even worse,

The Nave. Lichfield Cathedral.

demolition. In 1977/78, with the co-operation of local civic and church authorities, together with many private individuals, The St. Mary's Project Committee was formed. From this evolved the ambitious and imaginative plan to convert St. Mary's into the unique Community Centre which we have today.

The Guild of St. Mary's Centre.Lichfield. Tel: 01543 256611

It opened in 1981 and comprises: The original Dyott Chapel & Chancel which were retained as the Parish Church and thereby ensured the continuance of worship here for the future; a day centre for senior citizens; a gift shop; a coffee shop; the Heritage Exhibition & Treasury.

The Lichfield Heritage Exhibition & Treasury, being on a new mezzanine floor, has additional access by lift for the elderly and disabled and is based on the history of Lichfield through its people. Together with many other exhibits, it has two A.V. presentations, one entitled 'Lichfield - A Walk Through History' and the other 'The 1643 Siege of Lichfield Cathedral during the Civil War'. The beautiful Treasury houses many fine examples of the silversmith's art with collections of civic, church and regimental silver. The Muniment Room displays ancient city archives and charters. The latest attraction for visitors is a viewing platform 40m high in the Spire of St. Mary's which provides unique and spectacular panoramic views over the city and nearby countryside. This is proving to be a photographer's delight. Open daily 10.00am - 5.00pm except for Christmas Day, Boxing Day, New Year's Day and Spring Bank Holiday Monday.

Apart from the historic pleasure that Lichfield gives there is also large amounts of open water and green parkland to enjoy within the city. Beacon Park and Museum Gardens for instance where some seventy five acres of park encloses playing fields, a small boating lake and a playground. In the park there is a statue in the museum gardens to Commander John Smith, the captain of the ill-fated

Titanic. It was sculpted by Lady Katherine Scott, widow of 'Scott of the Antarctic'.

There are two wonderful pools, Stowe and Minster, the former is a large area of water used for fishing and sailing and is the site of the Festival fireworks display each July. The Minster Pool is beautiful, it was landscaped in the late 18th century by Anna Seward and is now a haven for wildfowl.

Anna Seward is one of Lichfield's famous sons and daughters. She lived in the Bishop's Palace and was a poet, letter writer, and centre of a literary circle in the late 18th century. There are many well known names to add to hers. Samuel Johnson, of course, but also Elias Ashmole the Antiquarian and herald whose collection became the basis of Oxford's Ashmolean Museum. He was born, like Samuel Johnson, in Breadmarket Street. Then there is Erasmus Darwin, the doctor, inventor, botanist and poet who lived in a house in Beacon Street on the corner of The Close. David Garrick probably the greatest actor-manager of the 18th century theatre, had a home which stands opposite the west gate of the cathedral.

Just behind the industrial units at Lichfield, out in the countryside you will find a rural gem at **Curborough Hall Farm**. The land here has been farmed by the Hollinshead family for many years and since 1989 the family have been steadily converting the farm outbuildings to create a variety of small craft workshops which will keep browsers fascinated for hours. Within one of these workshops you will find Frank Daysh, a highly skilled man who originally trained as a scientific glassblower, a job requiring highly precise skills. Since 1985, he has used these skills to develop his profession and visitors are welcome to watch him at work in his upstairs workshop. Frank is a lamp glassblower which means that rather than working from molten glass he reheats glass tubing and rod, modifying it to produce some simply exquisite pieces such as decorated perfume bottles and chess sets. The showroom also has an interesting range of glass by other workers including animal sculptures, paper weights, jewellery, glass domes and even a glass grand-daughter clock. The only dilemma for visitors is deciding which piece to choose as a memento! There is also a lovely tearoom and having enjoyed a look around you can relax in the tearoom garden, weather permitting, with a refreshing cuppa and a tasty homemade cake. For self-catering enthusiasts, the Hollinshead family provide excellent accommodation in four self-contained cottages at nearby Elmhurst Dairy Farm. All the cottages are equipped to a very high standard and graded Commended with a Three or Four Key rating by the English Tourist Board, a sure sign of the quality of accommodation you can expect. Opening times Wednesday to Sunday 10.30am - 5.00pm.

Curborough Hall Farm Craft Centre, Curborough Hall Farm, Watery Lane, Lichfield. 01543 262595

Situated on the **A461**, 100 yards from the **Muckley Corner** roundabout on the A5, **Copper's End** is an ideal touring base for this lovely part of Staffordshire. Lying just three miles outside historic Lichfield with its Cathedral and Heritage and Treasury Centre, not to mention Cannock Chase Country Park and Shugborough, the Earl of Lichfield's family home, there are numerous attractions within easy driving distance tempting you to prolong your stay. Copper's End was built during the 1930's as a police station, today it offers far more comfortable accommodation than the former cell which is now the lounge. The bedrooms are all very well equipped and tastefully furnished with guest comfort always a prime consideration and breakfast is a substantial treat that sets you up ideally for a day's exploring. All major cards taken.

Copper's End. Muckley Corner, Lichfield. Tel: 01543 372910

Dr. Johnson's Birthplace Lichfield..

On the way to **Tamworth** take a look at **The Museum of the Staffordshire Regiment (The Prince of Wales's)**, which incorporates the former South and North Staffordshire Regiments which were amalgamated in 1959. Its origins go back to 1705 when the 38th Foot, (later the 1st Battalion of the South Staffordshire Regiment), was raised at Lichfield. The museum exhibits a good range of uniforms, shako and helmet plates, belt plates and clasps, badges and buttons, and weapons from pistols to machine guns. There are relics from the Sikh Wars, the Crimea, Indian Mutiny, Zulu War, Egypt, Sudan, South Africa and both World Wars. You realise the bravery of the Regiment when you see amongst the medals no less than thirteen Victoria Crosses awarded to the men.

The Old Stables Farm Shop and Bakery, Packington Moor Farm,
Near Whittington, Lichfield. 01543 481223

Close by one 'hidden' place well worth seeking out is **The Old Stables Farm Shop and Bakery** at **Packington Moor Farm** near **Whittington**. To find your way here, take the Whittington turn off the A5 and the farm shop is situated midway between the **A5** and **A51**. The shop sells a wide selection of homegrown produce including meat, vegetables and dairy products such as cheese and ice cream and while you browse, children can play on the swings and make friends with the small farm animals. There is a bakery on the premises which produces delicious bread and cakes and in the tearoom and courtyard you can relax with a cup of tea and a tasty homemade snack. There are 'pick your own' fruits available in the summer months and you can book a 'childrens party in the Barn' should you wish.

Just south of Tamworth lies **Drayton Manor Park and Zoo**, another popular theme park in 60 acres. It has over fifty different rides, a Zoo and farm which combine to promise an action packed day out, especially for families. Entering **Tamworth** the visitor finds a young town with an ancient history. It straddles the famous Roman

65

Watling Street (A5) and has had a fascinating and turbulent past. The earliest reference is the 8th century when it was the capital of the Kingdom of Mercia and its king, Offa, built his palace here. The Danes managed to destroy the town twice and it was invaded later by the Scandinavians. You can see evidence of this in the names of streets such as Gungate. Alfred's daughter Ethelfleda was busy here too and there have been excavations in the town centre which produced Saxon fortifications.

Dominating the town is the fine Norman motte and bailey castle set in the Pleasure Grounds which have truly magnificent floral terraces. The sandstone castle and superb herringbone wall dates originally from the 1180's, having replaced a wooden tower on the present artificial mound constructed shortly after the Norman Conquest.

Daniel Defoe called Tamworth, 'A small but very handsome market town'. Much has gone but something of this can still be seen in the 18th century buildings of Market Street and Lady Bank. The Town Hall is charming with open arches and Tuscan columns below. It was built in 1701 and paid for by Thomas Guy, the local MP, who is famous for founding the London hospital which bears his name. He also gave the town its fourteen almshouses in Lower Gungate, which were rebuilt in 1913.

Tamworth's most famous son was Sir Robert Peel, who was Prime Minister under both William 1V and Victoria. In front of the Town Hall is a fine bronze statue of this great man. The parish church is vast,founded in 963, it was rebuilt after the Norman Conquest and again after the Great Fire of Tamworth in 1345. The splendid 15th century tower at the west end contains a most remarkable double staircase. The mixture of Victorian and modern stained glass is remarkably harmonious.

The bustling town centre's modern shopping facilities include a street market every Tuesday and Saturday and the attractive Ankerside Shopping Centre is a covered precinct opened by the Queen in 1980. There is a fascinating glass mural by John Lawson here which depicts Tamworth's past.

On a warm summer's day there can be few nicer modes of transport than by boat, travelling at a leisurely 4mph and watching the world go by. At Canal Wharf in Fazeley, **Debbie's Day Boats** give visitors the opportunity to experience this pleasure with a small fleet of 15 foot, luxury, all-weather cruisers which can be hired by the hour, half day, or full day. Run by Debbie and Tom Hayes, the business was set up in April 1993 following Debbie's prize-winning business plan. Seating up to five adults, the boats, all of which are named after members of Debbie's family, are easy and safe to drive, with full tuition provided before you set off. As a picnic venue they are ideal and the trip takes you past many canalside pubs.

Debbie's Day Boats, Canal Wharf, Fazeley, Tamworth.

We were enchanted as we drove through the village of **Alrewas** on the A38. Lining the main street are delightful black and white thatched cottages, some of which have stood since the fifteenth century. The village is surrounded by countryside and this makes a drive, very pleasant. The River Trent and The Trent and Mersey canal run through the village adding to its beauty. This canal links the River Trent near Derby with the Mersey at Runcorn, a substantial part of it being in Staffordshire.

We wrote earlier about Josiah Wedgwood and the Harecastle Tunnel but whilst the towpath has gone from Telford's tunnel, it is still used by pleasure boats, as is the whole of the canal. South of the Potteries, the Trent and Mersey runs close to the River Trent, passing the wild expanse of Cannock Chase and the busy **Fradley Junction** where there is a connection to the **Coventry Canal** before leaving Staffordshire by way of **Burton-on-Trent.**

The church of All Saints in Alrewas is as beautiful as the village. Doorways remain from a Norman church to which the beautiful chancel was added in the 13th century. The church is open every day from 9am -5pm.

King's Bromley is a little to the west of Alrewas and is one of Staffordshire's oldest villages. Lady Godiva lived here with her husband Leofric. It was also the scene of Leofric's death. King's Bromley was a crown property for many years after the Norman Conquest and it had other royal connections in the 12th century. Henry 1 loved hunting and stayed here, close to the forests. When Charles 11 needed to escape he was sheltered by the Lane family who were locals and it is they who engineered his route to freedom.

Yoxall is one of those villages which is designated a

67

Tamworth Castle

conservation area. It is a romantic sort of place and we were not surprised to learn that, according to legend, Robin Hood was lord of the manor and married Maid Marion at nearby **Tutbury.** There are some very nice buildings and the parish church is worth a visit. Visitors to this tranquil village will discover an excellent touring base at **The Moat,** the charming home of Pam Hopkins. The original manor house on this site was blown up during the battle of Burton Bridge during the Civil War and the present house was built about 100 years ago using bricks from the mill which stood next door. Standing in two and a half acres of beautiful landscaped gardens the house is surrounded by a dry moat dating back to the 13th century and believed to be the deepest of its kind in the Midlands. Pam is a welcoming hostess who provides very comfortable accommodation in three en-suite guest rooms. Awarded a Two Crown Highly Commended rating by the English Tourist Board, there are full facilities for the disabled including a chair lift and guests can be provided with an evening meal by prior arrangement.

The Moat, Town Hill, Yoxall, Staffs. Tel: 01543 472210

Ridware Arts Centre just outside Rugeley is within the Tudor walls of the ancient manorial site of Hamstall Hall and there we found a fascinating group of shops, studios and a restaurant. Everywhere there was activity. Demonstrations of the various skills of the occupants hold the visitors interest. There are always changing exhibitions at Ridware so it does not matter how often you come back as there is always something new to see. The Malt House Craft Shop shows an enormous variety of British craftwork including unusual porcelain, fascinating wood boxes, toys and turned bowls as well as some delightful domestic pottery which are collectors' items. In the Gate Barn there is a collection of plant containers from every corner of the world. All sorts, shapes and sizes to take plants small and large and designed to fit into odd corners of your home.

Rugeley gained an unhappy notoriety in Victorian times as the home of the poisoner, Dr William Palmer, who murdered his victims after insuring them. There is a walk through the town along a designated route. Leaving Market Square look along Anson Street to your left and note the interesting three-storey Victorian buildings and varied roof line. Opposite was the old 'Penny Bank' building.

Market Street has long been the main street of the town. In it is 'The Shrewsbury Arms', a former coaching inn dating from about 1810 although parts may be even older. It has changed its name once or twice. Between 1860 and 1967 there was a cattle market at the rear and a market bell was rung from the steps of the inn summoning the farmers back from lunch.

The Tudor House that you can see is one that was rented by the evil Doctor Palmer. He got his just desserts though and was publicly hanged in Stafford in 1856. A bit further down the street is The Red Lion, an attractive timbered building of about 1600. Inside one wall has linenfold panelling.'The Sycamores' is a much altered farmhouse built about 1600 and parts of the timber frame are still visible.

The Old Chancel across Station Road is Rugeley's original parish church, founded in the 12th century. The tower, chancel and north chapel which remain, date mainly from the 13th and 14th centuries. The nave of the church was demolished in 1823 to help pay for the new church. Next to the Old Chancel is Church Croft, a Georgian house where William Palmer was born.

Brook Square, back in the old town centre where it is worth a short detour up the narrow Upper Brook Street to Horse Fair. Until 1932 there was an annual horse fair here with dealers coming from all parts of the country, France and Ireland. A thousand and forty horses were recorded at the 1867 fair. On the far side of Horse Fair are a pair of 16th century timber houses and a restored 18th century stone wall. Lower Brook Street took us back to Market Square.

A few miles north of Rugeley is **Hoar Cross**. The church of the Holy Angels delighted Sir John Betjeman who said; 'The church of the Holy Angels, Hoar Cross, is the masterpiece of its late Victorian architect, G.F. Bodley'. Much of its beauty, indeed its very being is down to one remarkable lady, Emily Charlotte, eldest daughter of Sir Charles Wood, 1st Viscount Halifax and widow of Hugo Francis Meynell Ingram.

To write about Hoar Cross without mentioning the **Meynell Hounds** is like thinking about **Stratford** without Shakespeare. Meynell is perhaps, the most famous of all names in the world of Fox Hunting and for many years the hounds were kennelled at Hoar

Cross. In those far off days anyone who could beg, borrow or steal a horse was welcome to follow Meynell's hounds and share in the days sport. As well as this, such a large establishment of horses and hounds provided occupation for most of the people in this small community.

A delightful village to tempt the tourist is **Abbots Bromley**, a 13th century settlement, where, on the first Monday after the 4th of September, the villagers celebrate the annual Horn Dance. This ancient fertility dance is performed by many men wearing reindeer antlers, amongst other things!

After all this excitement you may need a drink and whilst in **Burton-on-Trent** do visit the **Bass Museum of Brewing** in Horninglow Street. Take a few thousand gallons of good Burton brewing water and combine it together with best English Malt in a traditional Mash Tun, then run the resultant sweet malt liquor into huge boiling coppers and add to the brew good old English hops. When it has cooled, run the wort (Malt liquor) into wooden fermenting vats and pitch in the breweries own strain of yeast. Seven days later the beer is ready to be racked off into casks. This is the traditional way that beer has been brewed for centuries, and here at the museum you will be offered the opportunity of seeing, sniffing and sampling!

They have restored the original Buxton-Thornley steam engine, scrapped in 1970 and are proud to have it back home and in steam again. They also have one of the largest 'bottled beers' collection in the United Kingdom. They are open all the year telephone 01283 42031 for more information.

On the edge of **Newton Solney** on the **B5008** from Burton -on-Trent you will find an excellent place to stay at **Newton Park Hotel.**

Newton Park Hotel, Newton Solney. Tel: 01283 703568

Built in Italianate style in 1798 by a wealthy local gentleman, this

71

delightful country house hotel enjoys a lovely setting, with wonderful countryside views and yet lies only three miles outside Burton-on-Trent. Traditionally furnished throughout, in keeping with its age and character, this impressive establishment boasts 51 en-suite guest rooms, all of which are equipped to the highest standards. The elegant restaurant with its ornate ceiling and oak panelling provides a relaxing setting in which to savour a fine menu of traditional English cuisine. Stained glass is a major feature, with glass panels on the main staircase depicting the seasons and months of the year, and in the Derbyshire Bar, further glass panels depicting attractive countryside scenes, enhancing Newton Park's distinctive charm.

On the main **A50** road three miles from Burton upon Trent lies **Tutbury**, a small market village, lying in the **Dove Valley** on the Derbyshire border.1989 was a special year as St Mary's Priory Church was founded exactly nine hundred years before by Henry de Ferrers. Its splendid Norman architecture makes the priory one of the most impressive relics of the Conqueror's England.

A beautiful village with many Georgian fronted shops, it has held onto the historical charm and character from this period in time. **Tutbury Mill Mews** is a shopping complex, originally an ironmongery and wheelwrights to Lord Burton.

The town of Tutbury had been renowned for glass making as far back as Mary Queen of Scots time. In 1980 when the old glass factory, was forced to close, sadly one hundred and fifty employees were to find themselves out of work. However, just two years later, the factory was to rise like a phoenix from the ashes, all due to five past employees, who took up the challenge of reopening the factory. This age old tradition synonymous with the ancient town of Tutbury has been brought back to life and it's all due to five enterprising and ambitious people. A visit to**Tutbury Crystal Glass** (Tel:- 01283 813281) will enlighten you to the process of glass making.

R.A.James M.B.H.I., 14 High Street, Tutbury.Tel: 0283 814596

On the High Street in the centre of Tutbury you will find a fascinating place with the impressive title **R.A.James M.B.H.I.** above the door. The James family have been horologists since 1918 and Robert James, the current owner, specialises in repairs and renovations of antique clocks, watches and barometers. He makes regular trips abroad where he is able to buy more unusual and interesting pieces with which to fill the shop, tempting the passer-by and habitual browser to call in. With pieces of every style you can imagine, there is something here to appeal to every taste and if your own clock or barometer is broken or has seen better days, Rob's skill as a craftsman can bring it back to its former glory.

At the end of the High Street in Tutbury, you will discover a first class restaurant called **Mulberry House.** This delightful 200 year old listed building boasts a mulberry tree in the centre of the rear patio which is also over 200 years old and has a conservation order to protect it. Inside, the restaurant has a cosiness and warmth which is enhanced by attractively laid tables, beamed ceilings and lovely dried flowers. Open for everything from morning coffee and cream teas to lunchtime snacks and a full à la carte dinner, Mulberry House offers an excellent menu of traditional homecooked fare throughout the day. You can enjoy a game of croquet on the lawn or purchase one of the gifts on sale, and for those wishing to stay, there are also four lovely guest rooms to choose from.

Mulberry House. 19 High Street, Tutbury. Tel: 01283 815170

Almost next door to Mulberry House is the fabulous **Crystal Studio** glass works, run by Geoff Press and Mike Underwood.

This is a real treasure trove and, as its name suggests, the studio specialises in glassware and crystal, which is handcut and finished on the premises. Mike and Geoff also produce crystal sports trophies and can make repairs and renovations to any glassware. The vast array of goods on show are of the highest quality, with something to suit every

Church of Holy Angels. Hoar's Cross.

taste and pocket. Beautiful vases, glasses, decanters and trinkets are all attractively laid out, leaving you spoilt for choice when it comes to choosing a memento or gift.

The Crystal Studio, 22 High Street, Tutbury. 01283-520917

In all Staffordshire is a much underated county with much to keep the visitor amused and occupied however long their stay. Leaving the county behind the scenery becomes much more industrialised, but there are still some fascinating 'Hidden Places ' to discover.

The Black Country

Dudley Castle

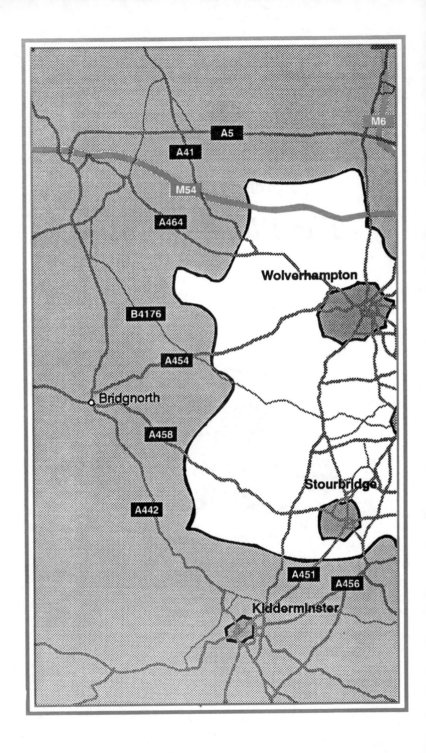

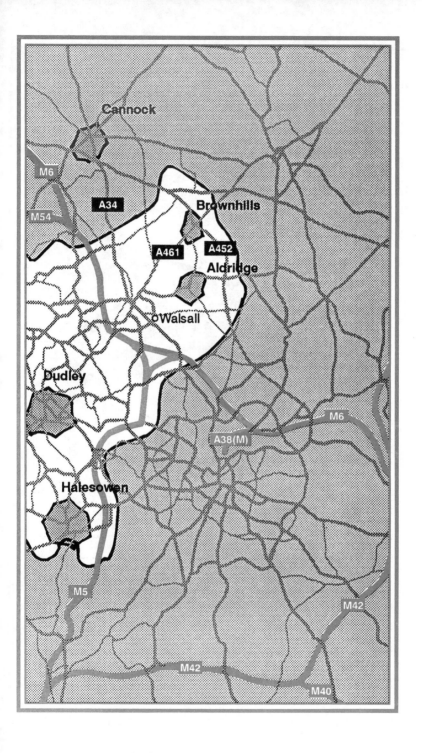

Interior.Chillington Hall.

CHAPTER FOUR

The Black Country

Our starting point in this chapter was something very different from what the term ' Black Country' conjures up in the mind. The name itself originates from the 19th century expansion of previously small iron and coal industries into more or less a continual conurbation. The pollution generated by the industrial expansion helped coin the name we still call this part of the country although it is now, without doubt cleaner. Dickens called the area a modern hell, *"....as far as the eye could see....tall chimneys,crowding on each other.....poured out their plague of smoke,obscured the light and made foul the melancholy air...........strange engines spun and writhed like tortured creatures; clanking their iron chains,shrieking in their rapid whirl from time to time.....and making the ground tremble with their agonies."*

Heading out of Cannock along the A5 going westwards and then turning to the left at **Horsebrook** brought us into **Brewood,** a village mentioned in the Domesday book. It was once the centre of the nail making industry. It is hard to believe that this peaceful place is only three miles from the M54 and just eight miles from **Wolverhampton**.

This small, but busy market town is a delight. It is of medieval origins and has the **Shropshire Union Canal** running through it. The Shropshire Union Canal is Telford's masterpiece. He was intensely proud of it and with reason. It leaves the Staffordshire and Worcestershire Canal at **Autherley Junction**, near Wolverhampton,and in Telford's inimitable fashion, runs north west to Nantwich in Cheshire often through deep cuttings, the most spectacular of which are at **Norbury** in Staffordshire, with its famous high bridge, and at **Tyrley**, with its sheer rock sides.

At Brewood, which is pronounced Brood, are two interesting works; the aqueduct over which Telford's canal crosses the same engineer's Holyhead Road (now the A5), and the ornamental bridge - or short tunnel - which he was obliged to construct to take the canal beneath the avenue to **Chillington Hall.**

You'll find this Tudor house on an unclassified road just before the

Bantock House Museum.

M54. It was rebuilt by Francis Smith of Warwick and later Sir John Sloane in the 18th century,its garden laid out by Capability Brown. Tourist Information will have details of its limited opening times.

There are some beautiful buildings including the Tudor Brewood Hall and Blackladies, an old monastery. If you like Queen Anne and early Georgian houses you will love Brewood. The parish church of St Mary the Virgin and St Chad date back to the 13th century and has a wonderful sense of peace about it as well as being extremely beautiful.

When we left Brewood, we drove along crossing the busy M54 until we came to the bustling village of **Codsall** which is only a few miles north west of Wolverhampton and is famous for its lupins. We were told that they are a result of the medicinal springs in the Codsall Wood area.

Just north of the village is **Pendrell Hall**, built in the 19th century. It is a weird architectural mixture, some Gothic and some Tudor style. The house sits on top of a slope and has the most superb views of the Welsh Marches, Cannock Chase, Wolverhampton and the Black Country. It belongs to Staffordshire County Council and is used as a residential college. The parish church of St Nicholas is well worth looking at. It has an impressive Norman archway and an Early English square tower.

It was during the Saxon times that the town was first recorded as a community. Ethelred the Unready gave a charter to a local lady, Lady Wulfruna. In 994 she gave a plot of land at the highest point of High Town for the construction of a monastery. It is on this site that St Peter's church now stands. Outside the church is the town's most ancient relic. It is a Saxon preaching cross which is believed to have stood there since the mid-9th century. It stands fourteen feet high, and isn't really a cross but rather a circular pillar with a decorated shaft that is worn almost smooth with age.

In Bantock Park, the **Bantock Museum** has some wonderful 18th century enamels for which neighbouring Bilston was famous, and First Period Worcester porcelain.

There are perfectly preserved examples of houses with the Civil War Connection. One such house is **Moseley Old Hall** which once stood in a remote part of Staffordshire, surrounded by its own agricultural estate. Today that remoteness no longer exists for the outskirts of Wolverhampton reach to within a mile of the house. The Hall once sheltered King Charles ll for two days after the Battle of Worcester in 1651. There have been innumerable accounts of the King's concealment there which have given the house its place in history.

Dudley Castle

You would be forgiven for thinking that the house belonged to the 19th century at first sight, but look more closely and you will see the two groups of Elizabethan chimneys, star-shaped in section,towering over the roofs. Little in the way of structural alteration appears to have been done to the house until about 1870, when the outer walls were covered in brick, and the Elizabethan windows were replaced by casements. Much of the original panelling and timber framing inside the house is still visible. In 1962, by the generosity of the Wiggin family, who had acquired the house in 1940, the Hall and one acre of land were transferred to the National Trust. The house was virtually empty then and almost all the furniture and pictures now shown have been lent or given to the Trust.

Further west **Boscobel House** has royal connections as it is where King Charles is said to have hidden in an Oak Tree while Cromwell's troops searched the house and grounds for him. Legend has it that the Royal Oak outside the house is a descendant of that original tree which sheltered the King.

Three miles west of Wolverhampton stands **Wightwick Manor,** pronounced Witick, this National Trust property is a half timbered and half bricked building built in the late 19th century by paint manufacturer Theodore Mander. Inside you'll see 19th century decor with Morris wallpaper and fabric, stained glass and examples of pre -Raphaelite paintings.

On the outskirts of the town, a long defunct Great Western Railway track bed now forms the Valley Park footpath along which walking is a great pleasure.

Dudley can justly claim to be the showpiece of what canals can offer visitors. **The Dudley Canal Trust** and its boat trip company carry over a hundred thousand visitors a year, deep underground beneath Dudley Castle, through canal tunnels into the caverns which supplied the Black Country iron foundries with limestone. A spectacular audio visual presentation with dramatic floodlighting brings back the days when the miners worked by candlelight in dangerous conditions to mine the limestone.

Adjoining the canal is the **Black Country Museum**. Apart from a wide variety of buildings which have been rebuilt to form a Black Country 'village' scene, including a Methodist Chapel and a canal pub, there is a faithful reconstruction of a narrowboat building yard and a restored wharf where limestone was loaded into boats from kilns.

Dudley Castle, perched on a limestone ridge dominates the town. It was first mentioned in the Domesday book in 1086. The first stone castle was built in the 12th century but was destroyed less than a hundred years later following the rebellion against King Henry ll.

Black Country Museum, Dudley

From the 13th century, rebuilding and extension work continued up to the 16th century. In 1554 the Duke of Northumberland lost the castle, and his head, for treason, and in 1575 Queen Elizabeth stayed here whilst travelling through the Midlands.

During the Civil War, the castle paid the ultimate price for being a Royalist stronghold, the Parliament ordered it to be 'sleighted' in 1647. This destroyed much of the keep, gatehouse, barbican and curtain wall, ensuring that the castle was useless for military purposes.

The Black Country Museum is already ranked as one of the nation's best 'living' museums. From the moment you enter the site your senses are kept busy. A vintage single deck tram ride takes you past a recreated Black Country Colliery, where you see the conditions of the early days of mining. The display has easy access. A series of concrete tunnels sunk into the ground with a walk - in facility providing a series of galleries featuring miners and their equipment.

In the village is a priceless collection of cottages and Victorian terraced houses which were carefully removed, brick by brick, from clearance sites all over the Black Country and rebuilt to their original design to create a typical Black Country street scene. All the houses are furnished and equipped in the original style with outhouses and small chain shops where the outworkers made chain for the bigger companies. Shops, too, form another fascinating feature in this time capsule of Black Country life as it was. Amongst the shops are a chemist, haberdashers, bakery and hardware merchants.

The Bottle and Glass Public House with its traditional furniture and real ales is exactly what you would expect to find in a pub of this age. The building was removed from its canal side site near Brierley Hill and rebuilt alongside the canal leading to the Dudley tunnel and the trip boats. Close by is the disapproving Methodist Chapel originally from Darby Hand at Netherton, complete with its original furniture and some times special services are still held here.

One of the museum's most prized possessions is a replica of the world's first **Newcomen Beam Engine** which was installed in **Tipton** to pump water from mine workings. The engine is not always in steam but for more information telephone: 0121-557-9643.

Did you know that **Willenhall** produces ninety per cent of all the locks we use in this country? Once here you are made very much aware that during the reign of Queen Elizabeth 1, the town was granted the exclusive right to manufacture locks for the state and has done so ever since.

Willenhall also has a very nice market place which is the centrepiece of a splendid conservation area resurfaced with blue brick pavements and cast iron kerbing, restoring it to its 19th century splendour.

If you love snuff boxes and little enamelled trinkets you will enjoy spending time in **Bilston.** Somehow in the midst of the Industrial Revolution and backstreet workshops, 18th century enamellers carried on their craft. They called themselves toymakers but they were not talking about children's toys. They provided society with such items as patch boxes, snuff and sweetmeat boxes, scent boxes, bonbonnieres following the fashion set by the French at Versailles. Their product was infinitely cheaper than the French because they worked on copper rather than gold or silver.

The museum at Mount Pleasant holds the world famous collection of Bilston enamels and it is a delight to see.

Glassmaking has been carried out in the Stourbridge area for nearly four hundred years. During that time the towns of **Amblecote, Wordsley, Brierley Hill** and **Stourbridge** have produced some of the world's most memorable glass. Stourbridge glassware has been supplied to stately homes and palaces throughout the world and is as much in demand today as it ever was. Modern technology has not replaced the actual skills of centuries ago which still apply in the final stages.

The glass industry dates back to the beginning of the 17th century when 'gentlemen glassmakers' originating from Normandy and Lorraine, in eastern France, settled in the area, attracted by the plentiful supplies of coal to fire their furnaces and fire-clay from which to make their melting pots.

We had noticed in our journeying from Wolverhampton, the **Red House Glass Cone.** In fact you cannot fail to see it. It is the sole survivor of dozens in continual use in the glass industry. The cone housed the circular furnaces which the glass makers worked around. Today, it is one of only four surviving in the country. It is imposing, almost 100 ft tall and was built about 1790.

A priceless collection of glass from Roman times up to the present day can be seen at the Stourbridge glass industry's museum at **Broadfield House,** Compton Drive, **Kingswinford**. The exhibits come from donations from individuals, private collections and glass manufacturers with particular emphasis on the dazzling range of coloured glass and crystal for which the name of Stourbridge became internationally famous.

To the west lies some attractive country for walking or simply a pleasant day picnicing. Kinver Edge is National Trust Property consisting of moorland and you'll find the remains of a hill fort there.Alternatively south of Stourbridge lie the Clent Hills, also

National Trust property and rising to a height of 1036 feet. Close by is **Hagley Hall,** built in the middle 18th century by a Sanderson Miller for the first Lord Lyttelton. The interior is rich with ornate plastering by Frncesco Vassali. In the gounds there is a sham ruin and a classic temple.

Visitors to **West Bromwich,** could be forgiven for thinking of it as just a thriving town created by the industrial revolution. Such thoughts are entirely incorrect. It has been in existence for well over eight hundred years and All Saints' parish church has been the site of religious worship for more than a thousand years. The Domesday Book lists the Manor of West Bromwich under the possessions of William Fitz-Ansculph, Baron of Dudley. The Manor House was rescued from dereliction in the late 1950's and is now a restaurant. The Great Hall of the house was built in the closing years of the 13th century. It is possibly the most complete example of such early construction.

In Oak Road is **The Oak House,** a magnificent Tudor house built in the reign of Henry Vlll which has survived intact. It was once the centre of a considerable estate owned by the Turtons. During the Civil War, the Turtons sympathised with the Parliamentary forces and legend has it that many Roundheads sheltered here. This lovely house is furnished throughout in the Tudor style as if the Turtons were still in residence.

Methodism played a large part in the history of the Black Country. **Sandwell** can claim a part in the growth of Methodism in the U.S.A. It was at **Asbury Cottage**, Newton Road, **Great Barr,** where America's first Methodist bishop, Francis Asbury, spent much of his childhood. He was apprenticed to a blacksmith named Foxhall at the Old Forge, at what is now Forge Mill Farm in the Sandwell Valley. He became active in Methodism and began attending West Bromwich Church. Eventually, he became a Methodist preacher and a friend of John Wesley. Meanwhile, Mr Foxhall's son had gone to America to become a wealthy iron merchant and eventually built the Foundry Methodist Church at Washington DC.

Sandwell Valley is a tribute to a foresighted Council, who prevented the urban sprawl engulfing it with factories and housing. It is wonderful countryside with a long history. One thousand years ago, an isolated hermitage stood in the valley close to pure spring water flowing from the sandstone rocks. It is from this ancient spring that the area - and eventually the Metropolitan Borough, gained its name, Sandwell. Today it is the home of sailing, fishing, horseback riding, playing fields, golf courses, working farms, forming Sandwell's major open space leisure area.

Around 1189, William Fitz-Wido, Lord of the Manor of Bromwich, founded a Benedictine Priory on the site of the old hermitage. The Priory was dissolved in 1525 and given to Cardinal Wolsey who, in turn, passed it on to what is now Christ Church College, Oxford. When Wolsey fell from grace in 1539, the King reclaimed the estate which the Crown passed to the Clifford family. They were succeeded by the Whorewood family who built Sandwell Hall in 1609 on the Priory site.

Walsall, dates back to the 11th century, it is an important place today at the centre of a large metropolitan borough but it is still dominated by the past in the beautiful shape of its 14th century parish church. Like most of the towns round the Black Country its open air market was established by Royal Charter. Walsall's came in 1219 and it was an important trading centre even then long before the industrial revolution arrived with its collieries, blast furnaces and ironworks.

Jerome K. Jerome was born in Walsall at Belsize House in Bradford Street. You might recall that he wrote 'Three Men in a Boat'. The house is now a museum and is quite fascinating. He was not the only famous son. General Booth, founder of the Salvation Army, was also born in Walsall.

The Museum and Art Gallery is one of the finest in the Black Country, and has a Garman-Ryan collection of art treasures, comprising some three hundred and sixty drawings, paintings and sculptures chiefly of the late 19th and early 20th centuries. Like other towns, Walsall's industry benefited from the canals but they were allowed to fall by the wayside and it is only recently that restoration work has brought them back to regular use and the pleasure of visitors and townsfolk alike. The towpaths are popular as walking routes.

A good walk is along the **Hay Head Nature Trail** at Longwood Lane, two miles from the town centre. The trail follows the final stretch of the old Hay Head branch of the Wyrley and Essington Canal through an area rich in wildlife.

Walsall Leather Centre Museum was is a different experience. You realise how important leather has been to life in Britain. From jugs and bottles, bridles and saddles to forge bellows, musical instruments, luggage and clothing, leather has always been a vital material. We had no idea that today over a hundred and twenty five Walsall companies are still involved in the manufacture of leather products. In this museum you'll see how leather is prepared and worked. Original workshops re-create the conditions, the atmosphere and even the distinctive smell of Walsall's traditional trade. Every day there are live demonstrations, special displays and frequently trade exhibitions are held here as well. It is a vibrant place and what is more there is no charge to go in!

We had such an enlightening and interesting time in the Black Country that we hope we have whetted your appetite as we did our own. There is far more to this area than its label 'The Black Country' conjures up in the minds eye and its easy access via many major road networks make it an ideal area to visit for both daytrippers and the hardened tourist.

St. Peter's Church, Wolverhampton

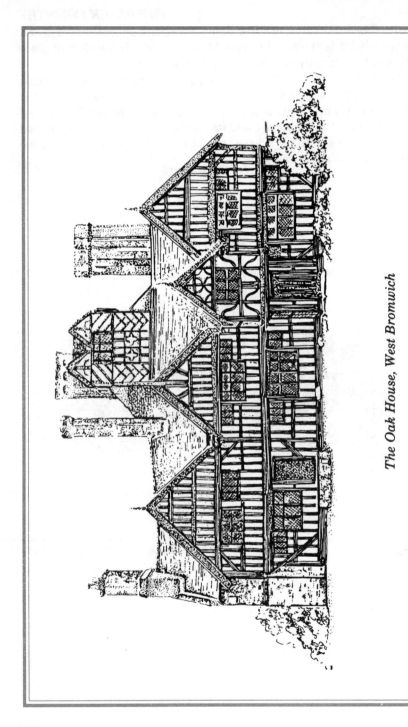

The Oak House, West Bromwich

CHAPTER FIVE

Birmingham To Coventry

Blakesley Hall

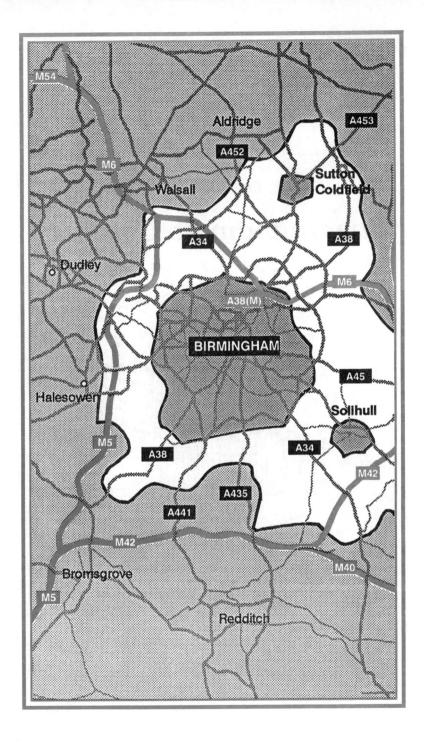

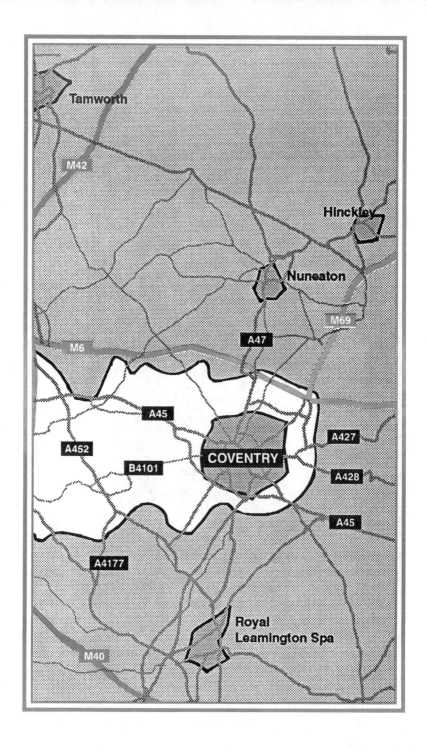

Narrowboats in Gas Street Basin. Birmingham.

CHAPTER FIVE

Birmingham To Coventry

A city a large as **Birmingham** would justify a book in itself but for obvious reasons we can only give you a 'taster' of this interesting city and its surrounding area which as the chapter titles indicates, includes Coventry.

The Domesday book tells us that in the survey of 1086, the hamlet of Birmingham was among the least prosperous manors in the area. As is often the case, geography played a large part in its later rise to prosperity, it was a dry site with a good supply of water and routes converged at Deritendford across the little River Rea. We know from our recently culled knowledge of the Black Country that there was easy access to coal, iron and timber.

Peter de Bermingham obtained rights of trading in a Market Charter granted by Henry ll in 1166 and in 1250 William de Bermingham was given permission to hold a four day fair at Whitsun.

By 1538 there were some fifteen hundred people in two hundred houses, one main street with a number of side streets, grain and livestock markets and mills for tanning. Already, the smiths were selling their knives and all manner of tools all over England. Lorimers and Nailers had joined the growing industry. This growth was helped by the demands of the Parliamentarians during the Civil War for pikes, swords and armour so Birmingham emerged with a strong reputation as a metal centre.

Less than two hundred years later the population had become twenty three thousand and by the 18th century during the Industrial Revolution, Birmingham had become the industrial, commercial and cultural Capital of the Midlands. This was largely due to the industrious

'Brummie' people and not much has changed in that direction today. Many more people of course, more nationalities and more industry make up the core of this humming city.

There have been many famous people over the centuries who have been able to call themselves Brummies. In the 14th century church at **Aston** there is an effigy to Ralph Arden, an early ancestor of Shakespeare, and a black marble and alabaster memorial to the 17th century knight, Sir Edward Devereux plus two unidentified armoured knights. In Birmingham's parish church of St Martins there are memorials to the two Lords of the Manor, the de Berminghams.

Whilst we are talking about churches do take a look at St Alphege in the Square at **Solihull**. This church was a favourite of John Constables who used to come here regularly to draw the enchanting window tracery, foliage and corbels in the 13th century chancel. The beautiful Chantry Chapel of St Alphege was built in 1277 by Sir William de Odingsells, who employed a priest to do nothing but pray for the souls of his parents. The priest lived on the job as it were, his home was the crypt below in which there was a fireplace installed to keep him warm. It must have been a daunting home. The church is open from 8am - 6pm Monday, Wednesday and Thursday and from 7am on Tuesday, Saturday and Sunday.

Just three miles to the north-east of Solihull is a lovely village in the heart of the ancient Forest of Arden. **Hampton -in- Arden** is said to have been the setting for Shakespeares 'As You Like It', something we could well believe as we wandered along the delightful streets taking in the pretty ornamented cottages and reaching our destination, the church of St Mary and St Bartholomew which graces the village. It has a perpendicular tower which until 1643 was topped by a spire. There is a Norman and 13th century nave and a Norman chancel. The chancel which is entered through an arch adorned with crockets and carved heads and has some medieval blue and white tiles in the floor. The icing on the cake here is the fine **Hampton Manor House** which has a most interesting pyramid clock tower.

You will find **Sarehole Mill**, inspiration for J.R.R.Tolkeins 'The Hobbit' and 'Lord of the Rings' about five miles south-east of the city centre and to get there we followed the Stratford Road (A34) to its junction with Cole Bank Road. We turned right into Cole Bank Road and continued over Sarehole Road. The Mill is on the right hand side and we found easy parking in the neighbouring recreation ground. The present buildings are mainly Georgian, having been rebuilt in the 1760's, and were in use, commercially, right up to 1919. The mill then fell into disrepair but was carefully restored to working order in the 1960's.

Visitors have the opportunity to see the interior ,and one of the two waterwheels is regularly operated, subject to the availability of water in the millpond. The process of corn grinding can be followed on all three floors of the mill, whilst in the adjoining building a reconstruction of a blade-grinding workshop showed us how the mill was partially converted to industrial use in the 18th century. The granary contains displays on local agriculture and rural life, illustrated by farm and craft tools, machinery and horse drawn vehicles. The engine house was added in the 1850's and contained a steam engine that supplemented the water power from the River Cole. The original engine was removed many years ago,but one of similar type was installed in the 1970's when the building was restored. A 19th century bakehouse faces the mill building across the yard a reminder that some of the flour produced at Sarehole was used by the miller.

For classical music lovers the **Birmingham Symphony Orchestra**, recognised as one of the front runners in the music world, often hold concerts in the classical Roman style **Town Hall** built by Joseph Hansom of the hansom cab and an E.Welch. Mendelssohn gave several organ recitals in here.

Sporting facilities are extremely good in Birmingham. The famous Belfry Golf Course is open to the public in Lichfield Road, Wishaw, near Sutton Coldfield attached to the Belfry Hotel which is a marvellous place to stay even if you are not a golfer. There are public squash courts at the Birmingham Squash Rackets Centre in Rotton Park, Edgbaston and at Wyndley Leisure Centre, Clifton Road, Sutton Coldfield to name but two. At Wyndley Leisure Centre there is swimming as well as many other sports activities. To get full details of these facilities do pick up one of the many guides that are available at the Tourist Centres. If you enjoy soccer then in the area Aston Villa, Birmingham City and of course not very far away Wolverhampton Wanderers, West Bromwich Albion and Walsall all provide opportunities to find a good match in the season.

There are no less than six thousand acres of parkland and open space in Birmingham and we are reliably informed that there are six million trees. The highlights are **Cannon Hill Park,** Edgbaston with eighty acres of flowers and ornamental gardens which are a joy to explore and the **Botanical Gardens** and glasshouses with an Aviary and tropical species thrown in for good measure. **The Nature Centre** with all its wildlife is a place of great interest,and at Edgbaston Reservoir there is every kind of water recreation you could wish for. County and Test Cricket is played at Edgbaston too, of course.

We haven't broached the question of shopping yet - the focus for

Birmingham Museum & Art Gallery

Botanical Gardens & Glasshouses.

the department stores is New Street, Corporation Street, The Bull Ring Shopping Centre and coming away from these areas are some very attractive Victorian arcades which house the smaller speciality shops. Birmingham traditionally is the centre of jewellery, indeed there is an 18th century church in St Paul's Square, from which it takes its name, known simply as The Jewellers Church. You will find jewellers still abound especially in the Hockley area. Gunsmiths are also to be found here, another craft for which Birmingham is renowned.

Poking around in indoor markets has long been a great pleasure to us and Birmingham is outstanding for this. It is a tradition that stems back to the first Market Charter some eight hundred years ago. You will find them close to St Martins church. The Rag Market is the place to spot a bargain whereas The Bull Ring Open Air Market and the Bull Ring Centre Market Hall deal in anything from food to household goods. Monday is the day to go looking for antiques in the Rag Market.

One would expect a city as flourishing as Birmingham to be a natural centre for Theatre and it is. **The Hippodrome** was once a music hall but it has become one of the leading opera houses in the country as well as a centre for musicals, international ballet and some wonderful pantomimes. The theatre has been restyled quite recently and without losing the magic of an old theatre it has become one of the best equipped anywhere.

More restyling and rebuilding has gone on to produce the **Birmingham Repertory Theatre** which has become celebrated for major musical shows, comedies, classics, Shakespearian and stage productions being tried out before their London runs. There is a smaller 'Studio Theatre' attached to it which pioneers new ideas in the theatre and encourages new writers. Touring companies bring classics and comedies and sometimes there are premieres of shows booked for the West End at the **Alexandra,** which is another great venue.

Once a year Birmingham has a **Jazz Festival** which attracts big name stars from the world of Jazz and there are never less than forty bands taking part. The weeks activities include over a hundred performances, many of them free, in pubs, clubs and hotels as well as open air concerts and street corner Jazz sessions.

It would be surprising if a city like Birmingham was not able to indulge anyone's interest in Art and Architecture. We found the 17th, 18th and 19th centuries represented in some super displays in the **Museum and Art Gallery** in Chamberlain Square, with one of the best collections outside London, including the world's finest examples of works by the Pre-Raphaelites. The contemporary art of sculpture has one of the best displays you can see. In fact there is costume,

101

silver, textiles and ceramics as well as works of Ethnography from around the world among which is a rare and very large copper Buddha from Sultangani.

In the City Centre your eyes will be drawn to the many murals on all sorts of subjects. In Colmore Circus the mural depicts a Civil War Battle,and another one of the Industrial Revolution. Holloway Circus has an enormous mural of 85'x 14' showing The Horse Fair of 1908.

When we looked up the facts we discovered that in spite of what seems a sparcity of old buildings there are some two thousand listed buildings, Elizabethan, Jacobean, Georgian, Victorian and more that have been beautifully restored. The 1879 built neo - Renaissance **Council House,** magnificently represents the achievements and successes of the city. Another colonnaded building is the **Curzon Street Goods Station** built in 1838 by Phillip Hardwick. Its Ionic portico seems to celebrate the wonder of the railways as they were then regarded then and which doesn't really say much about contemporary attitudes when you compare the building with the modern **New Street Station**.

It has been said that Birmingham has as many canals as Venice. some of the waterways have been neglected but if you ever want to get away from the bustle of the city, the **Gas Street Basin** is as good a place as any to start your escape. If you prefer a quiet stroll or even an energetic ramble, the towpaths are ideal. The Worcester and Birmingham Canal stretches to the south west from here and passes through the Norton Tunnel. You can also follow the path to the Worcester Bar, the centre of the English canal system. The canal heads north to Wolverhampton. The Birmingham and Fazeley Canal has thirteen locks that narrowboats have to pass through. There are many old buildings, locks, factories and cottages to see, as well as the plants and animals that live there. We watched several people just sitting behind an easel and either sketching or painting the very pleasant scenery.

The Cadbury World located in the heart of the famous **Bournville** factory, follows the story of chocolate, taking you through tropical rain forests to 16th century Spain and onto Georgian London before arriving at the beginning of the Cadbury story in Victorian Birmingham. When we enquired about it we were told that if we wanted to find out about the Milk Tray hero who is always taking incredible risks to please his love, or how Cream Eggs were made, then all the answers will be revealed at Cadbury World. Even the chance to sample the real thing from their own production line! Cadbury World is on the outskirts of Birmingham, close to the M5 and M42 and it is just as easy to get to by rail or bus. It is open every day except Christmas Day. If you want more details about visits then ring 0121-433-4334.

Blakesley Hall is about five miles from the city centre. You follow the Coventry road (A45) to the Swan roundabout at South Yardley and then take the A4040 Church Road northwards into Stoney Lane to Blakesley Road. Turn left into Blakesley Road and the Hall is on the right hand side. Birmingham Museum and Art Gallery own Blakesley Hall which is Birmingham's finest Elizabethan building. Built in 1590, the hall is an extremely attractive timber-framed farmhouse which has been carefully restored. Its rich decorative framing and jettied first and second floors reflect the wealth of its Elizabethan owner and builder, Richard Smallbroke, one of the leading merchants of the 16th century. A diminutive Long Gallery which is rare , survives, whilst in his bedroom the original wall paintings were uncovered in 1950. A more recent discovery is the original lavatory shaft beside the hall chimney!

You are able to imagine how the family lived there three hundred years ago. Some twelve of the rooms are furnished as they were in 1684 when an inventory of the house's contents was drawn up.

One special attraction is 'The Bailiff's Pots' from Temple Balsall, which represents probably the most important collection of early country pottery ever found. Excavated at Temple Balsall Old Hall, near Knowle, in 1981, the pots represent the discarded contents of the bailiff's household pottery and glassware, deposited in the cellar when his family moved house in 1741.

Having got to Blakesley Hall the next step was to explore the delightful **Old Yardley Village**, one of the city's outstanding conservation areas. It is within walking distance of Blakesley Hall and is truly remarkable with its medieval church and Trust School. Of particular note are the pretty Georgian cottages.

Aston Hall, just three miles from the centre of Birmingham, was one of the last great Jacobean country houses to be built in England. Like Hatfield House and Blickling Hall, it has a highly intricate plan and a dramatic skyline of turrets, gables and chimneys. It is also administered by Birmingham Museums and Art Gallery who have done much to make it such a memorable place to visit. The house was built between 1618 and 1635 by Sir Thomas Holte and remained the seat of the Holte family until it was sold in 1817. King Charles 1 came to Aston Hall in 1642 at the beginning of the Civil War, and it was later besieged and sacked by Parliamentarian soldiers. Much Jacobean decorative work of high quality, still survives, especially the moulded plasterwork. The house has the most wonderful staircase and long gallery.

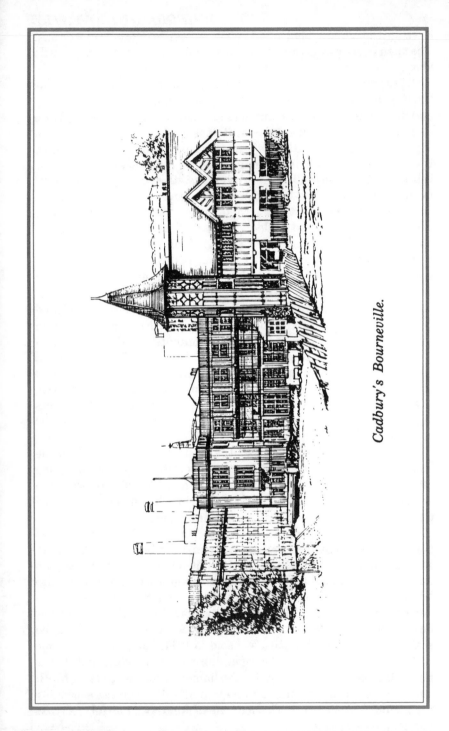

Cadbury's Bourneville.

Something totally different is a visit to **The National Motorcycle Museum** at **Bickenhill** which is opposite the National Exhibition Centre. It is a breathtaking collection of British motorcycles displayed in this purpose built complex. The purpose was to ensure that the sixty years of British motorcycle design and construction should not be lost to future generations. There are over seven hundred machines to see, each of which has been painstakingly restored to its original specification. Alongside the machines are a wealth of historic documentation and photographs, which certainly help visitors get the flavour of historic motorcycling. We got a great deal of fun out of this visit, not least from some of the odd names the motorcycles were given, like 'Slippery Sam', the winner of five production TT's on the Isle of Man. The complex has also been designed to provide seminar and conference facilities with the versatility to meet all types of business needs. Along with these facilities is some pretty high standard catering, you can dine sumptuously or merely have a snack.

While we are dealing with various forms of transport , an entertaining time can be had at **The Railway Museum** at **Tyseley.** You step back in time here to an era of fire-breathing steam locomotives, tiny tank engines, opulent Royal carriages and much more besides. On steam days, visitors can actually ride behind a steam engine. A special gallery allowed us to see the workshops where restoration and repair projects are taking place all the time. You really feel you are back in the old days and watching a traditional locomotive works. If you want further details write to the Museum at 670 Warwick Road, Tyseley, Birmingham, B11 2HL.

Going further south on the A41, **Solihull** is worth visiting. It began to grow in importance during the 1930's having been until then, a sparsely populated part of the country, today it is a Metropolitan Borough. Somehow the Industrial Revolution passed it by. Its motto ' Urbs in Rure' - Town in Country - is well deserved. The cottages and houses built in medieval times were characteristically attractive and blended well with the green vegetation which covers a large part of the region. As the number of buildings grew it still remained orderly and today the 17th and 18th century houses clearly demonstrate the good planning which has continued today.

Many historic buildings in the town have been carefully restored. Elizabethan **Grimshaw Hall** in **Knowle** is a fine example. **Chester House** is not far away and originally built in the mid-14th century it has been successfully refurbished and converted into a library offering a practical service to today's community. Another fine old house **Baddesley Clinton**, has been highly recommended for its excellent home-cooked food. This sounds as though it is just a good restaurant but that is not the case. It is another of the hidden gems

Blakesley Hall.

of the West Midlands. This romantic, medieval moated manor house is little changed since the 17th century. Set against the backdrop of the Forest of Arden, Baddesley has strong Catholic connections, shown in the house with a tiny chapel and secret priests' holes. Modern needs have not been neglected and there is an ice rink which is the second largest in the country.

Heading north you'll find by the M42 and A45, **The National Exhibition Centre**, now world famous so we do not intend to write about it but, what we would like to say is that Birmingham wants you to enjoy a visit to the full and to do so they have placed The Birmingham Convention and Visitor Bureau, which has a ticket shop and tourist information, right in the city centre and another one at the National Exhibition Centre. You will find, as we did, that the staff are friendly, helpful and knowledgeable. They will answer any questions and encourage you to visit the many wonderful places in the Big Heart of England. Stratford-upon-Avon, the Severn Valley, Warwick Castle and the Cotswold Hills are all within easy reach of the city. The Bureau will also book theatre and concert tickets for you and make hotel reservations.

Coventry is only thirty minutes away from Birmingham but it is a different world. Although on the fringe of the West Midlands conurbation, it is surrounded by some of the finest scenery and heritage in the country. It claims amongst many of its famous residents, George Eliot, who attended boarding school in Warwick Row and lived with her father between 1841 - 49 in Floeshill Road; more recently the controversial poet Philip Larkin was born in the city in 1922. Coventry is almost in the centre of England and lies at the heart of the national motorway network and on the main Inter-City rail route from the Midlands to London. It is only minutes away from **Birmingham International Airport** and also possesses its own local airport which caters for executive jet traffic. A busy place you may well say, this is true, but in amongst all the commerce are places and things of great beauty.

Standing in the ruins of the old 14th century **Coventry Cathedral**, destroyed by fire in the savage bombing of the city in World War II, can be a strange and moving experience. The altar is made of broken stones gathered from the night of horror on the 15th November 1940. It is surmounted by a cross of charred roof beams and a cross of medieval nails, behind which are inscribed the words from Calvary 'Father Forgive'.

The new Cathedral stands by its side and together they symbolise 'sacrifice and resurrection'. It is not only in the two cathedrals that Coventry has shown its indomitable spirit. It is hard to imagine that in the space of one night in November 1940 the city centre was

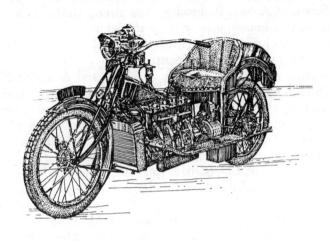

National Motor Cycle Museum, Nr Birmingham

Museum of British Road Transport, Coventry

gutted, forty six thousand homes severely damaged and nearly seventy five per cent of the industrial area was almost destroyed. The Cathedral Visitor Centre situated in the Undercroft is where you can see and hear 'The Spirit of Coventry', which tells the story of the historical events which took place in Coventry, including The Blitz and its aftermath and the cathedral's role in reconciliation world wide through the Community of the Cross of Nails. The Treasury in St Michael's Hall has many important exhibits and the Walkway of Holograms.

Whereas the magnificent Gothic tower of the old cathedral dominates, standing over three hundred feet, the new cathedral is dominated by Graham Sutherland's tapestry of Christ in Glory and John Piper's magnificent Bapistry window which beams a kaleidoscope of colours onto the nave as the sun passes over. Whatever one may think of the new, it works. The small chapels each have a dedicated purpose. The Chapel of Unity is where groups of different faiths meet, the Chapel of Gethsemane is an area for private prayer. The Chapel of Christ the Servant has become the Industrial Chapel.

The city's most famous legend tells of the story of **Lady Godiva** who rode the streets naked to reduce taxation on the 11th century town dwellers. A bronze statue in Broadgate has been erected to her memory. There are authorities however, who say that the famous ride never took place or that perhaps, she rode minus her jewels and was in that sense naked. Leofric should instead be praised, for it is he who started commerce and industry in Coventry as early as 1043, when he chose the small Saxon township as the site for a Benedictine monastery. He gave the monks land on which to raise sheep, laying the basis for the wool trade which made Coventry prosperous for over five hundred years. The story has it though, that this hard hearted man taxed the people too heavily and Godiva begged him to lessen the burden. She apparently took the precaution of sending her messengers to ask everyone to stay indoors behind closed shutters before she rode forth. Peeping Tom disregarded the request and was struck blind - or so legend would have you believe. The Earl, duly chastened, relented, the taxes were cut and no doubt Leofric and Godiva were reconciled. If you look at the clock in the arch over Hertford Street you will see the figures of Godiva and Tom re-enacting the legend hourly.

There are still many old buildings in this very new city; **Bond's Hospital** and **Ford's Hospital** are delightful half-timbered Tudor almshouses, still very much in use, while Bayley Lane and Hay Lane are places of peace and tranquillity reminding us of the illustrious past. A medieval cul-de-sac has been created in Spon Street, some of the buildings have been re-sited from other parts of the city.

Baddesley Clinton.

Coventry Cathedral

Medieval shops, taverns and dwellings abound in this living heritage of Coventry.

Across in New Union Street you'll find **Cheylesmore Manor House,** a half timbered building that was once owned by the Black Prince. Close by at Whitefriars Gate, the **Toy Museum,** has a collection of toys dating from the mid 18th century. Nearby on London Road stands **Whitefriars,** a renovated Carmelite friary dating from the 1342. Exhibitions of art, theatre and concerts are put on in this attractive building. Back in towards the centre and close to the cathedral is the **Herbert Art Gallery and Museum,** in Jordan Well. The ground floor has natural history displays, social history,which includes the story of Coventry and reconstructed rooms showing weaving or other skills that became associated with the city. Upstairs the galleries have 18th century furniture,silver and art that includes a collection of Graham Sutherlands sketches for the tapestry in the cathedral.

In Bayley Lane is **St Mary's Guildhall** where Kings and Queens have been entertained and Mayors appointed to their office since the 14th century. The medieval Guildhall contains a splendour of old glass, a wealth of carving and a delightful minstrels' gallery with the additional bonus of a unique tapestry. This is one of England's finest guildhalls dating back to 1342. Here we saw the Arras tapestry, the breathtaking Great North Window, the oak ceiling and many suits of medieval armour. It really is a stunning place and open daily from Easter to October with guided tours available.

Over the next two hundred years, clockmaking and silk weaving became Coventry's main industries but in the 19th century the French started exporting silks and the Swiss, clocks, which brought about a rapid slump. Faced with unemployment many families emigrated to America leaving behind those who were not adventurous enough or who had the wit to see that other industries could make them prosper once again.

Cycle making and engineering started the new wave of prosperity and by 1896 Daimler and Humber had opened the city's first car factories. It was not long before they were joined by other companies and Coventry became a magnet for labour from all over Britain. It was the city's skills in engineering that brought it to the attention of the German bombers during World War 11. Today the city is one of the most up to date of our industrial cities and now boasts the fastest growing Science Park in the U.K., based at Warwick University and potentially the finest Business Park in the country.

The Museum of British Road Transport is in Hales Street just a few minutes walk from the Cathedral and Shopping Precinct.

It is an excellent museum and houses a collection of transport

Fords Hospital. Coventry.

Coombe Abbey.

which portrays the enormous contribution made by Coventry to the transport industry. There are more than four hundred exhibits on show including bicycles, motor cycles, commercial vehicles and numerous makes of cars.

'Memory Lanes' is an exhibition concept which recreates the atmosphere of the formative years of motoring history. The 'Street Scene' presentation brings together the pioneering 'horseless carriages', the elegant Edwardians and those cars from the Golden Age of Motoring, the 1920's. Just by passing through doors and archways the whole development of the motor car unfolds before you.

The museum's collection of cycles now numbers over two hundred machines and includes all of the important machines from the original Hobby Horses right through to the B.M.X. of today. It has a rightful claim to be the finest technical collection of cycles in Western Europe. The creative display includes photographs, costume and period artefacts presenting the history of cycling as it has progressed through the ages.

Here too there is an exhibition called 'Royalty on the Road' with Queen Mary's 1935 Limousine and the King George V1 1947 State Landaulette which form the centre-pieces of a special exhibition showing the Royal family's contribution to the British motor car industry. The extensive photographic gallery includes copies of pictures from the Royal Archives, all in situations connected with road transport. The museum also contains Monty's Humber Car which he used when entering Berlin and an interesting display of the Coventry Blitz.

Coventry has places for theatre lovers too; **The Belgrade Theatre** (01203 225834), in Corporation Street was the first Civic theatre opened after the war and has a busy programme of plays and concerts to meet the needs of theatre lovers. Alternatively, the **University Arts Theatre** (01203 524524), four miles out of town in the University of Warwick has constantly changing attractions that also includes a film theatre. Tourist Information will, naturally, have details of the programmes on offer during your visit.

If you enjoy the fun of a medieval banquet or have never experienced one then do go to **Coombe Abbey** which stands in magnificent grounds which are part of a country park landscaped by Capability Brown. It is a wonderfully romantic spot. Only a few parts of the original monastery remain but its history goes back to 1150 when the land was given to the Cistercian Monks by Roger de Mowbray. Over the years the Abbey has been associated with the Wars of the Roses, Lady Jane Grey, the Gunpowder Plot and the

English Civil War. The monastery was dissolved in 1539 and was eventually sold to the Craven family who owned it until 1922.

So it is in this historic setting that the Baron and Baroness invite you to join them in the romantic candlelit splendour of the ancient Abbey.   You will be welcomed and attended by the gracious and talented ladies of the Court in their colourful medieval gowns, and served with Lindisfarne mead, wine and succulent dishes.   Once replete you will then be regaled with traditional medieval entertainment which is part of the evening too, presented by accomplished performers.To take part just ring Coventry (01203) 452406. To get there is not difficult either. The entrance to Coombe Abbey is through Coombe Country Park on the A427 Coventry to Lutterworth road or from the M6 (Exit 2) take the A46 Coventry road and turn on to the A4082 (signposted Coombe Abbey).

If you want to take a trip to Coombe Park in the daytime you will find it is delightful with three hundred acres of formal gardens, woodland nature trails, angling and paddle-boating for the children. There is also Birdland with its innumerable highly coloured birds of all sorts and sizes.

Coventry provided moments of sheer delight which was contrary to what we had expected. Being city dwellers sometimes makes you blind to the beauty and attraction of other large urban areas. Besides all that, Coventry and Birmingham are excellent bases for the very many wonderful places around them, more of which we shall reveal in the following chapters.

CHAPTER SIX

Shakespeare Country

Anne Hathaway's Cottage

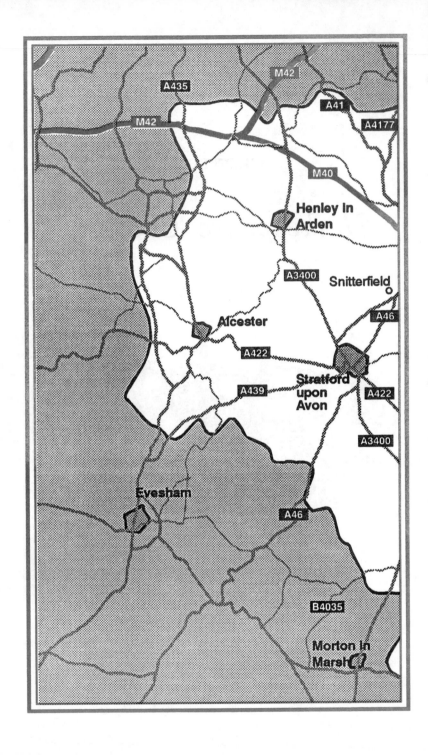

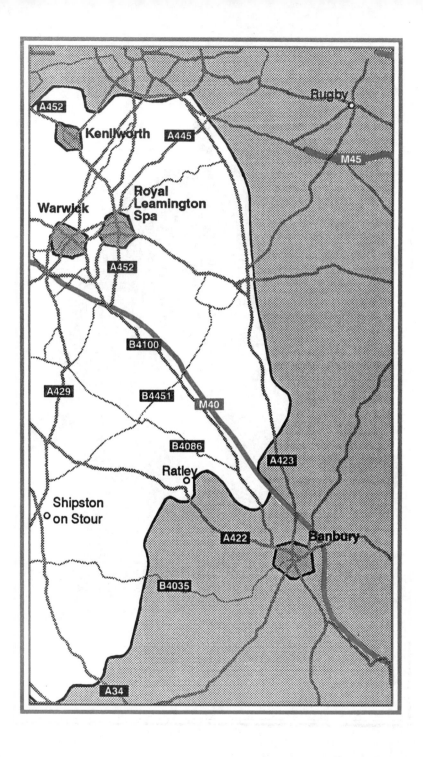

William Shakespeare.

CHAPTER SIX

Shakespeare Country.

When you think of England, and the very best of England, you might well be thinking about leafy Warwickshire, Shakespeare's country. The areas attractions draws an influx of tourists from all over the world. The county has much to offer with delightful contrasts from the rich vein of Tudor history at the heart of Warwickshire to **Royal Leamington Spa,** an elegant 18th century Regency town with wide tree-lined streets, imposing terraces and beautiful gardens. To the North, **Nuneaton** offers fascinating historical associations with George Eliot, one of England's greatest novelists. **Rugby** home of the famous public school which introduced the game Rugby is also close by. As if this were not enough, there is a great Palladian stately home at **Ragley,** the romantic ruins of **Kenilworth Castle**, **Warwick Castle** and a wealth of beautiful National Trust properties. Set in the geographical Heart of England there is easy access by the motorway network. Once off the high speed roads, experience a change of pace and explore the timeless qualities of the real England.

The Warwickshire heritage spans many generations and the Bronze Age King Stone standing on the high ground above Long Compton is one of the few surviving features of pre-history in the county, but when we come to Roman times remains are more plentiful. The final battle between the Roman Army and British troops led by Queen Boadicea in AD 60 took place at **Mancetter** and there are other Roman settlements at **Alcester, Chesterton** and **Tiddington**. There is little on these sites for visitors to see but at **Baginton**, a substantial part of the first century AD fort, known as **The Lunt** has been dramatically reconstructed. The Norman Conquest saw the establishment of Warwick Castle as a royal stronghold. In order to keep the local population under control, a number of smaller castles were also erected and a fine example can still be seen at **Brinklow**. The county has seen the hatching and subsequent discovery of the

Gunpowder Plot of 1605 and the first major battle of the Civil War was at **Edgehill** in 1645.

After the Commonwealth, when Oliver Cromwell ruled England as Lord Protector, there was a period of relative prosperity. Country houses such as **Ragley, Farnborough, Upton** and **Compton Verney** were built or extended, symbols of good taste, power and wealth. The 18th century saw the re-design of country estates, including Capability Brown's work at Warwick Castle, Charlecote, Ragley and elsewhere. At the close of the century Leamington Priors began to develop as a spa. At the other end of the social scale, Joseph Arch was born in 1826 at **Barford**. A pioneer of the farm workers union movement and later an MP, the Joseph Arch Inn at Barford must be one of the few pubs in England to be named after a trade union leader.

Even people living in Warwickshire may not be aware of the history they drive over; the hump back bridge can hide an altogether different world when seen from below. Waterways form an important and extensive part of the two thousand miles of Britains inland network. The Oxford and Grand Union Canals pass through the county as do restored lengths of the Stratford canal and the upper Avon.

We decided to start our tour of Warwickshire at the most obvious place, **Stratford-upon-Avon.** We found it difficult to know where to begin when attempting to describe all the many attractions on offer and although this is Britain's biggest tourist centre after London, they arrive because of one man, **William Shakespeare**. He was born here, found fame in London and retired here to die in 1616, some 500,000 visit Shakespeares birthplace alone. There has been interest in him ever since, and this ancient, prosperous town has been a backcloth to his genius and his life.

A short walk along Meer Street brought us to the very centre of the Shakespeare cult - his **Birthplace** in Henley Street. The two timber framed buildings consist a museum in the east half and the west half is furnished in the style of a 16th century home.

On High Street you'll find **Harvard House**, dating from 1596, this is where John Harvard's mother, Katherine Rogers, spent her childhood. The building was restored and presented to Harvard University in 1909. Further along on Chapel Street stands, New Place and **Nash's House.** This half-timbered building was inherited by Shakespeare's granddaughter, Elizabeth Hall, from her first husband, Thomas Nash. It now contains a museum of local history. By it you'll find the gardens on the foundations of New Place, the house that Shakespeare bought and retired to in 1611. The house was torn down by Reverend Francis Gatrell in 1759 after a dispute over rates with the Corporation. On the corner opposite is the **Guild Chapel** and

Harvard House.

Nash House & New Place Museum

121

beyond is the **Grammar School** where it is believed that Shakespeare was educated.

In fact you will not regret a visit to any of the fascinating old buildings in Stratford. The old market site in Rother Street has a history dating from 1196, when a weekly market was granted by King John. In the square is an ornate fountain-cum-clock tower, a gift from one G.W. Childs from Philadelphia in the jubilee year of Queen Victoria. It was unveiled by the famous actor Henry Irving who, when knighted in 1895, became the first ever "Sir of the Stage". Stratford has become the mecca of the theatre lover and they flock to enjoy an evening at one of the three theatres. On the walls of a pub called "The Dirty Duck" is a gallery of glossy signed photographs of familiar faces. These are of some of the actors and actresses who have appeared at the Royal Shakespeare Theatre just across the road, and popped in for a drink there. This attractive pub with its famous customers sums up Stratford, it manages to go about its busy life with thousands of visitors arriving from all over the world each year. The first celebration was organised by the actor David Garrick (of Garrick Theatre fame) one hundred and fifty years after his death, and people have been celebrating ever since. When the first Shakespeare theatre was burned down, George Bernard Shaw sent a one word telegram - Congratulations! Apparently the building was very ugly, but there are few such buildings in Stratford. Even the Marks and Spencers has the facade of a coaching inn with colonnaded entrances that once belonged to the Washington Irving Hotel.

The site of 17/18 High Street was once owned by the Guild of the Holy Cross and has seen much history from its early days as an Elizabethan town house to its present usage as the high class **Marlowe's Restaurant and Georgie's Bistro.** The 18th century saw the first use of the premises as an inn and in later years Marlowe's began its long association with the Royal Shakespeare Theatre as it was once the home of Denne Gilkes, a famous opera singer and actress who ran an actors' school in some of the rooms. Through the doors have passed may famous actors: Paul Schofield, Anthony Quayle, Vanessa Redgrave, Sir John Gielgud, Sir Alec Guiness, Sir Ralph Richardson and many others whose auto-graphed pictures now hang in the bar.

Entry to the restaurant is via a narrow alley off the High Street and up a flight of stairs. Here you will find a central patio area and to the left Marlowe's Restaurant, and to the right, Georgie's Bistro. Marlowe's is a silver service restaurant with a classy and intimate atmosphere. Meals are served in a grand dining room with open fires and wooden panelled walls. The excellent cuisine is deliciously varied and can be accompanied by wine from the extensive wine list. Bookings are essential for pre-theatre dinners and at weekends.

Georgie's Bistro, is a little more informal offering a menu that changes daily, and although the food is of the same excellent standard as that of the main restaurant, the dishes are less exotic and more competitively priced. Georgie's is open for lunch and in the evening, while Marlowe's is open in the evenings only (except Sunday when it is open for lunch).

Marlowe's Restaurant and Georgie's Bistro, 18 High Street, Strat-ford-upon-Avon Tel: 01789 204999

Also on the High Street, you will come across the delightful **Hathaway Tea Rooms and Bakery**. A building once stood here in the 1300s but apparently it burned down - the present building dates from 1610 and is typically Jacobean in appearance. The owner is Bill Gates who, with his son Paul, has built up a thriving and successful business. The tea rooms are open for morning coffee through the day to afternoon tea, with lunches on offer in between. The menu is varied and the food delicious, all having been made on the premises. Most items can also be purchased from the shop downstairs. This excellent food, combined with quality of service makes this a very special place.

Hathaway Tea Rooms and Bakery, 19 High Street, Stratford upon Avon, Tel: 01789 292404

Guild Chapel.

Anne Hathaway's Cottage

The Royal Shakespeare Company has a marvellous reputation both in the UK and abroad. To see Shakespeare performed at the Royal Shakespeare Theatre is quite possibly every theatre lovers dream. Perhaps Stratford has something just little more special in atmosphere than say ,the Barbican in London. However, wherever you see the RSC perform you are certain of witnessing performances of a high standard.

The company has operated in its present manner since 1961, but the history of Stratford and theatres goes beyond that. The first permanent theatre was built as a result of local brewer, Charles Edward Flower, who gave a two acre site on which to build a theatre in Shakespeares birthplace in 1875 and then launched an appeal for funds.

This theatre opened in 1879 with a performance of ' Much Ado about Nothing'. starring Ellen Terry and Beerbohm Tree. The season was limited to one week as part of the summer festival. It was so successful that under the direction of F.R. Benson it grew to spring and summer seasons and toured Britain in between. In 1925,because of the excellence of the performances and direction, the company was granted a Royal Charter. Sadly, a year later the theatre perished in a fire. The company, not deterred, continued by giving performances in cinemas whilst a worldwide campaign was launched to build a new theatre, which was opened on April 23rd, 1932, traditionally thought of as the Bards birthday.

A theatre tour gives you the opportunity to discover what's goes on behind the curtains. The itinerary for the tours vary according to rehearsal schedules and the incidence of technical work on stage but they are great value and usually include the RSC collection as well as both the Royal Shakespeare and Swan Theatre. Weekdays the tour times are 1.30pm and 5.30pm excluding matinee days and on Sundays at 12.30pm. 2.15pm, 3.15pm, and 4.15pm with just a slight variation from November to March when first tours start at 11.30am. The tours takes around 45 minutes. You can book by calling 01789 296655 or writing to the RSC.

The RSC collection has over a thousand items on view. The costumes, props, pictures and sound recording which illustrate changes in staging from medieval times to the present and compares past productions with the current season's plays. You can spend a fascinating time in the souvenir shop.

Disabled people have also been included in the lay out with front row seats for the disabled .There is also an audio frequency induction loop system in the theatres for the hard of hearing. Special parking spots are reserved for disabled drivers but it is advisable to inform the Booking Office as early as possible.

One of Stratford's finest inns, **The White Swan**, is also one of the town's oldest buildings still in use as an inn and dates from the early 15th century. Since these early beginnings little has changed about the building's appearance. The gabled medieval front remains, while the beautiful wall paintings in the lounge date from 1550. The paintings are very well-preserved having not been uncovered until earlier this century. The cosy bar area, popular with locals, features exposed beams and ancient wooden panelled walls. It makes the perfect setting for sampling a pint of local ale prior to enjoying a hearty meal in the restaurant where distinctive local specialities are served. The evening table d'hôte menu changes daily and features fresh local produce while the lounge menu, which is à la carte, changes weekly and offers a good variety of interesting dishes.

Although very historic and full of charm, the bedrooms have every modern convenience the visitor could require. All 37 rooms are en-suite and have a drinks tray, telephone and television. The White Swan can be easily found on Rother Street in the centre of Stratford.

The White Swan, Rother Street, Stratford-upon-Avon Tel: 01789 297022 Fax: 01789 268773

Holy Trinity Church, an inspiration for many poets because of its beautiful setting beside the Avon, is where Shakespeare is buried. Dating partly from the 13th century it is approached down an avenue of limes and the north door has a sanctuary knocker that, in the past, allowed any fugitive who reached it, thirty seven days grace. Anne Hathaway, their daughter Susanna and her husband are also buried here. The tomb of the great man himself carries a warning inscription:

> *Good friend for Jesus sake, forbeare*
> To digg the dust enclosed heare;
> Blese be ye man yt spares these stones
> *And curst be he yt moves my bones.*

Bancroft Gardens near to the fourteen arch Clopton Bridge is but a short walk from the centre of Stratford. This delightful leisure area contains the great Shakespeare Memorial which was designed by Lord Ronald Gower and built in Paris. The work took twelve years to complete and was finally presented to the town in 1888.

Only a few yards away is a preserved industrial tram, employed on the horse-drawn tramway connecting wharfs in Stratford with those in Shipston-on-Stour and Moreton-in-the-Marsh in Gloucestershire. The canal was completed in 1816 but fell into disuse with the advance of the railways.

South of Stratford is the village of **Alderminster**. Here, for a complete change - you could try out the 19th century Hayloft at **Bridge House;** it forms part of the splendid accommodation offered by Jane and Richard in their wonderful Georgian country home. It is to be found in the small village of Alderminster which has its origins in the 6th century. The house has uninterrupted views to the rear, across open countryside and nearby riverside walks along the River Stour. The rooms are very tastefully furnished where it is evident a lot of thought and care has been taken to create a high standard. Set your alarm clock early to cope with Jane's wonderful breakfast and if you feel the need, packed lunches and flasks can be provided.

Bridge House, Alderminster, Nr. Stratford upon Avon.Tel: 01789 450521

About a mile from Stratford in the village of **Shottery**, the birthplace of Shakespeare's wife you'll find the Elizabethan farmhouse, **Anne Hathaway's Cottage**. Incidentally Anne and William were married in 1582. We found it a delightful, though a popular spot and is everyone's imagined perfect thatched cottage. Hathaways have lived here since the 15th century until less than seventy years ago when the Shakespeare Trust decided it was time to allow public access.

The other notable house connected with the poet is his mother, **Mary Arden's House** in **Wilmcote,** about three miles from Stratford. This Tudor farmhouse is most impressive, but this maybe because it is slightly off the beaten track and doesn't attract the thousands of visitors which flock to some of the other attractions. There are guided tours available and a museum of farming and rural life. Notice particularly the bread oven doors, made of bog oak, which never burn and are only seen very rarely now in England. Perhaps, best of all though is the dovecote. Robert Arden, being lord of the manor, was the only man in the village allowed to have one. It has over six hundred pigeon holes and at nesting time would house about three thousand birds.

It is one of the few small villages left to retain its Victorian Gothic railway station. Alongside the railway runs the Stratford Canal. After years of neglect it has been taken over by the British Waterways and now carries many holiday boats on their way to join the Avon.

At the nearby junction of the A46 & A3400, lies the village of Bishopton and **Burton Farm.** Here, in contrast to the busy centre of Stratford upon Avon, is an opportunity to relax in a most peaceful rural .setting. The Farmhouse and barns dating back to Tudor Times, are set within a 150 acre corn, sheep and beef farm. In this lovely setting can normally be found, colourful gardens, and pools which support wildlife and a collection of birds and rare plants. Although Tony and Eileen have worked at their farm for twenty years, they opened their home to offer bed and breakfast accommodation a year ago. As you might expect, the interior offers plenty of character with old beams and flagstone floors. The accommodation is split between the house and converted outbuildings, all with immaculate en-suite facilities. Expect a lovely family atmosphere here and the wonderful customary farmhouse breakfast which you may struggle to finish.

Burton Farm, Bishopton, Stratford-upon-Avon. Tel: 01789 293338.
Also near to Stratford and worthy of an excursion is the village of **Alcester,** an ancient Roman town. Heading towards Alcester on the main A46 you will pass throught the village of **Redhill** where you will

find **The Stag at Redhill** .Present owners, John and Rosie Hunt came here only three years ago when the establishment was on its last legs and each year they have gradually refurbished and extended the property resulting in the outstanding condition that you will find it in today. Dating back to the 16th century the building was formerly a coaching inn. The entrance to The Stag is through a pretty pagoda with patio areas to each side.

The whole place is as pretty as a picture and the bar areas are full of character having unusual murals on nearly all the walls. The restaurant area has been created out of what was the archway through which carriages would have passed. Adjacent to this is a medieval banqueting suite which was, in days gone by, used by visiting circuit judges. Also at this time there were cells at the rear of the room and above the staircase, two of the original windows can still be seen. Prisoners that were found guilty would have been hanged nearby.

The menus here are really outstanding and the food is delicious, accompanied by well-kept ales to quench your thirst. The restaurant seats 70 people and it is advisable to book at weekends. A range of bar snacks and the specials board are available daily. There are eleven en-suite letting rooms which are all cosy and have lots of extra facilities. A comfortable residents' lounge features flagstone floors and exposed beams. The Stag is ideally situated to use as a base for visiting Stratford and touring the surrounding area. Excellent in every department and a credit to its owners

The Stag at Redhill, Alcester Road, Redhill, Nr. Stratford.Tel: 01789 764 634

South of the A46 where there is a marked trail through the woods at Oversley is **Exhall,** recorded in the Domesday Book, but its history probably goes back to Roman times as Roman coins have been found in a garden in the village. The architecture is varied, reflecting the history and development from Elizabethan to modern times. There are some interesting black and white half-timbered buildings and a farmhouse dating back to the 16th century. Most of the houses stand on steep banks on each side of the road and this adds much to the picturesque quality of the village. The parish church of St. Giles has a fine Norman door and the views from the churchyard are beautiful.

Whilst in the Alcester area we suggest a visit to **Ragley Hall**, a 17th century house with a magnificent great hall by James Gibbs. This is one of England's great Palladian country houses. The perfect symmetry of its architecture remains unchanged except for the massive portico added in 1780. The present owner, the eighth Marquis of Hertford inherited Ragley in 1940 when he was only nine. During the second world war the house was used as a hospital, and thereafter became almost completely derelict. In 1956 the Marquis married and he and his new wife set about making the Hall their home. All the main rooms have been redecorated in colours similar to the original ones and the process of restoring and improving seems to be forever ongoing.

The main formal garden, to the west of the hall, descends in a series of wide terraces, now entirely occupied by roses. The rest of the garden, covering twenty four acres, consists of shrubs and trees interspersed with spacious lawns providing vistas across the four hundred acre park. The lake, created in 1625, is now used for fishing, sailing, swimming and water skiing and the cricket pitch is in regular use. There is also a country trail of about two miles through the park and the woods ending at the very popular Adventure Playground.

The magnificent, black and white, **Broom Hall Inn and Restaurant** can be found in the village of Broom, just off the B4085 and only 10 minutes from Alcester. Dating back in its oldest parts to

1577, the hall was formerly a farmhouse, a youth hostel only in later years becoming an inn. The characterful interior retains an olde worlde atmosphere and is very stylish. The inn is renowned for its cask and real ales and people travel from far and wide to sample the traditional pub food. The bar menu alone offers over seventy dishes, and is available all day. There is a separate Restaurant which offers its own à la carte menu and a carvery, featuring Aberdeen Angus Beef. There are twelve en-suite rooms available for bed and breakfast accommodation - very convenient as you will probably find it hard to drag yourself away.

Broom Hall Inn and Restaurant, Broom, Nr. Alcester, Warwickshire Tel: 01789 773757.

Cutting across country we came to **Welford -on- Avon,** an attractive half timbered village with some outstanding houses and a maypole standing on the village green. If you are looking for somewhere to stay ,**One Acre**, is a real find. This is the home of Ken and Tina Clifton, a delightful couple, who personally run this bed and breakfast. A long drive leads to the house which has attractive cottage gardens to the front. The facilities of the establishment are excellent - to the rear of the house there is even a heated indoor swimming pool. There are three comfortable and cosy bedrooms , all non-smoking. Both Ken and Tina are qualified chefs and, as you would imagine, the breakfasts and evening meals are a real highlight of any stay.

One Acre, Barton Road, Welford-on-Avon,. Tel: 01789 750477

Further on we came to the village of **Long Marston.** Charles II stayed at a house here after his flight from the Battle of Worcester. The 14th century church has a half timbered turret and porch. **The King's Lodge** in Long Marston was once the Manor House of

Ragley Hall, Nr Alcester

this small, pretty village. It was purchased in 1577 by two yeomen, John Tomes and John Kecke, and remained the home of the Tomes family until its sale in 1976. Set in over 4 acres of gardens, the Lodge is an ideal centre for touring the Heart of England.

Having bought the property 20 years ago, George and Angela Jenkins fell in love with it and have enjoyed sharing their home with guests ever since. Although much has changed about the house since its early beginnings, its rugged charm and splendour remains. The rooms are all beautifully furnished and decorated and are very stylish. There are only three bedrooms available in the main house - one with a four poster bed, one a twin and the other having en-suite facilities. In a wing of the house there are now two self-catering apartments - Oxford, sleeping four people and Worcester sleeping six. Queen's Cottage, sleeping two, was converted from a semi-derelict barn and is adjacent to the main house.

King's Lodge, Long Marston, Stratford-on-Avon, Tel: 01789 720705

Across the B4632 and you'll pass **Meon Hill,** where are Iron Age Fort stood dominating the valley. Further along the road you'll come to **Ilmington,** at the foot of the Ilmington Downs; the north eastern Cotswolds. This village is eye catching with its old houses and church which inside has oak furnishings by Robert Thompson from Yorkshire which you pass through a 16th Norman arch to view.This is truly a 'hidden place', and certainly one of the most picturesque one could ever wish to find. Lying in the valley between the Campden and Foxcote hills, it is surrounded by green fields and Cotswold countryside. Here there are fine old stone cottages with roses around the doors, and gardens full of colour .

Ilmington, its name means "the elm grown hill", has only six hundred inhabitants. It was made famous on Christmas Day 1934, when the first radio broadcast by George V was introduced by Walton

Handy, the village shepherd and relayed to the world from **Ilmington Manor,** a fine Elizabethan house once owned by the De Montfort family. The remains of a tramway, once the main form of transport to the village, can still be seen. The nearby Ilmington Downs are at 850 feet, the highest point in the county and command fine views of the surrounding country.

Back on the A34 you'll find **Newbold-on-Stour**, and the **White Hart Inn** a good spot to aim for food and drink. You will find it on the main road. This historic Inn established around 1740, was originally farm workers cottages and retains many interesting features. A well established business whose owner is the Chef, offers special 'dishes of the day' and an extensive general menu of good wholesome food served in the comfortable restaurant; bar snacks are also on offer for those looking for a quick snack. Bookings are recommended at weekends. A good selection of first class ales along with a warm welcome awaits you.

The White Hart Inn, Newbold-on-Stour, Nr. Stratford-upon-Avon. Tel: 01789 450205

The A3400 crosses the old Fosse Way to the south , and by turning left you will very soon arrive at **Halford** and the historic **Halford Bridge Inn**, a lovely 16th-century coaching inn. Formerly known as the Bell, it is mentioned in many old documents 'where legal business was performed.' While retaining many old features, the Inn now offers accommodation and food to the traveller in comfortable surroundings. The old carriage entrance to the rear has been enclosed to make an attractive feature of the Inn. There are six comfortable letting bedrooms most with private facilities. A great choice of food is always on offer at the bar or in the lovely old beamed restaurant. Greta and Tony have between them 60 years experience in this business and so it's not surprising they are featured with the tourist board and in many guides. Certainly an ideal stopping point on your journey.

Halford Bridge Inn, Fosse Way, Halford, Shipston on Stour. Tel: 01789 740382.

Further south along the A3400 approaching **Shipston -on- Stour** stands **Honington Hall,** an interesting building reflecting the tastes of the late 17th and 18th century. There is limited opening for the house but you might be pleasantly surprised should you visit this delightful house. Situated in the heart of Shipston-on-Stour, is the magnificent **Horseshoe Inn**. This characterful establishment, a former coaching inn, dates back to the early 18th century although a building has been on the site since the late 17th century.
Inside you will find and warm, welcoming atmosphere and olde worlde, traditional decor. One of the many features to be admired is the outstanding collection of framed bank notes from around the world. Roger and Shirley Figures, the owners, came here six years ago and have worked hard to create the successful business you will find today. The inn boasts a delicious and varied menu supplemented by daily blackboard specials. The inn can seat up to 55 people comfortably so there is no need to book ahead. Add to this the fine array of excellent well-kept ales - what more could you wish for. There is more however, with bed and breakfast accommodation available in three cosy letting rooms. To the rear of the inn is a courtyard with seating and there is private car parking to the rear.

The Horseshoe Inn, Shipston-on-Stour. Tel: 01608 661225
Further down the A3400 and a short distance from the Oxfordshire
border is the village of **Long Compton,** close to which is a local
beauty spot at Whichford Wood . In the village itself you will find
The Red Lion Inn which dates from the 16th century and retains
all its olde worlde charm with open fireplaces and cosy corners, yet
offering all the modern facilities one would expect from such a
hostelry. The bar has a warm inviting atmosphere with exposed
stone walls and old oak beams. On offer is a fine selection of wines,
spirits and ales, and an excellent variety of quality bar food available at lunch times and evenings, seven days a week. In summer
months, the large attractive garden is ideal for alfresco drinking
and dining. Diners can relax in the intimate atmosphere of the
restaurant and enjoy a splendid candlelit dinner chosen from the
extensive à la carte menu. Jenny Parkin the resident proprietor
takes great care to provide all guests with a personal and friendly
service. The five bedrooms have recently been refurbished and
individually designed to give the comfort and facilities required by
the most discerning of guests.

The Red Lion Hotel, Long Compton, Nr. Shipston-on-Stour. Tel: 01608 684221

From Long Compton the back roads take you north away from the border through the little villages of Cherington and Stourton until you reach the B4035 near **Lower Brailes**. Here you will find **The George Hotel** which dates back to 1350, built, it is believed, to house the masons who built nearby St George's Church. During later years, in the days of the Royal Mail coaches, The George became a celebrated Coaching Inn.

Entering the George Hotel today is like stepping back in time to those early days. Owners Jane and Peter Brown came here only three years ago but together have more than 30 years in the licensing trade. They have carried out many alterations to the building but these have all been made sympathetically and in keeping with the original character. The main dining area features a magnificent fireplace which was only uncovered during recent renovations - carefully restored, it now serves as a focal point. This area is partly flagstoned and it is still possible to see the grooves where hob-nailed boots have left their mark. There is a lounge bar and public bar, both warm and cosy and with a welcoming atmosphere. Behind the hotel there is a very attractive garden, created mainly by Jane. It is a real old-fashioned cottage garden - well-stocked and lovingly tended.

Visitors to the George will find a good variety of home-cooked food all reasonably priced and served in good sized portions. To complement your meal there is also a fine array of real ales. Add to this the comfortable and cosy letting rooms and you have a first class inn.

Gatehouse at Charlecote.

The George Hotel, Lr Brailes, Nr. Banbury Tel/Fax: 01608 685223.

There is a surprising amount of interest around this area and a short distance to the North is the outstanding manor at **Compton Wynyates.** The estate has been in the hands of the same family since the 13th century , but it was Sir William Compton who built this magnificent manor as fine an example of Tudor redbrick construction as you will find. North of here and set just off the main A422, between Stratford and Banbury, within 100 acres of farmland and surrounded by beautiful countryside, is the impressive **Nolands Farm.** The outbuildings of the farm, which date back to 1870, have been carefully and sympathetically converted and enclose a courtyard which was once a stable yard. A magnificent building with letting rooms was built by owner Robin Hutsby six years ago and has real charm and character, being very cosy. All the letting rooms are of an excellent quality and all have en-suite facilities. There are also four poster bedrooms. The grounds are delightful with well tended gardens and pretty ponds with wild ducks. This is a wonderful place, a real 'hidden gem', and a credit to its owners.

Nolands Farm, Oxhill, Tel: 01926 640309 Fax: 01926 641662

139

Just off the A422 and on the border with Oxfordshire stands **Upton House,** a late 17th century National Trust property built of a mellow local stone. The house was remodelled in 1927-29 for the 2nd Viscount Bearsted, to house the growing collections, and also to modernise the premises. The collections in the house are the chief attraction; they include paintings by English and Continental Old Masters, such as El Greco, Brueghel, Bosch, Hogarth and Stubbs. Brussels tapestries, Sevres porcelain, Chelsea figures and 18th century furniture are also on show. In the fine gardens there is a typically English scene of white clad cricketers in summer and in winter, the Warwickshire hunt hold their meet.

A mile or so beyond is **Edge Hill,** where in 1642 the first and indecisive battle of the Civil War took place. Initially the Royalist cavalry routed the opposition but a lack of discipline saw their advantage lost. The Castle Inn pub stands above the battlefield and is reputedly the point where Charles I's standard was raised.

Only one road leads into **Ratley,** and none lead out of it. It lies in the folds and valleys over the crest of the Edge Hills on the border of Oxfordshire. The inhabitants will tell you that it is both the oldest and the highest village in Warwickshire and that during the war, from the hill that leads up behind the inn, they saw the fires of both London and Birmingham as they burned after the German bombings. The cottages here are built of the yellow-ochre ironstone indigenous to all these border villages and which looks so lovely when the sun throws shafts of light down on them.

Up from Ratley on the B4086 you'll come to **Kineton**, a market town that is now a quiet backwater. The village has an old Court house and several 17th and 18th century houses. The church tower is from the 14th century but the rest was rebuilt around 1755. Before crossing the Fosse Way, the Roman road that runs from Exeter to Lincoln you'll pass by **Compton Verney**. Although not open to the public, this delightful 18th mansion standing in a wooded valley is worth stopping to catch a glimpse.

Ettington used to have a public house called The Saracen's Head. It took its name from a legend which states that a knight and his squire returning from the Crusades stopped to drink by a spring, but their gory trophy, namely the Saracen's head, fell into the water and fossilised. The spring is said never to stop flowing even in times of drought, but it doesn't say what the water tastes like.

Just past Ettington **Park Leys Farmhouse** can be found on the Banbury road three miles from historic Stratford-upon-Avon, and is an ideal setting to 'Rest Awhile'! It dates back to at least 1700 AD and is bordered by a large pretty garden, which is surrounded by beautiful countryside. There is a relaxing homely feel to this Georgian house, and John, the owner, has lived in the area for many years and is well acquainted with the great variety of places to visit. Your stay in one of the comfortable en-suite bedrooms, together with the 'Farmhouse Breakfast' is a treat not to be missed!

Park Leys, Banbury Road, Goldicote. Stratford-upon- Avon, Warwickshire. Tel: 01789 740691 Fax: 01789 740501

A couple of miles due north from here is **Charlecote House,** the great house associated with the Lucy family. The house belonged to them from the 12th century until 1948, but only the gatehouse survives intact from the Elizabethan building. Inside there is no hint of the house Elizabeth I would have seen; the rooms are all 19th century, but no less impressive for this. The hall contains an interesting collection of family portraits including some by Gainsborough. It also houses a huge table bought from the Fonthill Abbey in 1823. More of the Fonthill furniture can be seen in the tapestry bedroom.

Also worth a visit is **Charlecote Mill** which is situated on the site of an earlier mill originally mentioned in the Domesday Book and valued at 6s 8d. In 1978 this 18th century building was restored with the help of numerous volunteers from Birmingham and the west water wheel was repaired at the expense of the BBC for their film "The Mill on the Floss".

To the east is the village of **Wellesbourne,** and if Country House style accommodation is what you seek then **Chadley House** is the place to make for, you will find it close to the village , equidistant between Stratford upon Avon and Warwick. This Georgian Farmhouse set in six and a half acres of grounds and bedecked with a climbing floral display, is the home of Caroline Powell and her parents, where all are welcome though there are no facilities for children. This

Warwick Castle.

Lord Leycester Hospital

impressive country house was built in 1730 and with its oak beams, wooden floors, guest lounges and log fires, offers a very peaceful and restful ambience. The nine letting rooms are all furnished in individual styles with character and comfort. All have private bath or shower rooms and colour television. The intimate and delightful farmhouse restaurant has Caroline as Chef; she is renowned for her excellent menus which are prepared only from fresh ingredients daily. Vegetarians and special diets can also be catered for by arrangement and booking is generally recommended. The Restaurant is closed on Sundays. *3 Crown Commended* by the tourist board and listed in *Michelin,* Chadley House offers a high degree of comfort and character in a setting with beautiful views. A hidden gem without doubt.

Chadley House, Loxley Road, Wellesbourne. Tel: 01789 840994

Warwick was our next destination and although separated from Leamington Spa by two miles, the two places have very different atmospheres. The castle which dominates Warwick is surely everyone's ideal of a medieval building. It is one of the few that still serves as a home and retains the greater part of its original masonry. Standing as it does by the River Avon, Warwick is in a good defensive position and became part of Crown lands as recorded in the Domesday Book in 1086.

Much of the castle was destroyed during the baron's revolt in 1264 by troops led by Simon de Montfort. The majority of the present castle dates from the 14th century. The towers at each end are very impressive, one known as Caesar's Tower is shaped rather like a clover leaf. The armoury houses one of the best private collections in the country and in the state apartments are some superb art treasures including work by Holbein, Rubens and Velasquez. The sixty acres of landscaped gardens were by Capability Brown with a famous display of peacocks.

A strong link with the castle is found in the Collegiate Church of St Mary, a fine landmark towering over the town. Of pre- conquest origin, the church contains the Beauchamp Chapel, built in the 18th century to house the monuments of Richard Beauchamp, Earl of Warwick and his family.

History of a different kind can be seen at **Oken's House**, an ancient building owned by Thomas Oken, a self-made businessman who died childless in 1573 and left his fortune to found almshouses for the poor. Today his home houses **The Doll Museum**, literally a hundred yards from the Castle. There are many displays here and the thing that strikes you most is the attention to detail in the dolls' costumes.

You will find among the displays the Joy Robinson Doll and Toy Collection, which has been at the museum since the 1950s and contains an incredible number of the pieces. In addition are dolls. toys, and games from Warwickshire Museum's own collection. Downstairs, the main collection of dolls is arranged according to material, age and maker which helps give an insight into costume history. (The museum is open from Easter to the end of September, Monday to Saturday 10.00am-5pm and Sundays 1pm-5pm. Winter months open Saturdays only 10.00am-dusk).

The Doll Museum, Castle Street, Tel: 01926 495546 or 412500

One of the most important buildings in Warwick is **St John's House**, dating from 1666 and considered a very good example of the period. Today the building houses a museum where visitors can find out how people lived in the past. The displays include a gallery of costume, a kitchen full of drawers to open and cupboards to explore, a parlour, and a schoolroom just waiting for Victorian

144

children. There is plenty to see and do and there are often special events and activities to enjoy. Upstairs there is the Museum of the Royal Warwickshire Regiment.

St John's House, St John's, Warwick Tel: 01926 412132

On the Market Place, in the centre of the town, you will find **The Market Hall**. Everyone is welcome to discover the displays of archaeology, wildlife and geology. There are exhibits of ancient jewellery, fantastic fossils, bees, bears and bugs. Find out about the early history of Warwickshire and look for the places you may know on the famous tapestry map. There are often special events to join in and even competitions to enter. The displays in the temporary exhibition gallery change every 4-6 weeks, so you'll want to come again to see what's new.

The Market Hall, Market Place, Warwick Tel: 01926 412500

The Tuckery , located in the Market Place opposite the Warwickshire Museum, provides the local people and visitors to the town, with all the best qualities of a family restaurant. Jayne Shorter, the owner, has been in business many years and her experience in the trade and the support of her excellent staff, have made The Tuckery a very special place.

The most evident feature of the restaurant is the varied menu with nothing being too expensive. Whether you stop for a cup of tea or coffee, a snack or a full lunch, you are sure to be impressed. There is also a good choice for children at reduced prices.

Please Don't Forget...

To tell people that you read about them in

The Hidden Places

The Tuckery, 21 Market Place, Warwick Tel: 01926 492171

At the top of High Street is the **Lord Leycester Hospital**, a beautiful collection of 15th century half timbered buildings; galleried courtyard, Great Hall and Guildhall was established as a home for retired ex-servicemen. The candlelit chapel dates from 1123 and the Regimental Museum of the Queen's Own Hussars are some of the things of interest in this medieval treasure.

The Black Horse Inn has stood in one form or another on the same site since the end of the 17th-century. In the early days it was a Blacksmiths forge with stabling. As time progressed the Blacksmith was granted a licence in the 1750s for the selling of ale. It became the Black Horse and through the years gained prominence as a Coaching Inn. After a period of closure, the present owners Polly and Joe acquired the Inn five years ago and through long-term endeavours, have created a successful business and brought the Inn back to its former glory. With ten newly created en suite bedrooms which are spacious and comfortable, an excellent choice of both traditional fare and Indian cuisine and a well stocked bar, you are sure of a happy stay with very warm-hearted people.

The Black Horse Inn, 62 The Saltisford, Warwick. Tel: 01926 403989

For somewhere convenient to stay, **Ashburton Guest House** offers a lovely family atmosphere where children are welcome, as are dogs but by arrangement. The Guest House is Two Crown Approved by the English Tourist Board and run by Pam Whitelaw. There are seven letting bedrooms two of which are family rooms; four with en-suite facilities and all nicely furnished. On a lower level from the main hallway you will discover a snug little bar where you can relax. Here too is the breakfast room to which you will be drawn by the aroma of Pam's cooking in the morning. Evening meals can be provided with prior notice and packed lunches too if required. The location is just ten minutes walk from Warwick town centre on the Emscote Road and private car parking is available.

Ashburton Guest House, 74 Emscote Road, Warwick. Tel: 01926 401082

The Seven Stars, near the racecourse in Warwick, is a magnificent 17th-century building offering old-fashioned hospitality with up-to-date facilities. The establishment is run by Audrey and John Flynn, who have created a rather special atmosphere that is much enjoyed by all who visit. They offer two letting rooms which are attractively furnished and comfortable - one even has a secret door which leads to another room! Back in the bar, you will find a good selection of home-made food, available every lunch time and evening, complemented by a range of real ales.

The Seven Stars, Friars Street, Warwick Tel: 01926 492658

Royal Leamington Spa is a very attractive town with its mixture of smart shops and Regency buildings. The Parade is undoubtedly the most handsome street in Warwickshire. It starts at the railway bridge, dives between a double row of shops and comes up with a rather startled air with a small stone temple announcing, ' The Original Spring Recorded by Camden in 1586'.

In 1801 very few people knew of the existence of Leamington but by 1838, the famous waters were cascading expensively over the many patients and the increasingly fashionable spa was given the title 'Royal' by permission of Queen Victoria. The Pump Rooms were opened in 1814 by Henry Jephson, a local doctor who was largely responsible for promoting the Spa's medicinal properties. Immediately opposite are Jephson's Gardens containing a Corinthian temple which houses his statue. The town's supply of saline waters is inexhaustible and a wide range of 'cures' are available under supervision.

If your journey takes you to Royal Leamington Spa, a very fine hotel can be found in a calm backwater close to the centre - **Eaton Court Hotel.** Its present owners Vince and Barbara Eaton, ably assisted by son Shaun, purchased the building in 1990 and after complete refurbishment opened later that year. It is a spacious hotel, very tastefully furnished with all 36 bedrooms having en suite facilities. The rooms are light and airy with a peaceful quality and all comforts; the owners ensure the high standards of service and quality are maintained. In the restaurant the tall windows and beautiful drapes make a lovely setting for your meal and the hotel offers a superb choice of table d'hôte and a' la carte menus; vegetarian and low fat dishes are always available. Some rooms are designated non-smoking. Three Crown commended by English Tourist Board, Eaton Court is ideally placed for both business people and family holiday breaks.

Eaton Court Hotel & Restaurant 1-7 St Marks Road, Leamington Spa. Tel: 01926 885848.

148

Packwood House.

Travelling on the A415 on the edge of Leamington Spa, the bright white exterior of **The Oak Inn** will certainly catch your eye. John and Linda took over the Oak Inn two years ago though have a solid experience in this industry in one capacity or another. The Inn dates back to the early 19th century and has over the years provided the weary traveller with refreshment and, until the mid 1900s, accommodation. During World War 2 the cellar was used as a Mortuary! The present owners have completely refurbished the Inn retaining its character and charm and in their two years here, John and Linda have projected their bright personalities into creating a successful business where locals and visitors mix freely. The Gatehouse restaurant is a recent addition with its exposed brickwork providing a pleasant feature. Additionally, food is available at the bar everyday until 7.00pm. Do call and try the delicious food and hand-pulled ale. The restaurant is closed on Tuesday evenings.

The Oak Inn, 89 Radford Road, Leamington Spa. Tel: 01926 429764.

To the east of the town continuing along the Fosse way, and almost equidistant from Warwick, Rugby and Coventry lies the impressive **Eathorpe Park Hotel** set in its own grounds of 11 acres of which 4 acres are magnificent gardens. Originally built for a wealthy family of Nottinghamshire Lace Makers in 1861, the hotel has many interesting structural features such as marble fireplaces, ornate ceiling coving and a grand wooden staircase. A truly splendid hotel run as a family concern by Rodney and Carol Grinnell with their daughter Yvette and son Simon, who ensure a professional approach and personal attention to all guests. Children are encouraged here and will find plenty of room to have fun. The eighteen en-suite bedrooms are spacious and stylish and supplied with all facilities.

Two very pleasant and cosy restaurants offer 'catering for the discerning palate'. Many activities take place at Eathorpe Park Hotel including Murder Mystery and Live Jazz Band evenings and outdoor events. Simon, Beverages Manager, prides himself on his real ales.

Eathorpe Park Hotel, The Fosse, Eathorpe, Leamington Spa, Warwickshire. Tel: 01926 632632

The towns of Leamington Spa and Warwick are very convenient as a base from which to explore the northern part of Warwickshire and on the A4177 northwest of Warwick is the village of **Hatton.**
Just off the A41/A4177 Solihull - Warwick road, you will find the premier tourist attraction of **Hatton Country World** where you will truly find 'all the fun of the farm'. There is so much to see and do here that your day out will offer a feast of attractions to enjoy within this 100-acre farmyard of fun. 'Hatton is dedicated to preservation of rare breeds of animals, the fostering of traditional crafts and entertainment of the public' - so says the guide to this wonderful attraction. Here you can find the largest collections of rare breed farm animals in Britain, the largest craft village in England and the longest flight of locks on the Grand Union Canal. Children get to feed and stroke the animals for hours in Pet's Corner and Guinea Pig Village is not to be missed. The adventure playground attractions start with the simple activity centre, to the commando slide, 'Fortress Hatton' and trampoline certain to keep them happy for hours. The Farm Park has a serious educational side too and thousands of children from hundreds of schools come on their special visits to learn about farm life. The craft village, winner of many coveted awards. was created from derelict Victorian farm building; the Craft Village has grown to house an extraordinary collection of craftsmen and women - some 35 workshops employing over 100 people. Make sure you don't miss Hatton Country World - a wonderful experience.

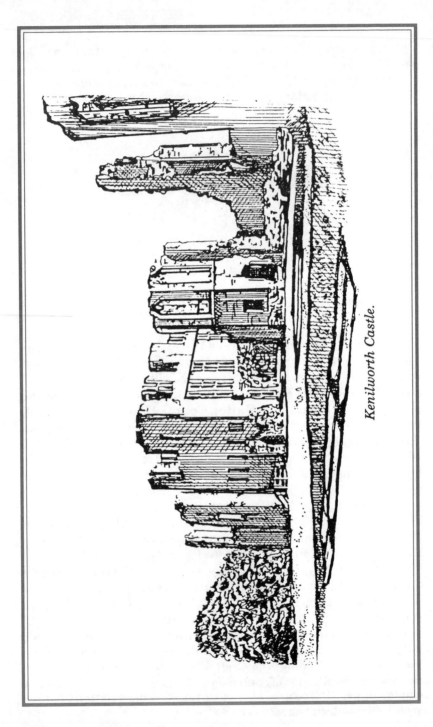

Kenilworth Castle.

Hatton Country World, Hatton, Warwick. Tel: 01926 843411

For a comfortable place to stay in Hatton well tended gardens and panoramic views greet you at **Northleigh House** . Here the most comfortable accommodation is offered to those visitors looking for a small Country House atmosphere. Sylvia Fenwick has a style and class of her own; Resident for 25 years and entering her twelfth year of business, Sylvia clearly knows how to create a high level of comfort at a very affordable price. All the rooms have been individually designed with colour co-ordinated furnishings and linen; the high level of facilities provided reflect her willingness to provide comfort in every way. Nothing is too much trouble and a request for any extra item or service will bring a helpful response. At Northleigh you can enjoy a smoke-free stay; breakfast overlooking the gardens; finding the secret door, and the warmest of receptions.

Northleigh House, Five Ways Road, Hatton, Warwick. Tel: 01926 484203

We travelled on to **Henley -in- Arden**, possibly the finest old market town in Warwickshire. Its mile long High Street is lined with almost every kind of English architecture from the 15th century onwards. Little remains today of the Forest of Arden, setting for Shakespeare's ' As You Like It '. The town, once a commercial centre

153

still has many old timber framed houses built from Arden oak. The forest was diminished during the 18th century when providing timber for the navy but nothing could diminish from the beauty of Henley. The town emerged initially,under the protection of Thurston de Montfort, Lord of the Manor in 1140. Beaudesert Castle, the home of the de Montfort family lies behind the churches of St John's and St Nicholas where remains of the castle mound can still be seen.

In the centre of Henley -in- Arden you'll find **The White Swan,** an inn that has been looking after travellers since 1350. Doctor Samuel Johnson regularly stayed here, there is a four poster bed named after him. His friend Boswell stayed as did the poet Shenstone.

The 15th century church of St John the Baptist has a tower that dominates the High Street where it narrows near the ancient Guildhall. The Guildhalls roof is supported by oak beams which were growing at the time of the Norman invasion and a wooden candelabra hangs from the ceiling. At one end of the hall is a huge dresser,displaying a set of pewter plates from 1677. The charter granted to the town has a royal seal embossed in green wax and is kept in a glass case.

The Court Leet still meets yearly with the Lord of the Manor at their head. Other members are the High Bailiff, the Low Bailiff, the Ale-Taster, the Butter-Weigher, the Mace bearer, the Town Crier, the Town constable, the Two Affearers and the Two Brook Lockers. In 1655 they noted, *" that usually heretofore there have been at Henley-in-Arden several unlawful meetings of idle and vaine persons about this time of yeare for erectings of May Poles and May bushes and for using of Morris Dances and other heathenish and inlawful customes, the observacon whereof tendeth to draw together a greate concourse of loose people."* The next parish **Beaudesert**, 'a beautiful waste land' is older than Henley and contains a few timber framed cottages and the beautifully restored Norman Church of St Nicholas.

The Bird in Hand is a great pub and although not very hidden, being located right on the A3400, it is easy to miss as you travel past. It is, however, well worth slowing down and stopping here. The establishment is a real credit to owners Mick and Irene Jarrett who, although having being in the trade for many years, took a chance on buying the Bird in Hand which was in a very poor condition. They have successfully renovated the building and turned it into something very special - all within six months. The overall impression is that of a very classy place and the atmosphere is equally warm and friendly.

It is said that is takes two to tango, and it takes two to make the Bird in Hand what it is. Irene is the cook, preparing a delicious variety of dishes served in good-sized portions and reasonably priced. Mick looks after the front of house where three traditional ales are kept in tip-top condition. Their bubbling personalities make this a place that you will really enjoy and want to return to again and again. A real credit to them both.

The Bird in Hand, Beaudesert, Henley-in-Arden, Tel: 01564 792689

Whichever way you approach **Wootton Wawen**, a couple of miles south of Henley, its situation in a hollow is dominated by its church. The name is part Saxon and the suffix Wawen was added to distinguish it from other Woottons and comes from the Saxon thane who held the land prior to the arrival of the Normans.

The village church of St Peter's retains its Saxon tower and is stands within a picturesque churchyard which has won the Diocesan 'Best Kept' award several times. The main building is actually three churches in one; there are three completely separate chapels tacked onto each other with total disregard for architectural design. It does not however, detract from its charm. Next to the church stands Wootton Hall, dating from 1637. Maria Fitzherbert, the wife of George IV, spent her childhood here and is thought now to return in the form of a ghost, the 'Grey Lady', that apparently wanders around the Hall.

Another real gem, **The Bulls Head** sits back off the A3400 as it passes through the village. This magnificent black and white, timber-framed inn dates back to the early 17th century by the end of which it had changed from a row of cottages to a coaching inn. The interior is as characterful as it appears from the outside, featuring flagstone floors and low ceiling beams. Every credit must go to owner John Willmott who has managed to retain the inn's character. On offer is a range of six real ales and the establishment has a reputation for its delicious and varied cuisine. In addition to the set menu there are daily blackboard fish dishes. The dining area is cosy and intimate and it is advisable to book ahead most evenings, especially at weekends. Outside there is a pretty patio area and children are welcome.

The Bulls Head, Stratford Road, Wootten Wawen, Warwickshire
Tel: 01564 792511

Wootton Park Farm is set within a 340 acre working farm with outstanding unspoilt views of the countryside. In the magnificent 450 year old half-timbered farmhouse, formerly a hunting lodge, Jackie and Ian-Roy have been providing bed and breakfast in their lovely home for the past eighteen years. There are three letting rooms one of which is on the ground floor; all are spacious and inviting. The atmosphere is very friendly and visitors can walk the farmland or sit and enjoy the picture postcard garden. There is a well-cooked breakfast to greet you as you rise in this most peaceful of settings and with so many local attractions nearby, Wootton Park makes an excellent base for a few days stay. Mine hosts will gladly recommend a selection of hostelries providing evening meals.

Wootton Park Farm, Wootton Wawen, Nr. Stratford upon Avon,
Warwickshire. Tel: 01564 792673

156

The main road through **Studley** is the Roman Rykneild Street, now the A435. Recorded in the Domesday Book in 1086 as the Saxon ' clearing for horses', it takes its name from the original farmstead hacked to form the edge of the ancient Forest of Arden. Before Henry VIII disagreed with the Pope, there was a Priory here but now the place of worship is the church dedicated to the Nativity of the Virgin.

It has Norman foundations and some original features survive the rebuilding that occurred in the 15th century and later. There is an early 18th century manor house with stone pilasters and columns, protected by striking iron gates. A castle once stood here but the massive Gothic building dates from 1834 and was home for Studley College.

We made our way to the village of **Coughton**, two miles north of Alcester and just a stones throw away from Studley. The parish church was built by Sir Robert Throckmorton between 1486 and 1518. It has six bells which were restored in 1976 but are still carried in their original wooden frame. Inside there are some interesting oddments; a faceless clock, fish weather vanes and dole cupboard from which wheaten loaves were distributed.

The crowning glory of this pretty village is the superb manor house, **Coughton Court**, which came into the possession of the Throckmorton family around 1409 and remained there for five and a half centuries until given to the nation in 1945.

Built at the end of the 17th century, **The Throckmorton Arms Hotel** takes its name from the family who played a part in the infamous Gunpowder Plot, and who lived at the historic Coughton Court which is located opposite this establishment. The inn became licensed in 1780 and present owners Brian and Sandra Betts arrived just 11 years ago. They have since sympathetically refurbished and extended the premises and have created an establishment of very high quality.

The lounge bars are traditionally decorated and furnished to complement the character of the building and provide a pleasant atmosphere in which to enjoy a drink and a meal. For something more, the intimate restaurant is ideal for lunches and candlelit dinners offering delicious food that is carefully prepared and presented. Based on both English and French cuisine, the hotel has an established reputation for taste, quality and good service. The ten bedrooms are en-suite and are of an equally high standard ensuring every guest a comfortable stay.

Set in the beautiful Warwickshire countryside the Throckmorton Arms Hotel is ideally placed for those seeking a relaxing break, equally for people on business in the Midlands. Situated in the village of Coughton, just north of Alcester on the A435. The hotel is within easy reach of the Midland's motorway network affording access to the business and commerce of the West Midlands, its cultural venues and the choice of city shops.

In contrast to this there is the magnificent scenery of the Vale of Evesham, the Cotswolds and the Malverns close by, as well as some of Britain's most famous tourist attractions including Shakespeare's home of Stratford-upon-Avon and the magnificent Warwick Castle.

The Throckmorton Arms Hotel, Coughton, Alcester, Warwickshire Tel: 01789 762879 Fax: 01789 762656

In **Hatton** you'll find the award winning **Hatton Craft Centre**, situated at George's Farm and described as 'a family trip in the Warwickshire countryside'. The farm was built by descendants of Sir Richard Arkwright of Spinning Jenny fame. It became known as George's Farm after a cowman with the same name in the 1920's.

As farming methods changed the small cow stalls, granary and carthorse stables became impractical so a new use was found. The old 19th century buildings were converted into craft workshops. Now in this flourishing centre you'll find workshops with jewellery, knitwear, ceramics, hand made furniture, toys, an art gallery, candlemakers, house signs, concrete ornaments and engraving. In addition to the workshops, there are farm trails, a Cafe, Farm shop, Garden Centre, One Stop Animal Shop as well as a farm park which features rare breeds of animals and poultry, a collection of agricultural machinery and childrens playground,all with access for the disabled.

Please Don't Forget...

To tell people that you read about them in

The Hidden Places

Nearby **Shrewley** boasts a marina on the Grand Union Canal and its well known landmark, the Hatton flight of twenty one locks that stretches for two and a half miles up Hatton Hill.

From Shrewley it is only a matter of miles to **Lapworth** where the Grand Union and Stratford canals meet.

Alongside the Grand Union Canal in the village of Lapworth, the appropriately named **Navigation Inn** is a old typical village pub. Not quite so easy to find these days after years of brewery modernisation. Lots of character here with flagstone floors and old beams. The blackboard menu offers a variety of well-cooked meals, all large portions and excellent value. The large garden has plenty of seating where you can take your time and watch the activity on the canal. Open everyday and all day on Saturdays. Well worth a visit.

The Navigation, Old Warwick Road, Lapworth, Solihull, West Midlands. Tel 01564 783337

Just a short distance from The Navigation Inn is **Packwood House**, lying in the Forest of Arden. The House is famous for its topiary gardens but less well known for the immense care in repairing,

159

restoring and addition of new buildings by Graham Baron Ash, the donor of the property to the National Trust in 1941. The house has a collection of furniture,tapestries and works of art.

Just east of Henley is **Claverdon** which is spread over a wide area now but there is evidence of a medieval village enclosed in a deer park during the 14th century. All that now remains to mark the site is Park Farm,which is near the church with its 15th century 'embattled' tower. In the church there are some fine monuments to the Spencer family.

The Crown Inn is just by the roadside near Claverdon on the A4189 from Warwick to Henley in Arden. In its early days the building was a butcher's shop, though it has provided refreshment for the traveller for over 300 years. Surrounded by trees, the inn presents a smart and inviting appearance, with fine leaded windows and clean exterior. Mrs Irene Young has been the owner of the Crown for eight years and you will find within, a characterful and cosy atmosphere, with low beamed ceilings, wooden Delph ledges displaying memorabilia and crockery from bygone days, while fine prints adorn the walls. Food is served everyday except Sunday evening and the menu offers Steaks, Poultry, Fish and Vegetarian dishes with some surprises on the daily 'blackboard'. There is a small children's play area in the beer garden and a private car park.

The Crown, Henley Road, Claverdon. Tel: 01926 642210

We ended this part of our meandering tour in **Kenilworth**, made famous by its Castle and also, in some part, by Sir Walter Scott's romantic novel ' Kenilworth'. Although the town was there before Domesday, Kenilworth's name is invariably linked with its castle. The keep, the oldest part of the ruins,was built in 1150 -75. After Simon de Montfort's death at the battle of Evesham in 1265, Kenilworth was held by his son. At that time the castle was surrounded by the Kenilworth Great Pool; a lake covering about 120 acres. Henry VIII's army failed in its attempt to storm the castle by using barges to cross the lake . Eventually the castle fell after six months siege when starvation forced de Montfort to surrender.

About three hundred years later Elizabeth I visited Kenilworth, then held by her favourite the Earl of Leicester. He laid on celebrations that cost around £60,000, in which the Queen was welcomed by the ' Lady of the Lake' floating on the lake.

The remains of the abbey can be seen in the churchyard of the parish church St Nicholas in the High Street. Much of interest was discovered during excavations, and there are many relics on display in the church, including a pig made of lead. It is said that this formed part of the roof at the time of Dissolution, but was then melted down and stamped by the Commissioners of Henry VIII.

Opposite the magnificent ruins of Kenilworth Castle and situated in the heart of 'old' Kenilworth you'll find the **Castle Laurels Hotel**. It's a fine looking Victorian house with some attractive half-timbered areas on the higher parts. Sue and Joe Glover came to this business in 1986 and made the hotel a quality establishment. It is set it pleasant gardens with private car parking. There are twelve en-suite bedrooms with differing designs; nicely furnished and decorated and one on the ground floor is suitable for a disabled guest. The Breakfasts and evening meals are all home cooked and the hotel is licensed for the benefit of residents. Well located for many amenities. Three Crown commended by the Tourist Board.

Castle Laurels Hotel, 22 Castle Road, Kenilworth. Tel; 01926 56179 FAX: 01926 54954

Situated in the main street of Kenilworth and close to the historic castle we found **Nightingale's Hotel & 'La Cicala' Ristorante.** A high class establishment by any standard, it is owned and personally run by Sally-Ann, her husband Piero with additional help from the family. Quality is the keynote with elegant furnishings and decor and excellent cuisine. The thirteen bedrooms are all different and are presented with thoughtful touches. Piero is the Chef presiding over the Ristorante renowned for its Italian and Continental dishes which are cooked specifically for the individual; closed only on Sunday evenings, bookings are preferred. You surely will want to return again to this lovely hotel.

Did You Know...
There is a full
Town and Village Index
at the back of the book?

Nightingales's Hotel & 'La Cicala' Ristorante, 95-97, Warwick Road, Kenilworth. Tel: 01926 53594

The Cottage Inn, on Stoneleigh Road, Kenilworth, dates back to the mid-18th century and become an ale house as far back as 1862. Present owners, Barry and Jackie English took over the property in 1987 and have since made many improvements, both inside and out. All alterations have been carefully carried out and are in keeping with the general style of the establishment. Today, the Cottage Inn can offer everything the tourist, visitor or local could wish for. The bar menu is varied and reasonably priced and senior citizens can enjoy discounts on certain days. Add to this the fine range of well-kept real ales and the friendly atmosphere which makes everyone feel welcome. There are, in addition, five en-suite letting rooms which are individually styled and comfortably furnished. All in all - a great place.

The Cottage Inn, 36 Stoneleigh Road, Kenilworth, Warwickshire Tel: 01926 53900

Finally, to the east of Kenilworth by the village of **Stoneleigh** stands Stoneleigh Abbey, a Baroque mansion by francis Smith of Warwick. The 14th century gatehouse and Norman doorways survive from the original Cistercian Abbey. The Royal Agricultural Show is held in July every year in the park. Leaving the southern part of Warwickshire our journey takes us northwards to the other half of the county.

CHAPTER SEVEN

North Warwickshire

Rugby School

Guildhall, Aston Cantlow

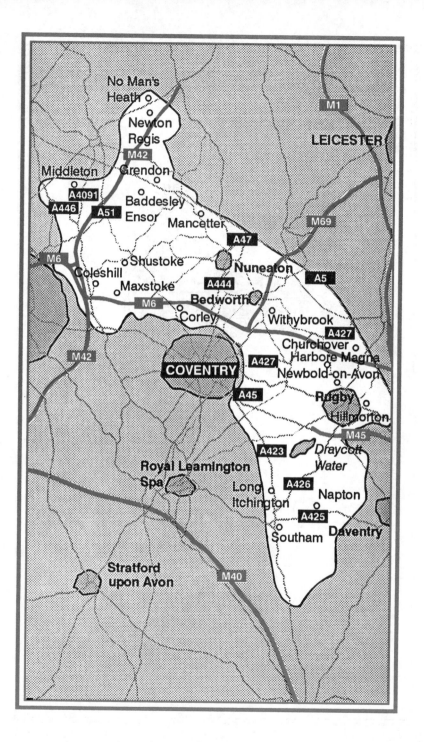

Rugby School.

North Warwickshire.

Rugby is the only town of any great size in north eastern Warwickshire. Its market place is a reminder of the towns origins during the reign of Henry III, surrounded as it is by old buildings Standing majestically in the centre of the market place is a clocktower that was erected to commemorate the jubilee of Queen Victoria The parish church of St Andrew in Church Street has an unusual tower which looks like a fortress with battlements and wall over three feet thick. It was built by the Rokeby family after their castle was destroyed by Henry II. The towns Roman Catholic church of St Mary's is attractive ,with its slender tower and spire reaching two hundred feet into the air.

Rugby is probably most famous for its public school, founded in 1567. There are many fine buildings, largely by Butterfield housing such treasure as stained glass,believed to be the work of Albrecht Durer, the 15th century German artist and engraver. The game of Rugby originated here when William Webb Ellis broke the rules during a football match in 1823 by picking up and running with the ball. His commemoration stone states that, *"with fine disregard for the rule of football as played in his time, first took the ball and ran with it, thus originating the distinctive feature of the rugby game."* Then of course the town is the setting for Thomas Hughes's 'Tom Brown's School Days'. Some of the schools illustrious pupils include Rupert Brooke, the First World War poet, Charles Lutwidge Dodgson better known as Lewis Carroll and the writer Matthew Arnold.

The school has not always been the calm and peaceful seat of learning that it is today. In November 1797 the Riot Act was read to a group of rebellious pupils who made a bonfire of books, pictures and other school property before retreating to the moated island in the school grounds. They were eventually captured by a large force of soldiers, school masters and volunteer civilians who waded through the water to the island.

The James Gilbert Rugby Museum.   Rugby.

If you are a rugby follower, then you will probably know about **The James Gilbert Rugby Museum** in St Matthew Street. The museum is in the building which, since 1842, the Gilberts made their world famous footballs.

Rugby is as far inland as one can get in the British Isles, yet it is an excellent centre for all kinds of water based activities. **The Oxford Canal** winds its way through the borough, providing many miles of scope for 'messing about on the river'. There are many places where you can hire a boat and enjoy the waterways. The Rivers Avon, Leam and Swift also pass through the borough and provide good angling, pleasant walks and places to picnic.

Another pleasant place is **Caldecott Park** which has an Organic Herb Garden. Unique in Britain and possibly the world, claims **Ryton Gardens** of their twenty two acres devoted to chemical free gardening. After strolling around this interesting garden you can enjoy a snack at their award winning cafe which uses only additive free produce for the food they have on offer.

Situated a couple of miles outside Rugby in the village of Hillmorton is The Red Lion public house. It's an attractive pub with an outstanding frontage. In the early 18th century the building was the home farm for a local estate, and later became the count house where beer was brewed and wages paid. Michael and Catherine have been the licensees for nearly 3 years and are obviously making a success of their business. Apart from an excellent range of ales wines and spirits the pub is open 7 days a week and has a busy restaurant. Also bar snacks and childrens menu. Beer garden and play area.

The Red Lion 73 High St, Hillmorton Tel: 01788 543028

When the Oxford canal was under construction, many workmen

170

needed to be housed, hence the building you will recognise today as **The Old Royal Oak.** This one time hostel for navvies fell into decline long after the canals were abandoned for faster modes of transport. Since it was last featured in *Hidden Places*, The **Old Royal Oak** has been outstandingly renovated and extended. It now forms part of Marston Brewery's very respectable chain of establishments known as 'Tavern Tables. In a lovely setting by the Grand Union Canal it provides moorings for visitors by water and a lovely outdoor setting for all to enjoy. The Inn now has seating for over 200 people in various rooms which are well furnished and comfortable, featuring lots of interesting bric-a`-brac, old prints and crockery. The adult and children's menu offer a good selection of fare and many interesting 'daily specials' are offered on the blackboard. The pub provides an excellent family room and indoor children's play area. All the family should enjoy a break here.

The Old Royal Oak, Crick Road, Hillmorton, Rugby, Warwickshire. Tel: 01788 561401

Tucked in between the railway and the canal, and standing apart from the village is the 13th century church of St John the Baptist; worth seeking out for the fine memorials to the Astley family who built it. The canal was built by James Brindley in 1769 but not completed until 1790. It skirts Rugby before arriving at **Newbold -on- Avon,** providing pleasant mooring for boats behind the Boat Inn just outside the village. Slightly isolated in a loop of the Avon is the parish church of St Botolph which like so many churches was improved during Victorian times.Tucked away in the neighbouring village of **Harborough Magna** is **The Old Lion.** This village Inn, owned by Marston Brewery, has a warm and friendly atmosphere not always apparent in managed houses. A converted cruck-style barn forms part of the attractive interior which is very well presented. There is an excellent menu with several interesting alternatives for the vegetarian diner. Daily specials displayed on the blackboard offer a variety of tempting dishes. A special children's menu offers good value too and the wine list has a popular selection at realistic prices. Well worth a diversion.

The Old Lion, Pailton Road, Harborough Magna, Nr. Rugby, Warwickshire. Tel: 01788 833238

To the Northeast of Rugby is the village of **Clifton Upon Dunsmoor** where you will find a haven of peace far removed from the hustle and bustle which is only a few miles away. Until a couple of years ago Pat and Parry Walters provided bed and breakfast accommodation at **Manor Farm**. A halt was called when they decided to convert the Old Granary into a new farm house which would also provide for four en-suite letting rooms. The new conversion will form part of the 175 acre working farm which the Walters family have farmed since 1937. Due to be finished later this year, Manor Farm's new accommodation will be a splendid place to stay for those wanting a homely atmosphere in a peaceful setting with lovely new facilities.

Did You Know...

The Hidden Places Series

Covers most of Britain?

For our full list see back of book

Manor Farm, Buckwell Lane, Clifton-upon-Dunsmore, Nr. Rugby, Warwickshire. Tel: 01788 544016

Churchover, close to the Warwickshire/Leicestershire border has less than one hundred dwellings. It sits on a hill, overlooking the Swift Valley and its church dedicated to the Holy Trinity, was mostly restored in the 19th century but still has a Norman front with a cover dating to 1673 as well as two interesting 16th century monuments. One of these commemorates the Dixwell family, who lived at the Coton House, about a mile outside the village. John Dixwell (1607-1689) was one of the signatories on the death warrant of Charles I. At the restoration of the monarchy, he was forced to flee the country and became one of the founding fathers of Newhaven, Connecticut. The church also has a 15th century tower and beautiful oak screen at the entrance to the chancel. It was erected by Queen Elizabeth, the Queen Mother, to the memory of her late godmother Mrs Arthur James, who, with her husband were tenants of the Manor House which now stands on the site of Coton House.

Not far from Churchover, and near Dow Bridge - known as Doves Bridge 300 years ago - is the site of Tripontium. Excavations started in 1964 have revealed extensive evidence of Roman occupation. Adjacent to the site is Caves Inn, now a farm but the birthplace in 1691 of Edward Cave, founder in 1731 of 'The Gentleman's Magazine'. The son of a cobbler, he was educated at the original public school in Rugby market place. He later became a printer and journalist; his magazine achieved a circulation of fifteen thousand copies during his lifetime. In 1732, Cave started publishing regular Parliamentary reports compiled by Dr Samuel Johnson, who was then sub editor of the magazine. Then, journalists were not allowed into the House so information was gained by sending in ordinary people who would report back. After the death of Edward Cave in 1754, the magazine continued to survive until the early years of this century.

Skirting close to Coventry in the triangle formed by the M6 M69 and A5 roads is the village of **Withybrook.**

Originally called Willowbrook because of the vast number of willow trees that grew alongside the brook. Withes were produced here and used for thatching the local homes and buildings. Back across the M6 where the Fosse Way meets the B4027 Coventry road, you will find **The Dun Cow** at **Brinklow**; a public house and restaurant run by a hard-working husband and wife team - Jeff and Rachel. This is an ideal family stopping point with a large safe garden at the rear with children's play activities. The Inn is open all day everyday, May to September excluding Sunday when it is closed 3 - 7pm. In the lounge area the Dun Cow has an extensive menu which includes fish dishes, Steaks platters you'll find hard to believe, homemade pies, a variety of others specials right down to the simple sausage. In the large and beautifully furnished Waterfall Restaurant you can choose from the carvery or a' la carte menu, the choice is quite exceptional and justly deserves the title used - ' No.1 for food'. The carvery has a choice of four Roasts and nine traditional puddings and sweets, while the a' la carte menu extends to four pages! As if that were not enough, there's still more on offer at the bar where traditional ale is available.

The Dun Cow, 6 Coventry Road, Brinklow, Warwickshire.
Tel: 01788 832358

From the Fosse Way turn onto the A427 to **Easenhall**. In the season you may enjoy the typical village scene; watching a local cricket match. Here also, is the **Golden Lion Inn** with its owners Jim and his lovely Argentine wife Claudia. The Inn has been in the family since 1931 with Jim in charge for the last twenty five years. The Golden Lion was built in the 16th Century and the surroundings take you back to those 'Olde Worlde' times with low oak beams and ceiling supports, narrow doorways and uneven floors; there is even a preserved 'Wattle and Daub' wall. The whole of the interior is very pleasing with tasteful decor and cosy environment, The Tourist Board awarded Three Crown classification for the accommodation which has four bedrooms, all with en-suite bathrooms and one with the real luxury of a Spa Bath. All other amenities are also supplied for your comfort. A good selection of wholesome food is supplied in the Restaurant with a Carvery on Sundays. Snacks are available at the bar where only the best Traditional Ales, wines and spirits are kept. Don't forget to say hello to the Charlotte the pet donkey.

The Golden Lion Inn, Easenhall, Nr Rugby, Warwickshire.
Tel: 01788 832265 FAX: 01788 832878

We journeyed south along the A423 to **Long Itchington,** the Anglo Saxon, ' Farm by the River Itchen'. Its population at the time of Domesday was larger than that of Coventry. The Church of Holy Trinity is a great interest here, its earliest part dating from 1190. The tower has only the remains of its original spire which collapsed when struck by lightening during a Sunday morning service in 1762. The carvings on the chancel arm of worth looking at, with a monkey and her young and the head and shoulders of what is commonly believed to be a jester. Also of historic note is **The Green Man Inn** which dates from 1674 and was formerly a farmhouse. In 1940 the building was found to have suffered from bomb damage and declared unsafe. Today, however, the building is perfectly safe, and the business side of things is in the safe hands of Sue and Barry Cramp who are the tenants. The interior is full of character featuring exposed brickwork and ceiling beams, reflecting its long history. Here, the visitor will find real ales on offer and a small menu of freshly prepared meals. outside there is a good sized private car park and a beer garden.

The Green Man, Long Itchington, Nr Rugby, . 01926 812208.

175

South of the church is the 15th century timber framed manor, now called Devon House, with its alternating diagonal and herringbone strutting. In 1572, Queen Elizabeth I was entertained in Long Itchington by the Earl of Leycester whilst on her way to Warwick Castle. She dined in the Tudor House facing the green, latterly owned but seldom used by the Sitwell family.

Southam was our next destination to see where Charles I spent the night before the Battle of Edgehill. The Roundheads also came into the town and Cromwell himself arrived with seven thousand troops in 1645. In the main street is the surprisingly named Old Mint Inn, a 14th century stone building that is said to take its name from an occurrence following the Battle of Edgehill. Charles I commanded his local noblemen to bring him their silver treasure, which was then melted down and minted into coins with which he paid his army. From here by travelling along the A425 Leamington Spa to Daventry road, a place look out for is the brightly painted, attractive **Napton Bridge Inn.** It is officially sited on bridge 111, on the South Oxford Canal. A picture-postcard of a place with outstanding country views and set alongside the canal. The owners, John and his lovely Italian wife Lydia, have been at the helm for twenty years now and the popularity of the Inn is clear evidence of how well they run their business. Before it was converted, the building now used for dining, housed the horses used to pull the canal boats. The menu offers a choice for every taste including Vegetarian and children's meals. Booking is advised at weekends. Three excellent well kept Real Ales are always available together with a large selection of other beverages.

Napton Bridge Inn, Bridge 111 South Oxford Canal. 01926 812466.
Following the canal southwards and near the Northamptonshire border is the village of **Priors Hardwick** where, in order to enjoy the very best in English and Continental cuisine, a pre-booked visit to

The Butchers Arms Restaurant in this tranquil and peaceful village is essential. This internationally renowned restaurant draws gourmet visitors from all over the world to sample the fine cuisine and simply beautiful surroundings.

The charming stone built inn with mullion windows has a history dating from 1375.

Lino Pires and his lovely wife Augusta came originally from Portugal and eventually purchased the Butchers Arms in 1973. A large open inglenook fireplace welcomes guests into the 14th century bar where stone flagged floors and ancient oak beams reinforce the historical atmosphere.

The silver service restaurant is tastefully decorated and well planned. An extensive a'la carte menu caters for every possible taste and is an invitation to a most memorable occasion. The freshly prepared food is selected from all over the country and is complimented by a range of over 200 wines.

This is where celebrities and politicians like to dine, as evidenced by the many signed photographs which adorn the walls of the conservatory. Mr. Pires will happily assure you that "English food is the best in the world" and there cannot be a better restaurant or setting to prove him right. Open 365 days a year, booking is essential. Easily accessed by either the A361, A423 or A425 between Banbury, Southam and Daventry.

The Butchers Arms Restaurant, Priors Hardwick, Warwickshire.
Tel: 01327 260504 Fax: 01327 260502.

Heading West if you turn off the A425 on to the B4452 near Leamington Spa, you can aim for the little village of **Harbury** wherein lies **The Dog Inn;** a very suitable resting place. Tricia and Bob who recently took over the inn, have applied a lot of their exciting ideas to create a very comfortable lounge and bar area. They have also created a Victorian themed restaurant with leaded windows, soft lighting and beamed ceiling and walls; those with an eye for antiques may admire interesting clocks. With Bob as Chef, good food is always available by way of the restaurant menu, blackboard specials, bar menu and a weekend carvery. There are two cosy letting rooms should you, not surprisingly, decide to extend your stay.

The Dog Inn, The Bull Ring, Harbury, Nr. Leamington Spa,
Tel: 01926 612599

Crossing the M6 into the final sector of this chapter is the town of **Nuneaton,** where we continued our tour. Originally an Anglo -Saxon settlement called Etone, Nuneaton is mentioned in the Domesday Book in 1086,and the prefix 'Nun' was added when a wealthy Benedictine Priory was founded here in 1290. The remaining ruins of the Priory adjoin the Victorian church of St Nicholas which stands on a Norman site which has a beautiful carved ceiling dating from 1485.

Coal mining began in Nuneaton as early as 1300, bricks and tiles were manufactured and label hand looms produced ribbons. Later, as communications improved, so did the prosperity of the textile and hatting industries. Today Nuneaton is still an industrial town with trades ranging from precision engineering to printing, car components to double glazing.

In **Riversley Park** there is a large recreation and adventure playground for children, a sports centre and boating facilities as well as conservatories and aviaries. You'll also find the **Nuneaton Museum and Art Gallery** here, where archaeological specimens from prehistoric to medieval and items from the local earthenware industry are on display. There is also a permanent exhibition of George Eliot's personal mementoes.

The daughter of a prosperous land agent she was born at Arbury Hall in 1819 and named Mary Ann Evans. She grew up to be a plain but serious and intellectual woman by the time she left Warwickshire for London. There she met George Henry Lewes, a 'bohemian type' who occasionally wrote and acted but also had a wife and three children. Eventually they set up house together, which in those days was quite a courageous act. As we know she became an extremely successful novelist during her lifetime, some of her better known works include Adam Bede, The Mill on the Floss, Silas Marner and Middlemarch.

A visit to **Arbury Hall** will fit another piece of the jigsaw of George Eliots life into place. It is only ten minutes from Nuneaton and is the ancestral seat of Viscount and Viscountess Daventry and the home of the Newdigate family for four hundred years. This once Elizabethan house was built out of the ruins of an Augustinian monastery and is now one of the best examples of 18th century Gothic architecture in the country. This was largely the creation of Sir Roger Newdigate who began the work in 1748. Prior to that, in the 1670's, Sir Richard Newdigate had built an impressive stable block - partly designed by Christopher Wren. However the character of the house originates from the 18th century. The opening times are limited so check with Tourist Information before making a visit to this lovely place.

A few miles to the north towards the Northampton border you'll find **Hartshill Hayes Country Park.** This is an ideal centre for exploring the developing rural tourism of the Midlands despite the fact that you are surrounded by a network of roads that soon take you into the major conurbations and attractions in the area. Woodland trails and walks, which give you the opportunity to appreciate the country and magnificent views. Hartshill itself was the birthplace of the poet Michael Drayton (1563-1631).

Situated close to the borders of Warwickshire and Leicestershire is the village of **Witherley** just off the A5. A good stopping off point for refreshment and where you will find **The Bull Inn.** This former coaching inn is renowned for delicious food and has plenty to offer either as a light snack, or main meal from the comprehensive menu which is supplemented by extra daily specials. The Inn is open all day, everyday, and food is always available   except between 2.0pm and 6.0pm For those with a powerful thirst, twelve different ales are on offer as well as the usual wines and spirits. To the rear of the inn is a well kept beer garden with tables and chairs and room for children to play.

The Bull Inn, Watling Street, Witherley, Nr. Atherstone, Warwickshire.
Tel: 01827 712323

Although the postal address is Warwickshire and it is only five miles from Nuneaton, **Manor Farm** in **Upton** is in fact in Leicestershire. For those with specific family requirements, **Upton Barn** is definitely a place to head for. Turn off the A444 which can be accessed from either the M42 or A5. Here, June and Arthur White and family have a superb holiday facility. Set within 33 acres of a former working farm, Upton Barn at Manor Farm has such a lot to offer the family. Nine letting rooms, five en suite, and full English breakfast is included in the price. There is a restaurant seating 30 people and offering a variety of food from snacks to a'la carte; a bar lounge in which children are allowed until 9.00p.m., a heated indoor swimming pool, games room, skittle alley and a lake of approximately 3/4 acre, well stocked for coarse fishing. A fun place to stay!

Upton Barn, Manor Farm, Upton, Nr. Nuneaton, Warwickshire.
Tel: 01455 212374.

Travelling on to **Bedworth,** a small town that was part of the North Warwickshire coalfield that was established at the end of the 17th century. It was local people who were largely responsible for the construction of the Coventry Canal which was built in 1769 to connect the fast growing town with the great new trade route, the Grand Trunk - now known as the Trent and Mersey Canal and to provide Coventry with cheap coal from the Bedworth coalfield.

It is also here that French Protestant families, fleeing from persecution sought refuge, bringing with them their skills for silk and ribbon weaving. The shopping precinct and open air market share the central area with the splendid Chamberlain almshouses in All Saints Square,founded in 1663. The Parish church, completed in 1890, is a good example of Gothic revival and outside there is a Scented Garden, designed for the blind. The **Bedworth Sports Complex** provides for more energetic pastimes and the Civic Hall has regular shows and concerts.

Mancetter now almost joins Atherstone due to sprawling urban development. This former Roman camp is situated on a rocky outcrop overlooking the valley of the River Anker and was one of a line of forts built as the Romans advanced northwards.

The village is chiefly associated with the Mancetter Martyrs, Robert Glover and Joyce Lewis, both of whom were burnt at the stake for their religious beliefs.

The martyrs are commemorated on wooden tablets in the fine church of St Peter, which is of early 13th century origin. The glory of the building is the rich glass in the east window of the chancel, most of which is 14th century and thought to have been made by John Thornton, builder of the great east window of York Minster. Between the manor and the church are two noteworthy rows of almshouses dating from 1728 and 1822.

Close by in the village of **Grendon** you'll find **The Boot Inn,** an 18th century coaching inn and the second oldest building in the village. Traditionally furnished throughout, the inn has two comfortable bars, adorned with pictures of stage coaches and horses; scenes synonymous with the life of this village.

Grendon once boasted its own mint owned by Sir George Chetwynd of Grendon Hall. It was this same Sir George who was enamoured with Lillie Lantry and who fought Lord Lonsdale in a fist fight to win her favours. He had a very extravagant lifestyle, spending a lot of time at race meetings and entertaining the Prince of Wales with the result that Grendon Hall had to be sold and was unfortunately pulled down in 1933.

Across from Grendon, divided by the old turnpike road which until recently still had toll houses standing, is **Baddesley Ensor.** In 1848 Baddesley's ancient church was pulled down and its old pulpit bought by the Wesleyan Methodists and installed in their chapel. This five sided black pulpit is claimed to be one from which the Protestant Bishop Latimer preached nearly four hundred years ago; the Bishop was burned at the stake during Mary Tudors reign. In 1772, when they were given the freedom to worship, Baddesley Quakers built a meeting house and up until 1931 Quakers from many parts of the Midlands made a yearly pilgrimage there.

Across to the east you'll find **Kingsbury Water Park** near to the M42, six hundred acres of landscaped park with over twenty lakes. It is by the River Tame and linked by miles of footpaths and nature trails through woodland,pasture and the waters edge. All sorts of water sports are pursued on the lakes and for those that own canoes and such this is an ideal place to practice their leisure pursuits. The Visitor Centre provides information about the nature trails, footpaths, bird hides and nature reserves as well as audio visual shows. Alongside it you'll find a gift shop and cafe which all together make this Park,that is open all year round, an ideal day out.To the west of the village lies **Middleton Hall** which was, until recently, the oldest inhabited building in Warwickshire. The oldest part of the house is Norman, and until the 15th century the property of the Marmions of Tamworth Castle. It was later acquired by the Willoughby family around 1528. It was a moated residence but in 1868 the moat was drained to reveal the skeleton of a rider in armour and a horse. It was believed that he was a courier in the Royalist Army, who when leaving the Hall in dense fog lost his bearings and ended up in the moat. The remains are buried in the churchyard and the gauntlet glove and helmet are on display in the chancel of the church.

We moved on along the A453 to **Newton Regis,** one of the least spoilt villages in North Warwickshire; it has been voted the ' Best Kept Small Village' several times and built around a duck pond which was once a quarry pit makes you understand why. The name Newton Regis probably derives from its former royal ownership by Henry II who reigned from 1154 to 1189. It has also been known as King's Newton and Newton -in-the- Thistles. The latter might have referred to the abundance of thistles or specially grown teasels which is used in the carding of flax fibre. Linen looms were worked in the house which is now The Queens Head Inn.

Alvecote Priory, just on the border with Staffordshire is an ideal picnic spot, where there is a distinctly religious atmosphere that emanates from the Benedictine Priory that was formed here in 1159. The 14th century remains include a fine moulded doorway and dovecote. The priory was founded by a William Burnett who built it as a penance after believing that his wife had been unfaithful during his pilgrimage to the Holy Lands. Alvecote Pools are formed by the River Anker in flood and are now nature reserves with specimens of many plants, insects and bird-life.

Back in a southerly direction we came to **Coleshill**, which derives its name from the River Cole, a clear and shallow waterway that passes under the lower part of High Street. It is a town of great antiquity, once being a royal manor during Norman times. It gained in importance when it became a staging post in coaching days along the main London to Holyhead route, boasting more than twenty inns.

Near the church are Coleshill's most known treasures, a combined post, stocks and pillory, the stocks were last used in 1859. One infamous inhabitant was John Wynn, owner of a cinema, who during the Second World War operated a transmitter from the roof of the building and was caught giving information to the Germans.

Maxstoke, some two miles to the east, is a privately owned castle but **Maxstoke Priory** is an early 14th century building which has two letting rooms. One is the old priors lodging and you'll take breakfast in the oak panelled dining room with its amazing armorial painted ceiling. The priory was nearly demolished during Dissolution but was rebuilt in the 1600's as a farmhouse without losing its sense of history.

Shustoke, a peaceful place close to Coleshill makes it hard to believe that you are only seven minutes or so away from the NEC and Airport. Here you'll find the old railway station has been turned into **Ye Olde Station Guest House.**

Not far from the village centre is Shustoke Reservoir which supplies some of the water for Coventry and where you'll find a sailing club and a place for enthusiastic anglers to enjoy the surroundings.

Furnace End, so named in 1700, takes its names from the furnaces of the Jennens family in the Bourne Valley. The present village is a group of older houses at a crossroads in an area of wooded countryside dotted with small mixed farms. The village boasts a post office, butchers and a pub plus guest house.

The pub is **Ye Olde Bulls Head,** a 16th century inn with a large bar and restaurant and ample car parking facilities.

Close by is **Corley**, where disaster struck in the 1920's with foot and mouth disease which was fortunately confined to the area. On a happier note it is here that you will find the historic **Red Lion Inn**, parts of which are over three hundred years old, The lounge side of the restaurant was at one time was used as a morgue, and at another time was the local carpenters cottage during which time it was shared with the blacksmith. Now, the Inn serves well kept Bass Bitter, Brew XI and Bass Mild traditional ales as well as lager. The restaurant side specialises in steaks, home made dishes and sweets. Children are welcome in the snug, which still has its original inglenook fireplace, though not in the lounge or main bar. However, there is a large garden outside with climbing frames and swings whilst perhaps best of all, an animal farm which has goats, sheep, rabbits, ducks and a large aviary.

The Red Lion Inn, Wall Hill Road, Corley Moor, Nr. Coventry.
Tel: 01676 540135

So we finally took our leave of Warwickshire and headed into the next chapter, Northamptonshire. We had found many places of interest both 'hidden' and not but we hope that our tour has helped give you an insight into an attractive and often surprising county in the Heart Of England.

CHAPTER EIGHT

South Northamptonshire

Canon's Ashby house

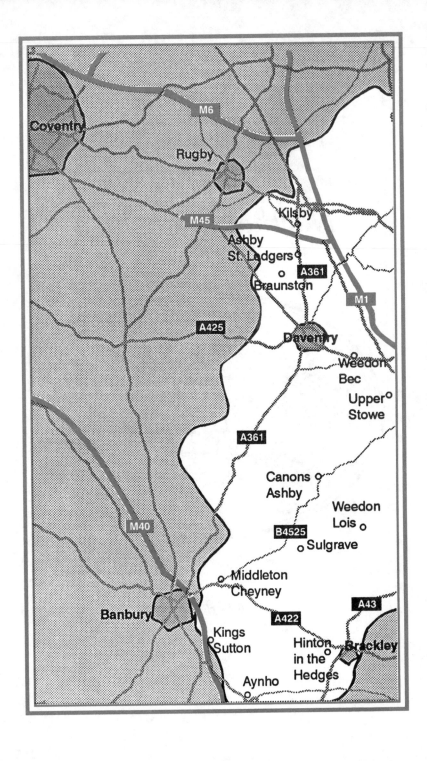

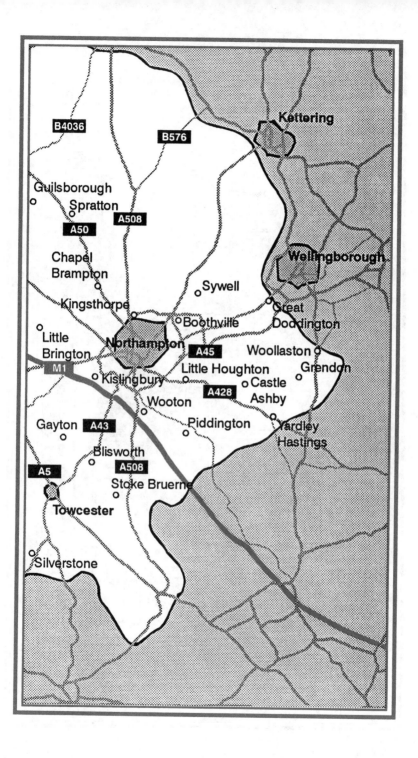

Entrance to Castle Ashby.

CHAPTER EIGHT

South Northamptonshire.

Northamptonshire is shaped like a laurel leaf and the **River Nene** is its most distinctive feature. Wherever you journey across the county you are never far from its banks and the reflection of the trees in high summer on its shimmering waters can be quite breathtaking. The alluvial soils and gravel terraces of the Nene Valley have been continuously farmed since Neolithic times and there are remains of many Anglo-Saxon settlements. Bones of horses, woolly rhinoceroses and mammoths have been unearthed giving some hint as to the kind of animal life Paleolithic man used to contend with. Polished stone axes indicate that their basic way of life was mixed farming.

During the Roman occupation, the Nene Valley lay within the most densely populated region of Britain, but we're only thinking in dozens here. Forts were built a days march apart round the Fens and towards the Trent and Humber. One such fortress, some thirty acres in size was discovered at Lonthorpe near Peterborough and as the legionaires advanced towards the north and west they built their famous straight roads.

The most impressive sections are those of Watling Street (A5), which enters the county at Old Stratford and runs in a rigid straight line for eight and a half miles to Towcester. The line of communication continues north through Watford Gap - now thought of only as a motorway service area. This route was followed by the Grand Union Canal in the 18th century, by the London to Birmingham railway in the early Victorian period; and by the M1 motorway in contemporary times. There can be few places that have played such an integral role in communications for over two thousand years.

The county abounds in steeples and it is unusual to see less than three at any one time. So graceful and abundant are these different styles of towers and spires that even the pylons and telegraph poles of todays landscape can hardly extinguish the effect. The Saxon church at **Brixworth** is the most impressive and has been described to quote the Tourist Information as *"probably the most imposing architectural memorial of the 7th century north of the Alps"*.

Whatever your taste in scenery there is something for everyone from rolling meadows to a spectacular view over seven counties. The main centres of population all have their own delightful corners, but the county is perhaps even better known for the many picturesque villages which dot the landscape. From **Harringworth** in the north to the equally lovely **Chipping Warden** in the south, Northamptonshire abounds with charm complete with true country hospitality in welcoming local pubs and cosy tea shops.

Both the **Grand Union** and the **Oxford Canals** run through Northamptonshire, meeting at **Braunston** where there is a large marina and a choice of canal-side inns.

If your interest is spectator sports, there is plenty to enjoy. The county town is host to a first-class county cricket team, a professional football club and a redoubtable rugby fifteen. Elsewhere in the county **Silverstone** hosts not only the best in Formula one motor racing, but also motor cycle racing and many club meetings. For the more ambitious, Silverstone also has a racing school with special race meetings for pupils, as well as providing instruction in advanced driving skills and skid correction techniques.

Brafield, near Northampton, caters for stock car and hot rod racing enthusiasts. For those whose interests lie on the race track, **Towcester Racecourse** is famous for its National Hunt meeting and horse trials are held at several venues around the county. If you prefer less nerve racking sports, the World Conker Championships are held at **Ashton** every year. Coarse, fly fishing and rough shooting are also available within the county. Add to these superb golf facilities and a wide selection of cultural activities, and it is easy to understand why Northamptonshire proves such a popular county for the young of all ages.

Our tour of Northamptonshire begins at the southern-most tip and our first port of call was **King's Sutton,** which boasts its own Anglo-Saxon saint called Rumbold, an extremely un-saintlike name we thought. The River Cherwell rises at **Charwelton** and its willow-lined course forms the boundary of the shire in its extreme south west corner as it goes south into Oxfordshire on its way to the Thames. The King's Sutton church of St. Peter and St. Paul has a 14th century spire rising from the handsome tower and a band of pinnacles is linked to it by dainty flying buttresses.

190

We travelled on to the pretty village of **Aynho**, six miles south west of Brackley. The parish church of St. Michael and All Angels has a wonderfully detailed 15th century tower which is rather startlingly attached to the church whose shape and symmetry give it the air of a villa. The body of the church was transformed in 1723 by a local carpenter-cum-architect called Edward Wing. It is furnished with a pulpit, box pews and a distinguished west gallery classically of the period. Aynho is picturesque with steep leafy lanes and apricot trees trained into fan shapes are a lovely feature, leaning against limestone cottage walls. The former manor house is called **Aynho Park** which gives a delightful character to this sleepy place.

Hinton-in-the-Hedges, is a village of thatched rooves and clipped yew hedges. The village green is triangular in shape and is still the centre of this tight settlement which has never grown beyond hamlet proportions. Here the Normans built a low tower, and from under its narrow parapet with a pyramid cap of the 13th century, eight heads peer down on each side. Three of the bells in the tower are older than the Reformation. We are, of course, talking about the church and inside there is a charming Jacobean pulpit supported on a finely carved pedestal.

The origin of **Brackley** is to be found in a cluster of farms two and a half miles to the north. Here was the centre of the old Saxon parish of Halse with a church mentioned in Domesday Book. This medieval seignorial borough grew to be quite prosperous in the early Middle Ages and then rather faded away.

The Saxon old town is distinguished by its huddle of houses round a tangle of streets. The prosperity brought by the marketing of wool in the broad High Street in the 13th century enabled the church of St Peter's to be rebuilt with its fine early English west tower and south aisle. Magdalen College School founded in 1548 by William of Waynflete incorporates the chapel of a Hospital of St John and St James, and the Town Hall, with its fine clock tower built in 1706 stands in High Street. The Duke of Bridgewater was responsible for the latter and its open arched windows on the ground floor used to be an open market place. The outsize station built in the 19th century is called Brackley Central whilst in fact it is on the northern edge of town.

Two miles west of Brackley off the A43 in the tiny village of **Steane,** is the little chapel of St Peter, built by Sir Thomas Crewe in his park in 1620. It has the appearance of being genuinely medieval although it isn't. The south doorway may have been added in the mid 17th century but it does contain good furnishings and fine monuments to his family and includes work by the Christmas brothers.

Moving north, and still on the religious theme at **Middleton Cheney,** about five miles beyond Brackley on the A422, you'll find the Church of All Saints. This 14th century church has a beautiful tower and perpendicular spire, its steeply roofed porch is built entirely of interlocking stones. Above all though, it has splendid stained glass by a galaxy of pre- Raphaelites - Morris, Webb, Rosetti - and includes the original Burke -Jones's ' Six Days of Creation'.

There would seem to be little connection between an Elizabethan manor house and the USA as we know it today. Yet it was from **Sulgrave** along the B4525 that George Washington's ancestors emigrated to a new life in the New World. **Sulgrave Manor** today is faithfully preserved and open to the public as a Washington Museum. The house was sold to Laurence Washington, George's great grandfather, in 1539, a distingiuished wool merchant and twice Mayor of Northampton.

The walls and ceilings have been stripped of their plaster and the panels of their coats of paint. The massive oak beams and the planks of the floors now gleam with a deep golden lustre as they must have done when Elizabeth I paid a visit. The seven feet wide fireplaces are fitted with medieval implements and there is a captivating miniature dresser with a child's play set of cups, plates and pots all made of shining pewter. George's black coat has pride of place and there is a fragment of Martha Washingtons wedding dress on display.

Outside the porch bears the family coat of arms, sometimes regarded as the origin of the 'stars and stripes'. The village church, St James the Less contains a memorial brass to Laurence Washington and his wife and the 17th century Washington family pew. It has also been enriched over the years by gifts from American pilgrims, one of which is a light oak tower screen with tracery picked out in scarlet and blue where the flags of England and the US hang side by side. Another gift is the organ donated by the colonial Dames of America. On the village green are the old stocks which actually pre-date the United States.

Just down the road from Sulgrave Manor, in the picturesque village of **Sulgrave** is the **Star Inn**. This three hundred year old former farmhouse is packed with interesting features, in the corner near the bar, for instance, you will meet an unusual 'regular', George the skeleton! The Star Inn is probably the finest in the county and has an outstanding reputation.

Caroline and Andy, the tenants, are justly proud of their inn, the food is superb and a good range of real ales, including Old Hooky and Hook Norton, is kept in perfect condition. Four beautiful ensuite letting rooms are available should you wish to stay a while in this delightful place.

The Star Inn, Manor Road, Sulgrave. Tel: 01295 760 389.

Due north of Sulgrave is another interesting stopover in the village of **Canons Ashby.** This pretty village contains the church of St Mary, which was once part of the Black Canons' Monastery church, although it is much smaller since the Dissolution by Henry VIII. Excavations in 1828 established foundations more than one hundred feet east of the present building. Recently the south west corner of the cloisters was uncovered. The population of Canons Ashby was recorded in Domesday Book in 1086 as sixteen and by 1377 had risen to eighty two.

Canons Ashby House was built from part of the priory after Dissolution. Home of the Dryden family since 1551, it is largely unaltered with Elizabethan wall paintings and outstanding Jacobean plasterwork. The terraced garden with yews, cedars and mulberry trees are delightful. The park has five pairs of gates and is stocked with a pure breed of spotted deer said to be unique in the country.

Heading towards Towcester we discovered the burial place of Edith Sitwell (1887 - 1965) in the hamlet of **Weedon Lois** then further east at **Slapton** the church's interesting 14th century wall painting. It is only a matter of miles before you reach **Silverstone,** its facilities we have already mentioned.

Britons, Romans, Saxons and Normans have all had a hand in shaping **Towcester** although little remains to testify to this. It does however, lie on Watling Street, and was during Romans times a walled town called Lactodorum. During the Civil War, it was the only Royalist stronghold in the area and later during the heyday of coaches it was an important staging post between Holyhead and London.

The history of the **Saracen's Head Hotel** stretches back more than

Sulgrave Manor.

Cannon's Ashby house

four hundred years, and today it still features prominently in the life of Towcester. The newly restored hotel offers a high level of comfort blended with the luxuries of the 1990's. The spacious restaurant has an arched ceiling which is now decorated with chandeliers made from the original bell of the local church. The surroundings are very comfortable and fine cuisine is served from either table d'hôte or a'la carte menu's. The Resident's Lounge has an original open fireplace and provides an ideal meeting place or a quiet retreat for a spot of reading. The Hotel has twenty-one en suite bedrooms some of which have beamed ceilings, they are tastefully furnished with all comforts. For a romantic occasion there are two four-poster bedrooms. On the other side of the original coach entrance, the Lounge Bar welcomes locals and visitors to relax over a glass as they have done for hundreds of years; light refreshments are also available. The Hotel's position on the A5 makes it easily accessible for Northampton and Milton Keynes. Towcester Racecourse is just half a mile distant while Silverstone's famous racing circuit is three miles from the hotel. Many picturesque areas and villages are nearby.

The Saracen's Head Hotel, 219, Watling Street, Towcester, Northamptonshire. Tel: 01327 350414 Fax: 01327 359879

The Towcester church of St Lawrence contains the work of many centuries; the crypt, reached by a doorway from the sanctuary is 13th century, and the arcades with their lofty piers originate from the 13th and 14th centuries. On the arch of the south chapel is a carved jesters head, probably six hundred years old. The massive ninety foot tower with carved angels and font are about five hundred years old.

To the east you'll come to the Grand Union Canal, constructed between 1793 and 1805, winding its way and taking its place in tranquil scenes until its waters are raised by seven locks and vanish into the Blisworth Tunnel, which is nearly two miles long.

Just off the main A5, a couple of miles out of Towcester, lies **Plum Park** Country House Accommodation, the home of Michael Fish.

195

There has been a house here for many centuries though the present building dates from 1895. Michael came here 20 years ago and then, in 1990, he opened his lovely house to guests. This is not just any hotel, guests are encouraged to treat the place as their home and become family friends. The house is surrounded by beautiful gardens where peacocks freely roam and there is a heated outdoor swimming pool for all to use. All the fourteen bedrooms are en suite and the dining room serves wonderful home cooked food. Look out for the staircase, it is well worth seeing!

Plum Park, Towcester Tel: 01327 811515

Just off the A5 still South of Towcester is the sign to **Paulerspury** formerly known as Parvelis Pery, where there is a gem of a place in the form of the splendid **Barley Mow Inn** and **Maltings Restaurant** which stands in this beautiful Northamptonshire village. Dating back to the late 17th century the inn was originally a Farmhouse and Count House of the day. It later became an alehouse and during the late 18th century it was licensed. The new owners Ray & Sandra who recently left executive positions in education, have, together with their Son Anthony, demonstrated a real enthusiasm and put in a lot of work to restore this lovely old inn. Clearly, they are going to make a great success here, and have already maximised on the character and features of the inn such as the low beams and superb open inglenook fireplace. The bar has a well stocked cellar with a fine selection of good ales, and expertly cooked bar snacks and meals, prepared and cooked by Anthony, are available each day. Attached to the Barley Mow is the wonderful Maltings Restaurant where in earlier times the malt was stored to allow it to breath. This characterful restaurant with half panelled walls and exposed stonework, displays old farming implements and memorabilia from bygone days. The menu offers a very good choice of food which should not disappoint, and to accompany your meal you can choose from a wine list which includes over twenty different wines. Sandra, Ray and Anthony have achieved a great deal in a short space of time, and with their welcoming approach and enthusiastic attitude will surely be very successful.

The Barley Mow & Maltings Restaurant, High Street, Paulerspury, Nr. Towcester, Northamptonshire. Tel: 01327 811260

To talk about a perfect venue for a top golf club, you would expect something special, almost unique - well that is certainly true of **West Park Golf & Country Club** situated amidst the beautiful and historic countryside of **Whittlebury**. The ancient park contains fourteen spring fed lakes and some of the oldest oak trees in the country. West Park consists of over 400 acres of gently undulating landscape where four courses are set in an area designated as being of 'Special Landscape Beauty', The 27 tournament standard holes have been constructed as three interchangeable loops of nine, to form several par 72 combination courses of over 6600 yards offering a challenge to players of all standards. In addition, the Golf 'O' Drome and practise Range adds another dimension for players.

The Country Club is designed to appeal to every member of the family; attractions such as archery, croquet, karting, clay pigeon shooting, tennis, bowls and fishing are some of the wonderful leisure facilities available. Of course, there's a Members' Clubhouse, bar,

Bistro, dining room and a great deal more on offer here with even more significant plans for the future. To get the full story, telephone the Club. Situated less than 15 minutes from Junc. 15A of M1 and Junc. 10 of the M40.

West Park Golf & Country Club, Whittlebury, Towcester. Tel: 01327 858092 Fax: 01327 858009

At **Stoke Bruerne**, old canal buildings have been converted into a fascinating Waterways Museum. Nostalgia for those times is aroused by replicas of gaily painted boats . Among the exhibits are an enormous padlock and key used to secure lock gates around 1770, but failed to shackle the famous escapologist Houdini one hundred and sixty years later.

The Boat Inn which stands on the Grand Union Canal at Stoke Bruerne is truly an old established family business. The Woodward Family has run the Inn since 1877 and is now into its fourth generation. Justifiably proud of their independent business and reputation, they offer hospitality second to none. The canalside bars with stone floors, open fires and murals offer visitors an insight into canal life and its busy trade. There's a room set aside for traditional Northamptonshire games, and a comfortable lounge bar. Available to all is a selection of fine beers, wines and spirits together with a an extensive menu of light meals and snacks. The Boat Inn's restaurant is housed in an extension to the old Inn overlooking the lock and offers a full a'la carte menu. Sunday Lunches and Saturday night Candle-lit Dinners are very popular. There's a Tea Room housed in the converted 'old stable' which was once the home of the canal horses used before motors took over. The Inn also has a very smart narrowboat which offers short and long duration trips through the locks and Blisworth Tunnel. A great family atmosphere and a wonderful place to spend the day

The Boat Inn, Stoke Bruerne, Nr. Towcester. Tel: 01604 862428 Fax: 01604 864314

While visiting the Canal Museum in Stoke Bruerne, pay a visit to the adjacent **Old Chapel Tea Room** owned and run by Sally Mays. This charming and bubbly lady has a great menu of delicious home made food available throughout the day. Enjoy scrumptious sandwiches, fresh homemade soup, lunch, cream tea or whatever takes your fancy. Formerly a Wesleyan Chapel built in 1879, it now bears no resemblance inside to its former use. Sally has created a superb tea room with a changing display of pictures by local artists within. Outside there are pleasant seating areas with a neat little surrounding garden. Call in at the **Gallery** next to the tearoom and meet people like John Moody, a local water colour artist; Stephen White, a professional photographer specialising in hand tinting and toning, and Sonya & Russell Cox who make hand painted, printed and embroided work. Open throughout the year.

The Old Chapel Tea Room, Chapel Lane, Stoke Bruerne, Towcester, Northamptonshire. Tel: 01604 863284

The Canal Museum at the heart of Stoke Bruerne, is housed in a restored canalside cornmill. Children can learn why canals were built, about the pioneering engineers who put so much research into the construction of the canals and the boats that worked on them.

Canal families have always had a lifestyle of their own and the museum gives an insight into the engines and range of colourful traditions. The exhibits include working engines, original photographs, waterway wildlife, workmen's and boatmen's tools and full size models of a boat horse and a traditional narrow boat cabin.

The Canal Museum, Stoke Bruerne, Towcester, Northamptonshire. Tel: 01604 862229.

At Stoke Bruerne you can explore both the flight of seven locks and Blisworth Tunnel, through which 'leggers' propelled narrow boats laden with twenty five tons of goods. In fact you will gain a fascinating insight into two hundred years of canal life on the Grand Union. The museum brings alive the vital part that the canal network played in the industrialisation of Great Britain. There is always plenty of activity on the canal. Boat trips are available and passing modern holiday craft contrast with the original working narrow boats moored outside the museum. Stoke Bruerne provides the perfect location for a family day out or for organised groups and school parties, who incidentally should book the time and the date of their visit with the Canal Museum Office (01604) 862229. An attractive tearoom serves morning coffee, lunches and afternoon teas whilst at the shop you will find a selection of souvenirs. In the summer the museum is open daily from 10.00am - 6.00pm including bank holidays. In winter, from October to Easter, it is open daily from 10.00am - 4.00pm except Mondays, Christmas Day and Boxing Day when it is closed. A short distance from all this is another place worth visiting at **Stoke Park,** a the great house standing in four hundred acres, built in 1630's and attributed to Inigo Jones, was the first in England to be built along the Italian lines. Only the two pavilions and a colonnade remain, but they are well worth seeing with the stately pool and its elaborate centre piece of statuary. Check before visiting as opening times are limited.

At the north end of the longest canal tunnel in England by which the Grand Union penetrates the hill from Stoke Bruerne is the pretty village of **Blisworth**. There are roses everywhere in summer; in the cottage gardens, in the Tudor and Jacobean houses, and forming a fragrant and colourful garland round the old grey 13th century church. It's most precious possession is a high screen of the 15th century complete with doors. The newel rood stairs which led to the top of it are still in perfect condition. There is an interesting tablet near the altar which tells the story of the wife of a sergeant-at-arms to Elizabeth I. She lived a maid for eighteen years, was a wife for twenty years and a widow for sixty one years, dying in her ninety ninth year.

The Blisworth Hotel is a carefully restored 16th century hunting lodge situated on the edge of Blisworth village opposite the site of the old station and yet it is just 3 miles from the busy M1 motorway. Owned and personally run by Florence and Larry Seale, who came here three years ago, this is truly an excellent establishment. All the nine bedrooms have en suite facilities and carefully decorated and furnished to provide guests with every home comfort. Both restaurants pleasant and intimate atmosphere in which to dine and the menus have skilfully blended traditional English cooking with classical continental cuisine. The self contained Banqueting suite is an ideal venue for wedding receptions, exhibitions and business conferences.

Blisworth Hotel and Restaurant, Station Road, Blisworth Tel: 01604 859551

Just across the busy A43 is **Gayton** where you will find a good stopping place particularly if you have the family in tow. Taken over, thirteen years ago by John and June, the **Queen Victoria at Gayton** has become South Northampton's most famous family steak restaurant.

The inn has a wonderful interior of character with many eye-catching features, furnishings and ornaments. An excellent range of real ales are kept in top condition and a selection of popular wines are

201

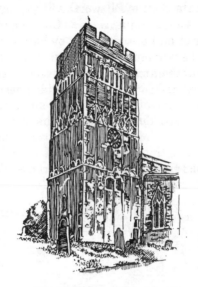

Earls Barton Church.

All Saints Church. Northampton.

always available. Within the Queen Victoria is the Cuttle Mill Steak House which boasts the finest, mature, prime Scottish or English Steaks. There is something to please all tastes and with a special section for children and a selection of freshly made soft ice cream desserts, you can't go wrong. John and June even offer a free collection and delivery service from the local areas in their 'Boozer Cruiser' mini bus service. Easily located off the A5, A43 or junction 15a - M1.

The Queen Victoria, 10 High Street, Gayton, Northampton. Tel: 01604 858438

Just down the road from The Queen Victoria, in the village of Gayton, lies the **Evergreen Riding Stables**. What started out as a hobby ten years ago has become a full time job for Rachel Billing and her two able assistants Emma and Vivien. In the heart of wonderful riding country, the stables, with fully qualified instructors, have plenty of horses and can cater for any age and ability.

Evergreen Riding Stables, High Street, Gayton Tel: 01604 858247.

Heading back towards Daventry at **Upper Stowe**, **The Old Dairy Farm Centre** offers a rewarding day out for all the family. Whatever the age group, there's something to interest everyone. Built around a working farm in the little village of Upper Stowe, not only do you get the chance to enjoy farm animals and pets in their everyday surroundings, there are craft workshops where a wide variety of skills are demonstrated, shops stuffed full of produce such as chutneys, old fashioned preserves superb cheese and traditional wine; Antiques, crafts and clothing and lots more to see and enjoy. The Barn Restaurant is open all day where everything served is home made. Enjoy a leisurely luncheon, indulge in a farmhouse cream tea or sample the wonderful freshly baked cakes and pastries. The centre is housed in a range of prize winning converted 19th century buildings and is one of the premier attractions of Northamptonshire. Location: half a mile from the A5 and ten minutes from Junc. 16 of the M1.

The Old Dairy Farm Centre, Upper Stowe, Nr. Weedon, Northampton.
Tel: 01327 340525

Following the Grand Union canal via **Upper Stowe,** and arriving at **Weedon**, which stands close to Watling Street, you will find the church which is approached along an avenue of limes, Built thirteen hundred years ago by the King of Mercia, whose daughter St Weburgh - buried in Chester - founded a nunnery among the swamps of the River Nene.

On the banks of the Grand Union Canal stands the historic **Heart of England Hotel,** built in 1740 and originally known as the New Inn, it continues to uphold a 250 year reputation for hospitality. Step inside this recently refurbished hotel where the character has been retained and a warm welcome awaits, with open fires for the frosty evenings. During the Napoleonic Wars the hotel became a military depot and remained as such until the end of the Second World War. Military memorabilia from both world wars can be seen in the oak-panelled bar area.

The bedrooms are a delight and have been furnished with care and individuality to offer a high level of comfort. All rooms have en-suite

The Round Church of the Holy Sepulchre, Northampton

facilities, television, direct dial telephones and hospitality trays. Traditional English cuisine is served and extra daily specials are featured on the blackboards. Children have an enclosed playground and outdoor barbecues are a feature in the holiday season. Set against one of the most picturesque waterways in the country with moorings at the side of the hotel. 4-Crown.

The Heart of England Hotel, Daventry Road, Weedon, Northamptonshire.
Tel: 01327 340335 Fax: 01327 340531

Situated on the main A45 road in the village of **Flore** is the magnificent public house **The Royal Oak**. Dating back over 200 years, the olde worlde charm of the building is a natural pull. This is a traditional family pub, with a warm and friendly atmosphere, that is full of character. Julie Trasler, your host, in her short time here, has turned this into a wonderful place to relax and enjoy a glass or two of fine ale and some delicious pub food. There is a full menu of meals and bar snacks and a daily specials board. Whilst visiting do watch out for Flappy, a magnificent Red Devil fish - the local character!

The Royal Oak, 28 High Street, Flore Tel: 01327 341340

The church at nearby **Dodford,**contains some interesting brasses and medieval monuments worth looking at whilst on your way to **Daventry.** Its streets of dignified Georgian houses follow the lines of the medieval thoroughfare and there is still a twice weekly market, held on Tuesdays and Fridays. In the High Street you'll see many fine old buildings and in the Market Place stands the **Moot Hall**, built in 1769 of ironstone, and home to Daventry Museum and the tourist information centre. Built as a private house, the building became Daventry's Town, or Moot, Hall in 1806 following demolition of the

Althorp House

original. The museum has a permanent exhibition illustrating the story of Borough Hill, the local trades, the local rural life and the development of Daventry. As one of the town's main education and cultural centres, the museum also has a programme of temporary exhibitions that are changed regularly and range from village life in Ghana to the work of professional artists on the ever popular theme of cats. Whenever you visit the Moot Hall, you can be sure there is something interesting to see and with the tourist information centre here as well, this is a place not to be missed.

Moot Hall, Market Square, Daventry Tel: 01327 300277

Why not follow your visit to the Daventry Museum with a visit to the pub next door, **The Plume of Feathers**. The building dates back to the 18th century and, in common with other buildings of its age, has been given a new lease of life having undergone a recent refurbishment and restoration. Great care has been taken to ensure that the character, charm and style of the original pub was not lost. The result is a great success. The interior is warm and inviting with oak beams, exposed brickwork and an impressive feature fireplace.

The pub opens early in the morning to serve a superb English breakfast, an excellent range of quality food and fine ale is available throughout the day apart from an hour or two in the
208

afternoon when the pub closes. The resident managers, Irene and Bill Turner are justly proud of the friendly atmosphere they have created.

The Plume of Feathers 19 Market Sq. Daventry. Tel: 01327 702378

Only a short distance from the centre of Daventry is the impressive Victorian style **Kingsthorpe Guest House** where the host, Lynne, strives to maintain a friendly, homely atmosphere. Fourteen cosy, well equipped, guest rooms of various sizes are available, all have en suite facilities. In the morning a wonderful breakfast awaits you, evening meals are available by arrangement. The guest house has a comfortable lounge with colour TV receiving Sky programmes. This is an ideal place to base a touring holiday or just to stop over for a night or two. Situated on Badby Road.

Kingsthorpe Guest House, 18 Badby Road, Daventry.
Tel:01327 702752

A hill fort lies on **Borough Hill,** six hundred and fifty feet above sea level and is the third largest fort of its kind in the country. Oval in shape, it is more than two miles round and covers an area of 150 acres. The hill is part of a range forming the great water divide of the Midlands and from this point you can see into seven counties.

Shakespeare mentions Daventry in his plays; once when Falstaff tells the tale of a shirt stolen from an innkeeper. It is said that Charles I spent his last six nights in the Wheatsheaf Inn before losing the Battle of Naseby and hence his kingdom. During the coaching era whip making was the chief industry of Daventry.

On the edge of Daventry, on the A45, stands **The Britannia Hotel.** A large and imposing modern building, everything about the hotel is on a grand scale, but do not let this put you off as the personal touch is very apparent. All the en suite rooms are modern, comfortable and well equipped and are guaranteed to ensure you have a restful stay. There are several different restaurant areas that serve exciting and varied menus at very reasonable prices. The interior of the hotel is lavishly decorated and furnished giving it a cosy and comfortable feel that is hard to find in so many large hotels. With several large function rooms available this is an ideal place to hold receptions and business conferences.

The Britannia Hotel, London Road (A45), Daventry
Tel: 01327 77333

Hellidon is a picturesque conservation village found on the Northamptonshire border with Warwickshire, sixteen miles from Leamington Spa and Warwick. It is well worth stopping off here to visit **The Red Lion Inn.** This lovely old-fashioned village inn has been owned and personally run by John and Jennifer Daffurn since 1985. It is a cosy and welcoming establishment where you can warm yourself by the open fires of the Lounge and Public bars with their old oak beams, country prints and good local atmosphere.

All eleven en-suite bedrooms are individual and pleasantly furnished complete with TV, radio alarm and other facilities. A variety of menus are available offering anything from a quick snack to full restaurant dining, available both lunchtimes and evenings. Residents have complimentary use of the local Tennis, Croquet and Fishing Clubs with Golf and Country Pursuits nearby - set in a lovely scenic area.

The Red Lion, Hellidon, Nr. Daventry, Northants. Tel: 01327 26120

Situated close to both the M1 and M40 motorways and lying between the villages of Hellidon and Southam is **Hellidon Lakes Hotel and Country Club**. Until five years ago this was farmland but Stuart and Jackie Nicoll have transformed 240 acres into a modern, well equipped hotel, restaurant and golf course with many other amenities besides. Everything about Hellidon Lakes is superb and it offers the ultimate in leisure facilities, accommodation and dining. As well as spectacular 27-hole golf course, with driving range and practice ground, there is a tennis court and fly fishing is also available. The leisure facilities include a sauna/steam room and solaium, a fully equipped gymnasuim with swimspa, and a snooker room.

In addition the hotel has two resident beauty therapists, excellent facilities for the disabled, a sports shop, conference, wedding and banqueting facilities, and a helipad. There are 45 luxury bedrooms and suites, tastefully decorated and furnished to provide all the modern comforts of the best hotels.

The Lakes Restaurant serves excellent á la carte and table d'hôte menus to be enjoyed in warm and intimate atmosphere enhanced by the wooden panelling and open fires. For less formal dining the Club Bar Restaurant offers a range of tasty snacks and full bar meals. In a wonderful position, with magnificent views for such an extensive establishment the personal touch is very much there.

Hellidon Lakes Hotel and Country Club, Hellidon, Near Daventry
Tel: 01327 262550, Fax: 01327 262559

The pretty village of **Badby** is situated just off the A361, three miles south of Daventry on the Banbury road. It is an excellent base from which to tour around many famous areas such as Stratford-upon-Avon, Oxford, Stoneleigh, Blenheim and Althorp Hall, Silverstone etc., and within walking distance of the Knightley and Nene Ways, Badby Woods and Fawsley Park.

What better place to stay therefore than **The Windmill at Badby,** a traditional Inn dating back to the 17th century, tastefully modernised, combining all the facilities of a modern hotel with the charm and character of the old and picturesque. The stone built and thatched inn has an inviting appearance, and inside, the log fires and flagged floors confirm the traditional warmth.

The recently created accommodation provides eight comfortable en-suite bedrooms with all modern facilities and there are special terms for Weekends and House Parties for which this Inn is ideally suited. The Windmill is personally supervised by the proprietors and many 'Speciality Evenings' are arranged with dancing and live entertainment. The Sportsman Dinners, with famous names from the World of Sport are particularly popular. A great variety of home cooked meals and bar snacks are served seven days a week including Sunday lunch and evenings. There are many specialities on offer such as Cajun Popcorn Prawns, Stilton Chicken and Vegetarian dishes, with the popular and easy foods for children all at very affordable prices. The choice of Real ales is extensive and includes Bass, Boddington, Flowers and Wadsworths. Telephone for details of offers on accommodation and special events.

The Windmill at Badby, Badby Village, Daventry, Northamptonshire.
Tel: 01327 702363

Following the border with Warwickshire northwards and across the **A45** lies **Braunston** an important junction on the Grand Union Canal. The canal links Braunston with the Thames, the Trent and the
212

Midlands. Nearby **Ashby St Ledgers** has a church with 14th century paintings and the manor house belonged to Robert Catesby and was used by the Gunpowder Plot conspirators as a meeting place. On November 5th 1605 he rode the eighty miles from London in seven hours bringing the news that the Plot had failed. Afterwards fleeing to Holbeach in Staffordshire he was tracked down on November 8th and shot dead after refusing to surrender.

The church, standing near the lovely three gabled Tudor Manor house was refashioned by John Catesby in the 15th century. Inside, there is much to see including Jacobean pews and a canopied chancel screen painted red and green with exquisite tracery and a frieze of foliage. There are many brasses of the Catesby's, a Norman font and on various walls the traces of medieval paintings among which you can make out the Last Supper, women at Christs tomb and the crucifixion.

The M1 effectively cuts the county in two and in order to explore the northeastern half of the area we headed south to junction 15 . Turning right off the A508 you will find **Wootton** and a convenient place to stop on your way in or out of Northampton. **The Queen Eleanor** is one of Scottish & Newcastle Breweries' 'Homespreads' providing friendly places to eat and drink. This inn is situated on the edge of the village of Wootton on Newport Pagnall Road West, and caters for families, tourists and local businessmen. In fact every effort is made to encourage families with provision of a separate family area and a wonderful children's play area which will excite any youngster. The Queen Eleanor is very nicely furnished and decorated throughout and unlike many larger establishments, maintains a person touch and a very warm welcome. Menus offer a choice for those just looking for a quick bite, to a relaxing meal for all the family with special menus for the young ones. Daily specials are displayed on the chalkboard and the tempting deserts will finish off the occasion.

The adjacent **Lodge Inn** has excellent quality accommodation with en-suite bathrooms many of which are ideal for families. Disabled guests are assisted wherever possible and may like to telephone in advance. Currently there are nineteen rooms with a further nineteen due to open in December 1995. Scottish & Newcastle Breweries are offering a combination of excellent facilities with good value.

The Queen Eleanor, Wooton, Northampton.   Tel: 01604 762468
In the tiny hamlet of **Piddington** which lies to the southeast of Wootton is the attractive **Spread Eagle** public house. Owned and personally run by David Nunn for the past 26 years, the inn dates back to the mid 18th century. Very much a meeting place for the locals, you can expect a good pint of real ale and excellent conversation. Every now and then outside influences touch this tranquil establishment as it is also the local polling station during local and general elections.

The Spread Eagle, Forest Road, Piddington, Northampton .
Tel: 01604 870053
From here the road wends its way between Salcey Forest and Yardley Chase arriving by way of the A428 at the little village of **Yardley Hastings,** which used to belong to a Saxon earl and then to William the Conqueror's niece, Judith. It can be reached through the

great beech avenue of Castle Ashby Park, remnants of the forest that once covered the whole of this countryside.

The building of **Castle Ashby** was started in 1574 in the area of a 13th century castle that had been previously demolished. The original plan of the building was in the shape of an 'E' in honour of Queen Elizabeth I, and is typical of many Elizabethan houses. About sixty years later the courtyard was enclosed by a screen designed by Inigo Jones. One of the features of Castle Ashby is the lettering around the house and terraces. The inscriptions, which are in Latin, read when translated '*The Lord guard your coming in*' and '*The Lord guard your going out*'.

Inside there is some wonderful restoration furniture and paintings of the English and Renaissance schools. The building of these great dwellings was one of the extravagance of the time and the hospitality offered continued to act as a magnet to royal company and the court in the age of Elizabeth I.

On a much smaller scale the old manor house makes a delightful picture by the church; it has a dungeon and there is a 13th century window with exquisite tracery set in the oldest part of the house near a blocked Norman arch. The poet Cowper loved to wander amongst the trees, some of which are said to have been planted by the Countess Judith herself. The tree that attracts the most visitors is called Cowper's Oak, the branches of which spread twice as far across as the tree is high. There is a tradition that it will never die because Cowper stood beneath it one day during a heavy thunderstorm and was inspired to write his famous hymn: '*God moves in Mysterious Ways*'.

At Castle Ashby visitors can discover the unique combination of civilised country shopping and walking in the gardens of a Stately Home with a visit to **Castle Ashby Rural Shopping Yard, Gardens and Restaurant.** The Gardens are set in 200 acres of unspoilt parkland with a mile long avenue offering views of Ashby Castle, the ancestral home of the Marquess of Northampton. Follow the 18th century carriageway through towering trees to the lake. There is much to explore and enjoy here. The Yard is open all year and you can explore the shops and watch the Craftsmen at work. Look in at the Country Collection for Knitwear, clothing, leather goods and accessories, and in Castle Ashby Pottery a wide range of practical Stoneware, Porcelain and Terracotta is made on the premises. The Bronte Furniture Co. offer custom built kitchens, bedrooms, bathrooms and lots more. Visit to the Fine Foods shop where you can buy fine cheeses, home made dishes, fresh fruit etc. in this fine Delicatessen. The Gallery has 19th & 20th century British Oils and Watercolours for sale as well as contemporary art, Sculptures and many items of interest. See Peter Rose in his workshop handcrafting a large selection of Wildlife and Fantasy pieces, while in Nightingale Jewellers, traditional and modern handcrafted jewellery is a speciality. With so much to see here, a break in The Buttery Restaurant will be welcome. Based in the former dairy it offers a delightful combination of creative home cooking with friendly and comfortable surroundings. Open all year (closed Mondays except Bank Holidays). Easy wheelchair access and free parking areas. Located close to the A428 & A509 south east of Northampton.

Castle Ashby Shopping Yard, Gardens & Restaurant, Castle Ashby, Northampton. Tel: 01604 696250

A few minutes away from the Castle is **The Falcon**, a traditional 16th century country inn of distinction, privately owned and managed by the resident proprietors Jo and Neville Watson. For the owners, "finding The Falcon was like a dream come true", and if your real enjoyment comes from the best food and accommodation, in the ambience of a quality country hotel, then it could be your dream come true. The Falcon is warm, cosy,and comfortable, and everywhere in the hotel, there's evidence of the personal touch; applied for example, to the charming rooms where fresh flowers abound; several languages are spoken for the well-being of guests, and nothing seems too much trouble. All sixteen bedrooms are very tastefully furnished with individual style, and have private bathroom or shower en-suite, colour television, direct dial telephone, hot beverage tray, hairdryer and electric trouser press. In the summer, the pretty restaurant, seating 60, and pavilion marquee overlook the lawn surrounded by trees. In the chillier days a blazing log fire draws you in where the menu may be perused at leisure over pre-dinner drinks. People come from far and wide to the restaurant where Chef Neil Helks serves modern English cuisine with an accent on good value. On Sundays a traditional roast is offered. In addition to an extensive wine list, Neville has introduced a good selection of interesting half bottles.

216

Booking for the restaurant is usually essential. This award winning hotel has a great deal to offer, and has special weekend and holiday breaks covering Art, Falconry, Ballooning, Flying and more. Awarded 4-Crown Commended by ETB and an AA rosette for the restaurant.

The Falcon, Castle Ashby, Northampton. Tel: 01604 696200 Fax: 01604 696673

The church in Castle Ashby is as old as William the Conqueror and still has in its walls stones laid at the same time as he gave this piece of England to Judith. A couple of miles north east of Yardley Hastings you pass the stone cottage and houses that line **Grendon's** long and twisting main street. The village is built on a slope, and the brown and grey tower of the 12th century church is one of the best known landmarks in the River Nene valley. It pokes up from between thatched and slated roofs, and overlooks an orderly patchwork of outlying fields. The church has been added to every century and the latest addition is a striking, black and white marble floor put in by a rector in 1914 in memory of his three children.

Grendon Hall is a Queen Anne mansion, once the home of earls and marquises of Northampton. The hall, now owned by the County Council, still has rooms with early 18th century panelling. Two other notable houses in Grendon are the Grange built in 1850, with a lantern cupola on its roof and the gabled 17th century Manor Farm House.

Nearby **Wollaston** is separated from its neighbour **Great Doddington** by the gently flowing Nene and there is a local industry making mats from the rushes of the river. Beacon Hill gives us a wide and lovely view, in which it is said, some twenty seven towers and spires can be seen on a bright sunny day. There are many 17th century houses built of the local brown ironstone and the spire of the church has eight sides of rich 14th century tracery in its openings. In

1737 most of the medieval church fell to the ground but part of the transept and the beautiful central tower still remain.

The magnificent **Stags Head** stands in Great Doddington, just a couple of miles out of Wellingborough and within easy reach of the main A45. Formerly thatched, it was built in 1693 and has a real picture postcard look, especially during the summer when the hanging baskets and troughs of flowers are in full bloom. Owned and personally run by Bob Rendle and his charming wife Gerry, the atmosphere is both warm and lively. Tastefully and sympathetically decorated in a style in keeping with the building's age, the pub retains its olde worlde feel. The inn boasts a fine selection of fine real ales and outstanding, delicious food. The cosy restaurant is very popular and booking is preferable at all times and essential at weekends. The menu is a mouth-watering list of traditional English fare with a tasty mix of continental and more exotic dishes. All in all a wonderful place, with plenty to offer.

The Stags Head, Great Doddington, Wellingborough
Tel: 01933 222316

From here there is a lovely walk by following the path of the river for a few miles as it meanders through this lovely part of the world on its way to the county capital, Northampton. The next stop heading towards Northampton and a must if you are in the area , is the village of **Earls Barton** where there is the most impressive Saxon church tower in the country, not just Northamptonshire, and there are some pretty impressive churches here. It looks today as it did a thousand years ago with its mass of decorations by medieval craftsmen.

In 1934 workmen found, embedded in the wall fifty feet from the ground, a horse's tooth. There was a pagan belief that the burial of horses' skulls improved the sound acoustics and that the skulls of forty horses were once laid in rows between the joists with the idea of improving the tone of an organ which stood over them. That wasn't here though - so maybe the tooth was meant to improve the sound a little bit, or more likely a horse belonging to one of the workmen had eaten too many lumps of medieval sugar.

The remarkably well preserved Norman doorway is one of the treasures of this lovely old church and is dated 1180. But it is inside that a profusion of colour can be seen where the chancel screen gleams as if encrusted with jewels. Set into this 15th century gem are hundreds of dazzling butterflies on the wing and beside the screen stands a wonderful heavily carved, black oak Jacobean pulpit. In West Street the **Earls Barton Museum** of local life is well worth a visit to see the exhibits of local industries including shoe and lace making. Just outside Northampton and south of the A45 is the village of **Cogenhoe** which overlooks the Nene Valley, and where, set high on the hillside, are delightful Tudor and Jacobean farmhouses. One gabled house bears the date 1684 and the initials of the builder. Just west of here is **Gt Billing** where you will find a great place to visit or use as a base for touring the area in the form of **Billing Aquadrome** which has to be one of the most accessible parks in the country. Well signposted from all the major routes,the park offers a wide range of leisure facilities including swimming pool, angling and boating as well as offering parks for tents and caravans and moorings on the Marina. There is everything here for a great family holiday.

Did You Know...

There is a full list of

Tourist Information Centres

at the back of the book?

Billing Aquadrome, Crow Lane, Great Billing, Tel: 01604 408181
The Westone Hotel is situated in **Weston Favell**, Northampton, a few minutes drive from the M1 and Northampton town centre. Its impressive stone frontage overlooks the terrace and lawn in a peaceful location. The Hotel was originally built as a country house in 1914 designed by G H Stephenson, a prominent architect of the day. The Westone today offers 66 bedrooms all with private bathroom, colour television with satellite channels, radio, direct dial telephone and all modern facilities. There are some suites which are ideal for families. The Hotel is well known for its excellent food and is an ideal venue for

private functions and wedding receptions. A hotel which maintains a very friendly and caring standard of service. Part of the Queens Moat House Group with many hotels in the U.K. and in Europe.

Westone Moat House Hotel,Ashley Way, Weston Favell, Northampton. Tel: 01604 739955 Fax: 01604 415023

We next came to **Little Houghton** where the poet, John Clare would often come on the walks he was allowed to take from his asylum in Northampton. There are traces of the moat of the old manor house near the 13th century church, and nearby are the village stocks.

There are many 17th century houses built of the local brown ironstone and the spire of the church has eight sides of rich 14th century tracery in its openings. In 1737 most of the medieval church fell to the ground but part of the transept and the beautiful central tower still remain.

In the square you can admire Sir Thomas Tresham's House, one of the trinity of buildings associated with his name; the others are the Lyvedon New Building at Brigstock and the Triangular Lodge at Rushton.

Heading towards Northampton on Bedford road and a mile before the centre is the **Courtyard by Marriott Northampton** one of the biggest and best equipped in the area. The hotel has a very welcoming and personal atmosphere and is a good base from which to explore the area's many places of interest.

As you would expect from a hotel of this calibre all 104 guest rooms are very well appointed and have en suite facilities. In addition the elegant 'Beeches' Restaurant provides a wide choice of delicious food throughout the day. Guests are also able to use the hotel's fitness room. Ample free parking. Exit M1 at junction 15, take A45 towards Wellingborough, then A428 towards Bedford. The hotel is 100yds away on left hand side.

Courtyard by Marriott Northampton, Bedford Rd.,Northampton Tel:01604 22777

Before entering Northampton itself there are a number of little villages on the approaches to town which are worth of mention and exploration.

Sandwiched between Earls Barton and Northampton is **Ecton** , where the ancestors of another famous American, Benjamin Franklin lived. Traditionally, for three hundred years, the eldest Franklin son was always the village blacksmith. During his visits to England Benjamin searched the Ecton registers and found a Franklin there from 1558, when records were started, and discovered that he was the youngest son of the youngest son for five generations. His father, Josiah, took his wife and three children across the Atlantic in 1685. There he had four more children and, on the death of his wife, he remarried and had another ten. Benjamin said that he remembered thirteen siblings sitting at the table at one time.

Today, unfortunately, the smithy and the Franklin home have disappeared and until 1910 there was nothing in the church to commemorate this world famous citizen, when a group of pilgrims provided a bronze tablet and bust. The inscription is from one of his speeches; ' *The longer I live, the more convincing proof I see of this truth, that God governs in the affairs of men.'* Opposite the church is **Ecton House** built in 1778. **Ecton Hall,** not to be confused with Ecton House, takes the place of the old nunnery and was rebuilt in 1756 and extended about 1880 all in the Tudor Gothic style. In the wooded grounds is an avenue still known as the Nun's Walk, and a summerhouse which has been there for several generations.

A few miles north is **Sywell** and the **Sywell Country Park** which has delightful waterside walks and a picnic meadow where you are able to observe a multitude of wildlife. There is a visitors centre; free admission and free parking.

Sywell is also where you will find **The Horseshoe**, a charming country pub. Its character and style befits the building's age and the olde worlde atmosphere is very apparent. The low beamed ceiling blends with some exposed brick work and the plate racks around the walls display interesting items from a bygone age. Pleasantly decorated with plenty of comfortable seating, there is also a wonderful, secluded beer garden for warmer days. Here you will find a good range of real ales and to fill that gap either at lunchtime or in the evening, there is a smashing selection of delicious meals listed on the blackboard. All in all this is a stylish, traditional village pub and they are getting rarer day by day.

The Horseshoe, 2 Overstone Road, Sywell, Northampton .
Tel: 01604 642286
Westward across the A43 is a village which has a church at one end of the village and a chapel at the other.
Hidden in the village of **Moulton**, but only a couple of minutes from the main A43, lies the **Artichoke Inn**. The inn was built in 1608 on the site of a meeting place for knights about to go off on the Crusade. During the mid to late 17th century is was a farmhouse and the village inn and it has also been a coaching inn on the main Northampton to Kettering coach route. Since early 1994 this historic pub has been run by Kerry Knight, the licensee, with the help of her sister-in-law, Angie, who runs the restaurant. Open all day everyday the bar offers a wonderful range of real ales including John Smiths and Speckled Hen. Food is available in the bar each lunchtime and the restaurant is open Thursday to Saturday evenings and Sunday lunchtime where you can choose from an excellent a la carte menu or, on Sunday, a traditional roast. The emphasis is most definitely on fresh, home cooked

dishes. This first class establishment is certainly a credit to Kerry and Angie.

The Artichoke Inn, Church Street, Moulton, Northampton Tel: 01604 643941

Heading towards Northampton along the A43 will bring you to the suburbs of Boothville, and you will easily spot the wonderful **Lumbertubs Inn and Restaurant** with its old farm cart full of flowers (in summer) on the green. Like a number of this Breweries' 'Homespreads' inns, it has recently been re-furbished and in keeping with its age has wooden floors, exposed beams and memorabilia from a bygone age. As with other 'Homespreads', Lumbertubs is especially welcoming to families. Recognising the needs of parents and children alike, the inn provides a 'families' room, a great children's play area and splendid beer garden. Menus feature a good selection of main course dishes with options for Vegetarian and lighter meals with smaller portions available for children. Under 7's get their own Funky Forest menu.

Lumbertubs Inn & Restaurant, Boothville, Northampton. Tel: 01604 644916

It is well worth spending a day in the county town of **Northampton** for there is much to see. Most of the town was destroyed by the Great

Fire of 1675, but is was rebuilt in such a spacious and well-planned way that Daniel Defoe (1661-1731) called it, *'the handsomest and best built town in all this part of England'*. This thriving market town offers a fascinating mix of historic and modern attractions. Fine Norman churches, Victorian architecture, museums, an art gallery, modern shops and entertainments will spoil you for choice. Northampton's history goes back beyond the Romans, certainly to the Iron Age as settlements have been found in and around the town. The Market Square is reputedly the second largest in England. The most distinguished building is **Welsh House**, rebuilt in 1975 to its original 16th century form. It is a relic of the days when Welsh drovers brought their cattle to the market. The focal point is the Victorian Gothic Guildhall, with its intricate carved statues outside depicting scenes of Northampton history.

There is a fine **Central Museum and Art Gallery** in Guildhall Road, with a collection which includes Italian art of the 15th to 18th centuries,ceramics and sculptures, some of the work is by local artists. There is also what is believed to be the finest collection of footwear in Europe. A room has been fitted out as an old home cobbler's shop before the days of factories. On display there is a wide variety of footwear including some Roman sandals, Queen Victoria's wedding slippers and Margot Fonteyn's ballet pumps. The strangest item is a huge boot worn by an elephant which was taken across the Alps in 1959 in a re-enactment of Hannibal's crossing.

Further down Guildhall street is the **Royal Theatre,** home of the Northampton Repertory Company. The modest exterior belies the gorgeously decorated auditorium which was designed in 1884 and was then known as the Opera House. A short walk away is the oldest building in Northampton, the **Church of the Holy Sepulchre** in Sheep Street. One of the four surviving round churches in England, it owes its character to the inspiration of the Crusaders and is a replica of the original in Jerusalem. The Nave was built in 1100 and is completely round. The choir section was built half a century later and the result is a disjointed exterior, but the interior has all the fascination of rarity.

All Saints, in the very heart of the town, is also most striking. Rebuilt after a fire, its entrance is reminiscent of St. Paul's Cathedral in London. The architect, Henry Bell used Christopher Wren's chief plasterer during the reconstruction. The great Portico is crowned by a statue of the dissolute Charles II who gave one thousand tons of timber for rebuilding. He stands above the open parapet wearing the bizarre mixture of Roman toga and an English wig! We were reminded sadly of another figure who used to sit in the shadow of the huge round columns, the poet John Clare. He would wander down from the asylum and sit here for hours watching the throng go by. Born in 1793 in a cottage in Helpston he lived for forty years within the countryside and county that was to inspire him.

In the heart of Northampton, in the pedestrian area of the town, is **The Fish Inn**. The Inn, built during the mid-18th century, takes its name from the street in which it stands which was once the town's main fish market. During the 'Hungry 1840s' the Fish Inn was part of a club that bought corn and flour to make bread. Things are much improved since those hard times and you can be sure of plenty of food and drink whenever you step into this lively inn today. Sympathetically renovated and redecorated the Inn has twelve comfortable en suite bedrooms with full modern facilities and there is a small, private car park for residents. The Inn is also well known in the town for the excellent quality and value of its meals and the wide range of real ales that it has to offer. This is an establishment that you will find difficult to equal.

The Fish Inn, 11 Fish Street, Northampton Tel: 01604 234040

Ever since King John bought a pair of shoes here for ninepence in the early 13th century, the boot and shoe trade has flourished mightily and Northampton has become famous throughout the world for its footwear. Names like Barratt and Mansfield are just two of the huge chain shoe shops that started life here in a small way. Cromwell's Parliamentarians, with whom the town sided during the Civil War, were sent one thousand five hundred pairs, and many other famous armies over the years have been supplied with footwear made here.

The other great Northampton industry is lace-making and no-one is quite sure how far back the tradition goes. The influx of lace-makers from the Continent in the 17th century exerted a great influence. They were Protestants seeking sanctuary from religious persecution and this transfer of skill enhanced the industry considerably. For three hundred years nearly every village in the county had its lace-makers. As agricultural wages were low, the skilled wife could often earn more than her husband.

Wherever you look in Northampton there are lawns and trees, a meadow or park. It has four hundred acres of open spaces and playing fields and there is a disused racecourse on the highest ground from here to the North Sea. There is also a delightful children's lake, one of the most spacious open-air pleasure centres in the county and no less than three excellent golf courses. Still close to the centre is a convenient place to stay at **St Pauls Guest House** which is family run, has a friendly atmosphere and provides a high standard of accomodation. The 17 bedrooms are a variety of sizes and all are well equipped. Breakfast is a feast, so allow yourself extra time to enjoy it to the full. The guest lounge and licenced bar receive Sky television. Excellent evening meals are available on request. Situated on St Pauls Road, just off the A508 near the centre of Northampton.

St. Pauls Guest House, 37 St. Pauls Road, Tel:01604 718886

Alternatively ,in the same part of town,is an excellent place to stay on the A508 just one mile from Northampton, heading towards Market Harborough. **The Langham Hotel** has been run by Mary and her sons Michael and Robert for the past 21 years. They pride themselves on providing a first class service with a warm and friendly atmosphere. The comfortable single, double and family rooms are fitted with central heating, en suite facilities, colour TVs, direct dial telephones, hairdryers and tea & coffee making facilities. There is a choice of either English or continental breakfast in the morning and a varied selection of evening meals.

The Langham Hotel, 4-5 Langham Place, Barrack Road, Northampton. 01604 39917

A little further on lies the privately owned **Barratts Club**.
Entering the club is like taking a step back in time. The Victorian-
style bar area is tastefully decorated with plenty of comfortable
armchairs and lots of gleaming brass rails to add to the
atmosphere. Langtry's, the Club's restaurant, is an ideal place for
business people and family get togethers alike. There is a tasty
three course menu that is accompanied by a fine selection of wines.
However, the Club's major and most popular activity is snooker
and there are 23 tables carefully laid out in the large snooker room
as well as three private snooker rooms. With a family room to
cater for the younger members this is popular place.

Barratts Club, Kingsthorpe Road, Northampton Tel: 01604 715703
Arriving in **Kingsthorpe** itself and right on the main A508
Market Harborough road is **The Frog and Fiddler**, an
impressive public house full of character and charm. It is over 150
years old and was originally called the Old Five Bells until just two
years ago when it was taken over by McManus Taverns and
completely refurbished. Since then it has unsurprisingly grown
very popular indeed. The Frog and Fiddler is open for fine ales and
a selection of good food all day, seven days a week. Children can
have fun in their own separate room called 'Tumbletown'. The pub
was deservedly voted 'Pub of the Year 1995' by the local Chronicle
and Echo paper.

*The Frog and Fiddler, Harborough Road, Kingsthorpe,
Northampton .Tel:01604 711099.*
Also on the outskirts of Northampton, but this time to the west
betweeen junctions 15 & 16 of the M1 you will find the magnificent

Sun Inn in **Kislingbury**, a 'hidden place' not to be missed. The name of this wonderful inn is really quite apt as its atmosphere is as warm and cheerful as a sunny day. This picturesque thatched roofed building is probably the prettiest in Kislingbury, with its eyecatching hanging baskets and tubs full of blooms, it presents a colourful spectacle all year round. The beautiful exterior is well matched by the traditional and characterful interior of the inn. Barry and Kim, the owners, have over the last few years undertaken a thorough and sympathetic renovation of the property and this has proved to be a great success. A fine selection of real, hand-pulled ales and a wide range of cheeses and wines is always on offer. During the summer the inn's beautifully designed and well kept garden plays host to the occasional barbeque, it is the ideal place to enjoy a quiet drink. This superb inn is well worth a visit.

The Sun Inn, 6 Mill Road, Kislingbury. Tel: 01604 830594

From Northampton there are also a number of interesting villages which lie to the north and west of Northampton . Taking the A50 brings you to the village of **Chapel Brampton** and the historic **Spencer Arms**. This public house takes its name from the Spencer family, whose family home, Althrop House, where Lady Diana grew up, lies only a mile or so away. The traditional country style of the inn is reflected in the interior decoration and furnishings. There are flagstone and quarry tiled floors, low oak beams, a large open brick fireplace and plenty of comfortable pew style seating. Open all day, the pub serves a range of real ales and has a full menu of tasty traditional bar meals along with salads, pasta dishes, daily blackboard special and a menu suitable for children. A very English country pub in the heart of some delightful countryside.

The Spencer Arms, Northampton Rd, Chapel Brampton
Tel: 01604 842237.

Also close by you'll find **Holdenby House,** a Tudor building that was used to hold Charles 1 as prisoner in 1647.

Situated in its own 16 acres of wooded and terraced grounds, **Broomhill Country House Hotel** in the village of **Spratton** lies on the edge of the Althorp estate. The house was built in 1872 as a farmhouse for a local businessman and it is an excellent example of opulent rural Victorian architecture. Owned and personally run by Sue and Joe Kelly, they have, since 1984, created a unique integration of Victorian elegance and modern comfort in a high class hotel. Comfortably decorated throughout, the en suite bedrooms are spacious, and certainly accommodate all guests' possible needs. The attractive restaurant, open to non-residents, is an ideal place to enjoy a leisurely meal, where the menu is a designed to tempt the most discerning of palates. All in all this is a gracious establishment, with a friendly and tranquil atmosphere, surrounded by some panoramic countryside.

Broomhill Country House Hotel, Holdenby Road, Spratton,
Northampton Tel: 01604 845959

Continuing west, the road reaches the A428 and from here the next stopover, especially for those interested in our Royal Family, is the family seat of the Princess of Wales, **Althorp House**. It is popular for visitors, especially those who are after a glimpse of the Princess's earlier life but the house itself originates from the 16th century with alterations added the 18th century. Inside you'll find an interesting collection of paintings,ceramics ,and furniture.

The estate was bought in 1508 by John Spencer a sheep farmer and the house begun in 1573. The entrance hall is lofty and impressive, with a magnificent ceiling of hundreds of flowers set in six sided panels. In 1786 the red brick house was refaced with grey-white brick tiles and the moat filled in as the gardens were remodelled by Samuel Lapridge, Capability Brown's assistant.

Just west of Althorp lies **Great Brington** where the tombs of the

Spencers and Laurences - ancestors of George Washington - can be found.

Situated in the hidden village of **Little Brington,** approximately six miles north west of Northampton, lies **The Saracen's Head** pub. Built in about 1765, this charming red sandstone inn retains many of its original features including inglenook fireplaces, exposed stone walls and dark stone floors. Inside there is an old fashioned style red telephone box and the toilets are an architectural feast not to be missed! The bar is well stocked with fine hand pulled ales and there is a mouth-watering menu offering a wide range of home cooked dishes, hot and cold, to suit every taste, with daily specials chalked up on a blackboard. With a beautiful beer garden this is a warm and friendly pub full of character that would be hard to beat.

The Saracen's Head, Little Brington, Northampton
Tel: 01604 770640

Heading North from here the road reaches the A428 and if you are in the area of **West Haddon** where the A428 crosses with the B4036, a short distance from junction 18 of the M1, a visit to the **Sheaf Inn** is a must: their motto is - "The happy little mad place which specialises in great food and wine at sensible prices". This 300 year old pub and former manor house is a place where seemingly everyone mixes in well and all receive the same attention from the proprietors Annie and Derek; - "Annie supervises the cooking, Derek does the running around".

The front bar has lots of character and looks as though it hasn't changed in years. Its full of atmosphere and serves a good variety of hand-pulled ales and a selection of bar meals. For those requiring a quieter venue, guests can relax in the lounge bar which is adjacent to the restaurant. There you will be offered not only a full a` la carte menu but an exciting selection of daily dishes comprising of starters, main course and sweets, explained to you in detail. The food is really superb and beautifully presented. with forty years in the business the expertise shows. Oh, and in case you are wondering - the restaurant is closed on Sundays - (Derek stops running around and Annie feeds him).

The Sheaf Inn, West Haddon, Northants. Tel: 01788 510328
Also in the area if you are looking for perhaps a place to visit where you can relax for a while then it is well worth visiting **Coton Manor Garden** ,a traditional old English garden in the hamlet of Coton close to Ravensthorpe Reservoir. With yew and holly hedges, extensive herbaceous borders, rose garden, water garden, herb garden and its famous bluebell wood this is a delight not to be missed. The old Head Grooms Cottage has been converted into a wonderful restaurant and tea rooms serving home made cakes and light meals. There is also a small craft and gift shop and many plants featured in the garden are also for sale.

Coton Manor Garden, Near Guilsborough Tel: 01604 740219
There is an air of dignity and prosperity about the wide streets of **Guilsborough**, flanked by 18th century houses of brick and ironstone. The vicarage here used to be Guilsborough Hall, where Wordsworth

came to stay and it is said that he bought with him from the Lake District the yellow Cumberland poopy that grows profusely here. The church has lovely windows by Morris and Burne-Jones. The nearby **Guilsborough Grange** has a wildlife park and a pets corner for children. Its acres of grassland, pond and streams make the Grange an ideal picnic spot.

Naseby played a significant part in the course of English history as this was where on June 14th 1645 the battle was fought that decided the outcome of the Civil War with Cromwell's defeat of Charles I. Here, Cromwell and Fairfax with fourteen thousand Roundheads faced the Royalists forces who advanced outnumbered two to one. Charles's right hand man, Prince Rupert, positioned his army first on Dust Hill; Cromwell drew in his army on the opposite side of the valley, on Red Hill and the first attack came at 10.00am. After heavy fighting, Fairfax won a resounding victory, capturing all the King's baggage, including about £100,000 in gold and silver. Eleven months later Charles surrendered in Newark ending the Civil War.

Today Naseby is one of the least spoilt of English battlefields and in it a large obelisk, erected in 1823, states that the battle had been,' *a useful lesson to British Kings never to exceedthe bounds of their perogative'.* A more modest memorial records the position of Cromwells cavalry before their decisive charge.

Naseby Battle and Farm Museum (01604 740241) contains a minature layout of the battlefield with commentary as well as relics from the battle. It also has on display a collection of bygone agricultural tools and machinery. The actual site of the battle is marked by a column erected in 1936.

Situated in the village of **Welford,** on the main A50 road on the edge of the Leicestershire and Northamptonshire border, is **The Wharf Inn**. This interesting building with its castleated top stands alongside the East Midland Canal. It has character and charm and is furnished and decorated in keeping with age.

There are six excellent bedrooms, five of which have en-suite facilities and it provide an ideal base for those touring in the area or makes an ideal stopping off point for users of the canal. Food features strongly at The Wharf and there is a wide range of food on offer from bar snacks to a'la carte menu for lunch or dinner. A fine range of ales are kept in top condition and there's a good and varied wine selection.

The Wharf Inn, Welford, Northamptonshire. Tel: 01858 575075

East of Naseby is **Kelmarsh Hall** which was built in 1728 by James Gibb, a follower of Sir Christopher Wren. The church is colourful with polished granite piers in the nave and in the chancel, the walls, floor, reredos and altar rails are of many coloured marbles and mosiacs brought from Rome.

To the west of Naseby lies **Cold Ashby**, the highest village in Northamptonshire at seven hundred feet above sea level. From **Honey Hill** a mile away you get fine views across into Warwickshire and Leicestershire. **Sibbertoft**, lies at the northern end of the tableland where the Battle of Naseby was fought. The River Welland, rising nearby, flows a little to the west before beginning its eastward journey, forming the northern boundary of

Northamptonshire. In a wood to the north east are extensive earthworks though to be a Norman motte and bailey castle. The medieval church is restored and the vicar here for twenty one years was the botanist, Miles Joseph Berkeley.

Finally, we cane to **Marston Trussell** on the Leicestershire border. After the Battle of Naseby many fleeing Royalists were surrounded and cut down here, their remains are in the churchyard. Four cedars have cast a shadow over the church for many centuries and both doorways into this 13th century place of worship are medieval.

Inside there is a statue of Mark Brewster who made a fortune in Russia from piracy. He donated four shillings to the poor and forty pounds to the church for a new bell .He returned to England to retire on his ill gotten gains but the long finger of the Tsar tapped him on the shoulder. He was taken back to Moscow where he was tried and executed in 1612. The 17th century hall refashioned in the last century stands in beautiful grounds with an island studded lake.
On that note we left this part of the county and continued our journey northwards.

CHAPTER NINE

North Northamptonshire

Memorial Chapel, Oundle School

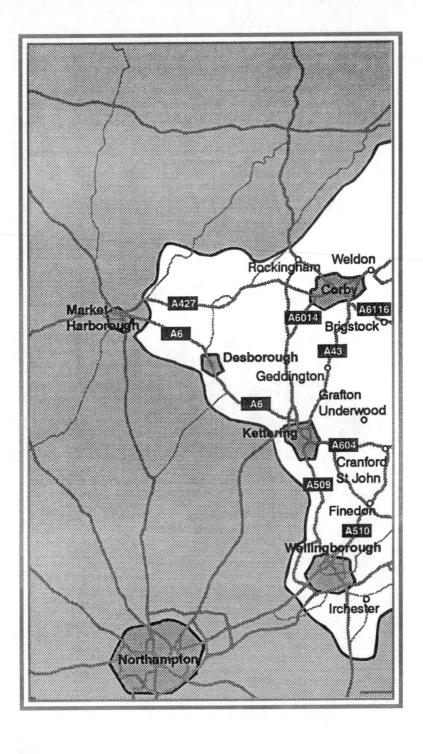

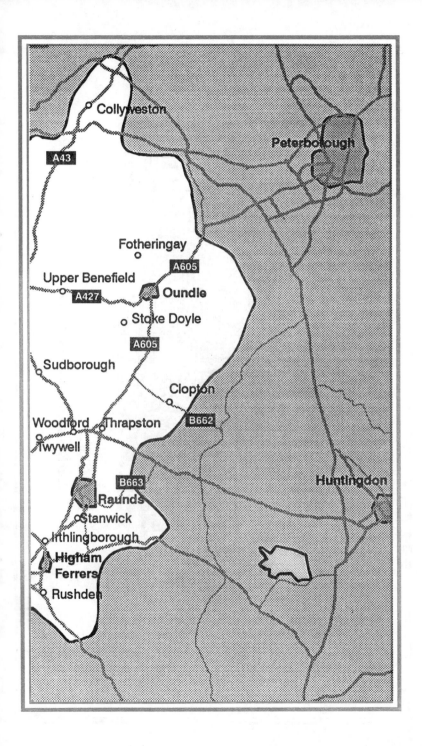

Market Square Higham Ferrers.

North Northamptonshire.

We started our tour of North Northamptonshire in **Irchester** originally a Roman settlement; a walled Roman town was uncovered last century and known as The Burrows. It is eighteen acres in area and part of the eight feet thick walls can be seen. Saxon England has also been discovered here, an extensive cemetery was found with four hundred graves all facing east. Many of the coffins were stone and in one eight bronze vessels were found packed into a bucket. Norman England is evident in the church where there are some columns and piers resting on Norman plinths. The six arched bridge, which crosses the River Nene, is 14th century and bears the crossed keys of Peterborough Abbey and the wheel of St Catherine.

There is a country park just outside Irchester which is on the way to **Wellingborough.** The town sits near the point where the River Ise joins the Nene and the medieval church spire can be seen for many miles. There are fine avenues of trees leading to the town which has, over the years, swallowed up the smaller villages surrounding it. Wellingborough is noted for its industry of iron mills, flour mills and tanneries.

In and around the Market Square there are several interesting old buildings. The Hind Hotel with its gabled roof and handsome windows looks out on the square. It has a 17th century oak staircase, a fine stone fireplace and a room furnished inn oak and called the Cromwell Room because it was being constructed whilst the Battle of Naseby was being fought. There is another fine old house called **Croyland Abbey,** with dormer windows in the five hundred year old roof. Near to it, in public grounds, stands an old tithe barn, stone walled and thatched, seventy feet long and twenty two feet wide. It was built in the 15th century and has two great doorways at either side, one of which is thirteen feet high. All these buildings escaped a great fire which razed most of the town in fours hours in 1738. The handsome 13th century tower and spire of the parish church of All Hallows rises amongst the trees in the centre of town. The great tower seen from across the Nene is that of St Mary's, a modern church built between 1906 and 1930.

To the east is the delightful old town of **Higham Ferrers** on the outskirts of the footwear manufacturing town of **Rushden.** Its long main street widens into Market Square complete with a market cross where the three story building of **The Carriage House** is easily found. In its time it has been a girls school, a gentlemans club and during the last war was requisitioned for housing soldiers. Step inside and you will find it is larger than it appears from outside; here Betty and Sid will greet you with a warm welcome. They have over seventeen years experience in the business and took over the Carriage House about a year ago. The restaurant has seating for approximately eighty people and offers many popular dishes on the a'la carte menu, while lighter snacks can be ordered at the bar along with a good selection of well kept ales. There are nine letting rooms of varying sizes and styles. Make a point of seeing the old carriage to the rear of the building.

The Carriage House, 13 Market Square, Higham Ferrers, Northamptonshire. Tel: 01933 314769

Just off the market place is a narrow lane leading to the church and a group of medieval buildings. One striking house has a great stone panel along its front, with fiery dragons linked to each other. Henry Chichele was born here in 1362; he progressed from bakers boy to Archbishop of Canterbury, a post he held for thirty years until his death in 1443. He never forgot his birthplace and his statue looks down from the church tower, and the house of charity he built, called Bede House is in the churchyard.

Irthlingborough is a small town thriving on leather and iron industries. It has two fine bridges across the Nene, one built in the 14th century and the other in the 20th. The medieval bridge has ten ribbed arches and the arms of an ancient monastery carved on one of its stones suggests that the bridge was built by monks from
240

Peterborough. The modern bridge running parallel to the old is a landmark with great arches stretching for half a mile over the low land by the river. Across the wide valley the handsome tower of the medieval church can be seen with its double rows of battlements, turrets and many windows.

Stanwick, just east Irthlingborough, is set high on a hill, its glorious 13th century church and spire soars high above the Nene Valley. On each side of the belfry are window arches which allow the sound of the bells, one of which is dated 1360, to be heard for miles.

Raunds is known chiefly for the manufacture of army boots and its dolls. In May 1905, Raunds came into the national consciousness when two hundred men marched to London in protest at the low rates of pay for bootmakers. They arrived in the capital to find a crowd of ten thousand supporters waiting. After ten days, concessions were finally made and the strikers victorious.

To the east **Finedon** has a character of its own. It has a well known inn called The Bell, which,by tradition occupies the site on which there has been an inn since 1042. The much restored old Hall with some Elizabethan rooms, a handsome rectory, a charity school built in the reign of Queen Anne and some ironstone houses of the 17th century are well worth noting. The school has a fine doorway and the inn, built in 1872 is a good example of the Gothic revival. Hereabouts, there is an odd tower which stirs the curiosity of the traveller, called the Wellington Tower. It is said that the Duke of Wellington used to stand on this spot when visiting a friend and point out where the countryside around resembled the field of Waterloo.

Finedon Hall, the near neighbour of the church, has a courtyard with embattled walls and an ancient covered walk like a cloister, but the house, with its fine ornamental gables, is mostly 19th century. This is the handiwork of the former squire who rejoiced in the name of William Harcout Isham Mackworth-Dolben.

Following the river north you arrive at **Woodford**, where within the Norman church a human heart was found in one of the columns during restoration work in the 19th century. It was presumed to be the heart of one of the Traillys, Lords of the Manor seven hundred years earlier. It's though to be the heart of one of the family who died during the Crusades and brought back by his followers so that he may rest with his ancestors. It is now enclosed in a cloth and in a glazed recess in the pillar in which it was found. There is also some medieval brass and over one hundred carved oak figures in the church.

Woodford's most unusual and possibly fittest inhabitants was a Josiah Eaton, who was born towards the end of the 18th century. He was only 5 feet 2 inches tall, but he accomplished feats of incredible endurance. In 1815 he started a marathon walk around Blackheath, completing a mile every hour. Apparently he did this without stopping for six weeks! Eventually he covered an astonishing eleven hundred miles.

Thrapston by the A604 and A605, stands on one of the loveliest reaches of the River Nene which flows under the towns medieval bridge. It is surrounded by fine pastureland, created when the flood waters and rich mud subsided following the two ice ages. Since the days of King John, the quiet of Thrapston has been disturbed on market days with farmers coming to sell their cattle and produce.

The castle has vanished and much of the church has been modernised, its main attraction is the stone tablet on the west wall which bears the stars and stripes. It is thought that the American flag was designed with this tablet in mind, it being the coat of arms of Sir John Washington who died in 1624. Thrapston and more specifically the church have become part of the George Washington pilgrimage made by many Americans. Not far from the church is **Montagu House**, believed to have been the home of Sir John Washington.

Within a short walk from the centre of Thrapston and set in five acres of pleasant countryside on the banks of the River Nene is the **Mill Marina Caravan Park**. All you need for an enjoyable caravanning holiday is here. There are 45 pitches on level grass meadows mostly with hook-up facilities, showers, toilets, laundry room, payphone and a licensed bar. Along the banks of the river are 25 moorings and also a slipway; coarse fishing is available from half a mile of riverbank and there is fly fishing two miles away. In the heart of England, a wide variety of wildlife can be observed from your caravan windows and there are many interesting places within easy reach. This is a family-run riverside park offering a friendly atmosphere in which to relax.

Mill Marina Caravan Park, Midland Road, Thrapston.
Tel: 01832 732850

Twywell is perhaps the last place you'd expect to find with links to Africa. Yet two Africans, who helped carry explorer David Livingstone's embalmed body eight hundred miles to the sea on its way to Westminster Abbey, lived here whilst the Livingstone Journals were being prepared for publication.

In the church there are three stones from Calvary in the window by the altar. These were sent by the rectors friend, General Gordon who wrote a letter saying that he hoped to visit the Pope on his way back from Palestine. The letter can be seen in the vestry and the choir stalls are carved with animals including a lion, a hippo, an elephant and other carvings depicting chained and yoked African slaves being driven towards the Cross.

It seems appropriate to find a pub called **The Old Friar**, in the village. Named after a nearby monastery this pub is steeped in history and was once popular with American servicemen flying out from Grafton Underwood on bombing raids during the Second World War. This family run pub welcomes children and has a large selection of non alcoholic drinks along with its fine ales, wines and spirits. The Carvery Restaurant seats seventy and you can also choose from an a la carte menu. The oak beamed ceilings, stone walls and open fireplace give the pub a rustic feel that enhances its informal friendliness where you will be made to feel welcome as soon as you arrive.

The Old Friar, Lower Street, Tywell, Near Kettering.
Tel: 01832 732625

At **Grafton Underwood**, three miles away, you'll find a memorial to the crews of the B17 flying fortresses who were based here and just a mile or so beyond is the delightful village of **Cranford St John**.

Rushton Triangular Lodge

At one time known as the Cathedral Steps due to its magnificent entranceway, **The Red Lion** at Cranford St. John has a characterful interior with some exposed brickwork and low beamed ceilings. Here you can quench your thirst by sampling one of the traditional real ales. Bob and Nuala have been at the Red Lion for thirteen years and have a good regular clientele for their busy 35 seat dining area. The food is reasonably priced and offers plenty of choice where you could tuck into Ocean Cocktail with Greek yoghurt sauce, followed by Duck breast in orange liqueur sauce served on a bed of warm salad leaves and finish off with something from the home made sweet menu. There is a pleasant patio area and garden and meals are served seven days a week. Half a mile from junction 11 on the A14.

The Red Lion, Cranford St. John, Kettering,   Tel: 01536 330663

Travelling west brings you to the second biggest town in the north of the county, **Kettering.** It stands above the River Ise and the name is familiar far and wide, for its produces clothing and shoes. It is here that the missionary William Carey and the famous preacher Andrew Fuller founded the Baptist Missionary Society, which gave a new impetus to the cause of foreign missions all over the world.

Kettering's great parish church, built of Barnack stone is one of the most impressive in the country. The tower and spire, rising one hundred and seventy eight feet, are a landmark for miles around. Much of the old town has disappeared in its rapid growth, but a few old houses linger in narrow lanes.

Hands-On Heritage is on offer at the **Kettering Heritage Quarter** and well worth investigating. Explore the local history at the **Manor House Museum** where both permanent and temporary exhibitions are held. Many regular activities take place and visitors of all ages will find plenty to interest them. A constantly changing programme of exhibitions ensures there is always something new to see at the **Alfred East Gallery.** Every few weeks brings new exhibitions

Deene Park., Nr Corby

recognising local talent with the work of artists, photographers sculptors and many more. You can pop in and enjoy a lunchtime talk or the occasional concert. Discover other interesting areas and sites in the region by visiting the Tourist Information Centre adjacent to the Museum - a good place to shop for gifts. In between times, enjoy a quiet break in the Heritage Gardens. Ring the Centre for further information.

Manor House Museum & Alfred East Art Gallery, Sheep Street, Kettering, Northants. Tel: 01536 534219 & 531381

Whatever you reason for visiting Kettering, you will find a warm friendly welcome from Helen and George at the **Headlands Private Hotel.** Situated in a quiet conservation area a few minutes walk from the town centre there is easy access to the tourist information centre, swimming pool, theatre, restaurants and shopping centre.
The hotel owners are on hand at all times and maintain high standards of facilities, service and cleanliness.
Many of the twelve bedrooms have en-suite facilities and all have colour television and tea/coffee making facilities. The hotel is beautifully furnished and decorated throughout.
In the dining room is a most interesting display of china and probably the largest collection of footwarmers you are likely to see anywhere. A delicious English breakfast is served and evening meals can be arranged; vegetarians and special diets can be catered for. There is a private car park. ETB 3-Crown, AA & RAC listed.

Headlands Private Hotel, 49-51 Headlands, Kettering, Northants. Tel;01536 524624 Fax: 01536 83367

A couple of miles north of **Rothwell** which stands by the A6, at the **Rushton Triangular Lodge**, you'll find a fascinating piece of pious eccentricity built by Sir Thomas Tresham. He owned Rushton Hall, and he built a folly in 1593 to symbolise the Holy Trinity, and everything about it related to the number three or multiples thereof - it has three sides, three stories and is twenty seven feet high. Each side has three windows and three gables and the theme is continued in the triangular decoration. It even has a three-sided chimney. It is difficult to understand the full meaning of Sir Thomas's personal philosophy, but the building is nevertheless quite beautiful. In a way it still partly fulfils his original idea, for it certainly provokes the visitor to think about this strange embodiment of religious fervour. Nearby **Rushton Hall** was Treshams home but is now school of the Royal Institute for the Blind.

Desborough is a small town with old ironstone houses ; it used to be a Saxon settlement and many treasures have come to light in recent years. Three massive stones have been unearthed in the Rectory gardens, the biggest carved on two sides with Saxon scrollwork and a crude picture thought to represent Daniel in the lion's den. Also found here was found the grave of a Saxon lady still wearing a beautiful necklace of thirty seven gold beads with a pendant cross of gold. It is one of the earliest Christian crosses in the country and is now in the British Museum. In another grave a Celtic bronze mirror exquisitely engraved with a spiral design, and an elaborate handle six inches long was found. The church has been here for seven hundred years, though its pinnacled tower with a fine spire is early 16th century. The church house dates from about 1700 and the Market Cross, at the north end of the High Street, was built in the 18th century.

The impressive **George Inn**, also on the High Street is old and, as your hosts Steven and Julia Stratford are proud to relate, has interesting associations with boxing. Very much a local pub, the
248

sporting links are strong today and each evening a variety of traditional pub games and pastimes are laid out for anyone who wants to try their hand. The bar is well stocked with a host of real ales and freshly filled sandwiches and cobs are available at lunchtimes. This is a friendly pub, with plenty of character, that makes a relaxing place to pause for a drink.

The George Inn, 79 High Street, Desborough Tel: 01536 760271

The fields outside **Geddington** bear the remains of more than seventy miles of trees. They were laid out in the 18th century by the 2nd Duke of Montagu, nicknamed John the Planter. He had an idea to plant an avenue from Boughton House all the way to his London home, but when his neighbour, the Duke of Bedford, refused to let the trees cross his estate he planted avenues of equivalent length on his own estate. Unfortunately, Dutch Elm disease destroyed much of his work but the present owners, Boughton Estates, are gradually replacing the old trees with limes and beeches.

Just north of here is evidence of one of the most poignant of love stories, namely that of King Edward I and his wife Eleanor. They enjoyed thirty happy years of marriage during which time Eleanor's devotion was exhibited in her risking her life for her Lord by sucking the poison out of the wound he received from a poisoned arrow. Many years later, the King was on his way to see her after she became dangerously ill but he arrived too late and, heartbroken, he embarked on the one hundred and fifty mile funeral procession to London. At every place her coffin came to rest each night, an **Eleanor Cross** was later erected. Out of twelve built, only three are still remaining; at Geddington, at **Hardingstone** near Northampton and at **Waltham Cross** in Hertfordshire. The Cross, now overseen by English Heritage, stands in a triangle near the church where three roads meet, rising from seven steps to a height of nearly forty feet. It is elaborately carved with statues of Eleanor gazing down upon the passer by.

Still further north on the banks of a tributary of the Nene called Harpers Brook is the Saxon village of **Brigstock** in the Rockingham Forest. The church of St Andrew has a substantial Saxon tower built and its bell used to be tolled three times a day as a guide for travellers through the forest. The forest itself was once the hunting grounds of Norman aristocracy but evidence has been unearthed to show that Brigstock had been settled during the Iron Age and during Roman occupation. The village has delightful old stone cottages, and a 16th century manor house. By the little tree-covered green a quaint Elizabethan cross stands on four steps and is carved on four sides. On the top stands a ball weather-vane.

About a mile away is **Fermyn Woods Hall**, a house which has grown through the centuries from the 14th to the 19th. It was a forest hunting lodge six hundred years ago, its gateway was brought from the house known as the Old Building (or Bield) at Lyveden and bears the coat of arms of Sir Lewis Tresham, second son of Sir Thomas the Builder.

His New and Old Buildings at **Lyveden** are about two miles from Brigstock; one a farmhouse, the other a ruin, bearing witness to the erratic devotion and architectural interest of their creator.

A good time to go to **Corby** is during the colourful 'Pole Fair', but as this only happens every twenty years, you will have plenty of time to plan your holiday. But beware, for on the day of the Fair any stranger may be carried off astride a pole and placed in the stocks where he must stay until a toll is paid - apparently its a Danish custom.

Even as a tiny village, Corby has been in contact with the mainstream of British history. It has been recorded very briefly since the time of King Edgar in the 10th century and there is evidence of pre-Roman and Roman occupation. The actual town itself is rich in open woodland, a surviving reminder of the once great Rockingham Forest. Kingswood, a nature reserve, Hazel Woods and the East Carlton Country Park offer natural habitat on the doorstep.

The latter contains the **Steel Making Heritage Centre** and tells of Corby's connection with that industry. There is also an attractive boating lake with small boats and canoes available for hire and fishing facilities in season. Alongside the Civic Centre, the Festival Hall and Theatre and the indoor swimming complex is the Lodge Park Sports Centre, offering exactly what you would imagine. The Corby Festival takes place over a week in July every year; events include drama,

Memorial Chapel. Oundle School.

Fotheringhay Church.

puppets, art exhibitions, folk and jazz 'happenings', concerts and poetry readings and programmes of popular music.

Weldon is an attractive village situated near to Corby and surrounded by marvellous places to visit. We found the village had a whole host of nice restaurants and pubs as well as good shop and post office. The history of Weldon is interesting because it has its own industry, quarrying the stone which bears its name. This stone was used to build **Rockingham Castle, Old St Paul's** and **Great St Mary's** in Cambridge. The village has a variety of good stone houses dating from the seventeenth century to today, some with date stones. Haunt Hill House for example was built at the time of Charles I. On the green adjacent to the school is the windowless 'Round House' which was used as the Parish lock-up. St Mary's Church, with its backcloth of tall trees, is reached from the village by a raised walk over the bridges across Willow Brook.

North East of Corby, we came across **Deene Park** standing amid gardens filled with old-fashioned roses and rare trees and shrubs. Originally a medieval manor, it has been transformed over the last four hundred years into a Tudor and Georgian mansion by successive members of the Brudenell family. Today Deene Park contains fine examples of period furniture and beautiful paintings. The oldest visible part is an arch circa 1300 in the east of the house which comprises a Hall of about 1450. The Great Hall was completed at the end of the 16th century and has a magnificent sweet chestnut hammerbeam roof. The most famous member of the Brudenells was James, 7th Earl of Cardigan, who led the charge of the Light Brigade at Balaclava and interesting records and relics are on display.

Kirby Hall, now an English Heritage property, dates from 1570 was given by Elizabeth I to her favourite courtier, Sir Christopher Hatton. 17th century alterations have been attributed to Inigo Jones and despite the house being abandoned during the following century it is still a fine example of Tudor and Renaissance influenced design and construction.

Three miles north west of Corby is **Rockingham** which, according to Domesday Book, was wasteland when William the Conqueror ordered a castle to be built there. Today, as in Norman times, the castle stands sentinel-like on the tree clad slopes of Rockingham Hill with the thatched and slated cottage of the village's wide main street spread out below. At Rockingham it is possible to trace the development of English domestic life and cultural taste over nine hundred years. Entering between the Norman towers it is not difficult to image the royal cavalcades thundering in the Middle Ages. The armour in the Tudor Great Hall reminiscent of the Civil War, when Rockingham was captured by the Roundheads. Indeed the castle was used by the

Elton Hall, Nr Oundle

Garden at Deane Park

BBC during filming of the series 'By the Sword Divided' where it was renamed Arnescote Castle.

The Royal George Inn at the nearby village of **Cottingham** is situated in the aptly named Blind Lane. The attractive Inn is built on different levels, and with its neat appearance and colourful window boxes you could mistake it for a private house though its appearance is deceptive, being much larger than is apparent.

Colin and Wendy Reed and family have been the proprietors of the Royal George for the past twenty years and know all about good innkeeping. Customers return on a regular basis to enjoy the home cooked food of which there is an extensive selection. The dining area seats about 50 people and bookings are advised at the weekends. Of course, the bar has a good selection of wines and spirits but the full range of Real Ales and quality food keeps this lovely inn busy most of the time.

The Royal George Inn, Blind Lane, Cottingham, Market Harborough, Leicestershire. Tel: 01536 771005

Situated in the wide Welland Valley between Rockingham Castle and Stamford is the picturesque **Harringworth.** A conservation village of mainly stone and thatch, it still remains unspoilt.

In this pretty village , lies **The White Swan,** a 15th century coaching inn. Owned and run by Chris Sykes, the inn has been totally renovated and also provides seven bedrooms (six en suite) which are all individually decorated in an attractive country house style. Enter the bar and you step back in time: with the old beams, stone walls and traditional furniture this could be the age of the stage coach but the photographs and flying memorabilia bring you back to the 20th century.

The restaurant, offering lunch and dinner seven days a week, offers a constantly changing menu and list of daily specials that above all ensures that whatever you choose the dish will arrive freshly prepared from the best of local produce and seasonal foods. A first class establishment full of character and with a friendly atmosphere that is a delight to visit.

The White Swan, Seaton Road, Harringworth, Corby, Northants.
Tel: 01572 747543 Fax: 01572 747323

Oundle is famous far and wide for its public school, its fine stone houses, its noble church and its old inns. It has been described as the most delightful town in Northampton and you might be inclined to agree, with its pleasant pastoral setting near the Fenlands and the River Nene flowing on three sides. We entered the town across the North Bridge which used to have thirty arches until it was destroyed by a tempest in 1570. There are some famous old inns in Oundle and they are each well worth a visit.

The Talbot, the oldest hostelry in Oundle, was built in 1626. Formerly known as 'The Tabret', (a form of Tabard - a sleeveless coat worn by heralds), it originates from 638 A.D. when a group of monks founded it as a hostel giving food, drink and shelter to the pilgrims and wayfarers. The inn's historic character has been retained throughout its many improvements made over the last 350 years. Today, its ambience is of quiet luxury, comfort and service. The hotel is well known for its delicious choice of cuisine which can be sampled in the timbered restaurant, whilst the Snug Bar is cosy and makes an ideal retreat for quiet conversation and perhaps a pint of local ale. The high standard of furnishings and facilities throughout the hotel are also reflected in the en-suite bedrooms where you can enjoy all the comforts of home. Children's needs are catered for and the hotel additionally provides a listening service. 4-Crown Highly Commended by ETB.

256

The Talbot, New Street, Oundle, Nr. Peterborough, Northamptonshire.
Tel: 01832 273621 Fax: 01832 274545

The Ship Inn is a family owned free house situated in this delightfully picturesque market town. The inn's original character is immediately evident from the low hanging ceilings, original oak beams and large inglenook fireplace. Frank, Dorothy and family took over the inn ten years ago. Through careful restoration the inn has been transformed and returned to its historic appearance retaining all the character from its 15th century origins.

Accommodation is provided in the quaint cottage adjoining the Inn and the converted Coach House and Barns. Both have been completely modernized and offer luxurious bedrooms most with en-suite bathrooms. For the romantics, one room features a corner bath and full four-poster bed. All rooms are fully heated, triple glazed and are tastefully decorated and furnished.

They all have colour television, complimentary tea/coffee tray, hair dryer and trouser press. Other facilities include a breakfast room and a cosy lounge with fire and television. The Ship is listed in the Good Beer Guide and provides a fine selection of real ales to choose from.

An extensive menu offers a wide range of delicious home made meals at very realistic prices, including such tempting dishes as sailor pie, jacket potato and toasted Stilton, and various soups and puddings of the day.

There is a large car park to the rear of the inn which enables residents to leave their vehicles close to where they are staying. An interesting place to stay in homely surroundings. ETB 3-Crown recommended.

The Ship Inn, 18 West Street, Oundle, Nr. Peterborough, Northamptonshire.
Tel: 01832 273918

The town has three sets of old almshouses, and some charming private houses. The two churches, one medieval, one relatively modern, and the old school buildings make a fine spectacle. The school was founded by Sir William Laxton in 1556 and an inscription to his memory is written above the 17th century doorway in Greek, Latin and Hebrew. The medieval church has a magnificent tower with a spire two hundred feet high. All the walls are about eight hundred years old and it is certainly one of the most impressive churches in the country.

Just outside Oundle there is a country park, a marina and a golf course and then **Fotheringhay** which used to have three castles. The first was probably built around 1100 by the husband of William the Conqueror's daughter Judith. The famous castle was built in the 14th century by Edmund of Langley, 5th son of Edward III. Henry VIII gave Fotheringhay Castle to Catherine of Aragon in their happier days and later it became the prison of Mary, Queen of Scots. She was brought here in bands of steel and executed in 1587 in the Banqueting Hall.

The castle was pulled down in 1627 and two hundred years later a gold ring was found with a lovers' knot entwined around the initials of Mary and Darnley; it is thought that it fell from her finger as she was executed. It is now a peaceful scene that surrounds the site of the vanished castle with the river winding through the meadows. Thistles still grow in the grounds where they were planted by the tragic queen and they thrive every year reaching a height of eight feet or more.

Nearby **Elton Hall** dates back to 1474 and is a fascinating mixture of styles reflecting the tastes and interests of succeeding generations. It has some wonderful furniture, fine paintings and books and lovely gardens.

258

Two miles west of Oundle in the little village of **Stoke Doyle** is the wonderful old 17th century **Shuckburgh Arms,** named after a friend of the present owner's great great grandfather who helped him finance the purchase of land. Shuckburgh is a real picture of an old English Inn, clad in ivy and set in the wonderful Northampton countryside. Inside you'll find a quiet, comfortable, wood-panelled bar with Chesterfield sofas and inglenook fireplace where real ales can be enjoyed. A cosy Dining Room serves good home-cooked food, and excellent bar snacks are available at most times; you could for example try the Wild Boar casseroled in red wine, port and brandy. Table booking are advised particularly at weekends. The Shuckburgh has five very pleasant en-suite bedrooms with television and complimentary hot drinks tray. Children are catered for and the large garden has a special play area for them. 3-Crown Commended by ETB.

The Shuckburgh Arms, Stoke Doyle, Nr. Oundle, Peterborough, Northamptonshire. Tel./Fax: 01832 272339

South of Oundle on the B662, **The Red Lion Inn and Motel** at **Clopton**, proclaims itself to be "large enough to employ top quality staff and small enough to provide a personal service". So whether on business or holiday, guests should feel comfortable with the amenities of the Red Lion which enjoys a rural situation while being only five miles from the historic city of Oundle. The two bars with log fires are the ideal meeting place to relax or enjoy a pre-dinner drink. The restaurant enjoys a good local reputation and offers a very comprehensive menu covering every taste and appetite. A traditional family lunch menu is served on Sundays and booking is strongly advised particularly at weekends. The Motel has all modern facilities with en-suite bedrooms, each with TV, telephone and hospitality tray. The rooms face open countryside away from any traffic noise. Morning will bring a friendly greeting and a hearty breakfast.

The Red Lion Inn & Motel, Clopton, Nr. Kettering, Northants.
Tel: 01832 720611 or 720296.

We headed towards are final part of Northamptonshire past yet another fine building some three miles north west of Oundle, **Southwick Hall**. It has examples of 14th century, Tudor and later building work but again be aware of its limited opening times. Situated on the A427 in Upper Benefield, midway between Corby and Oundle, is the outstanding **Benefield Wheatsheaf Hotel and Restaurant**. Dating back to the early 17th century, the building was formerly a farmhouse with a charming courtyard and outbuildings that have been sympathetically refurbished and now house some excellent letting accommodation. In wonderful, stylish surrounding, this establishment has a warm and friendly atmosphere created by your delightful hosts, Jane, Rolf, Debbie and Graeme. The intimate, bistro style restaurant serves delicious, imaginative, home cooked and freshly prepared dishes that melt in the mouth and the a la carte restaurant, The Regency Dining Room serves unique dishes by candlelight. A special feature of the hotel is its continued association with the local, but now closed, RAF and American World War II air bases and there is plenty of memorabilia about the place.

The Benefield Wheatsheaf Hotel and Restaurant, Upper Benefield, Near Oundle Tel: 01832 205254

Situated in the picturesque village of Brigstock, south of Upper Benefield, is the very impressive **Olde Three Cocks Inn**. Personally run by Archie Macnish for the past 16 years its known locally as 'Archie's Place'.

Dating back nearly 400 years, this popular inn has had several different names including, the New Three Cocks! A meeting place for the local hunt for many years, during the Second World War the inn played host to several Hollywood celebrities including Clark Gable and Jimmy Cagney, who came to stay whilst they entertained the American troops stationed at the nearby US air force bases.

The inn still boasts seven excellent letting rooms, available all year round. With a range of real ales, excellent home cooked food and a warm and friendly atmosphere this is a lovely place to stay that has an interesting past.

The Olde Three Cocks, Brigstock, Kettering Tel: 01536 373214

Our final stop was in the delightful village of **Collyweston**. Its houses are a picturesque mixture of 17th and 18th century stone-walled buildings roofed with stone slates, bounded for some distance on the west by the lovely winding River Welland. The village changed counties in the re-organisation of 1974 and is now in the north eastern sector of Northamptonshire. There are many 17th century houses built of the local brown ironstone and the spire of the church has eight sides of rich 14th century tracery in its openings. In 1737 most of the medieval church fell to the ground but part of the transept and the beautiful central tower still remain.

We now move on to the neighbouring county of Leicester and hope we have given an insight into a much underrated county prompting you to explore it for yourself.

Leicestershire

Old Grammar School, Market Harborough

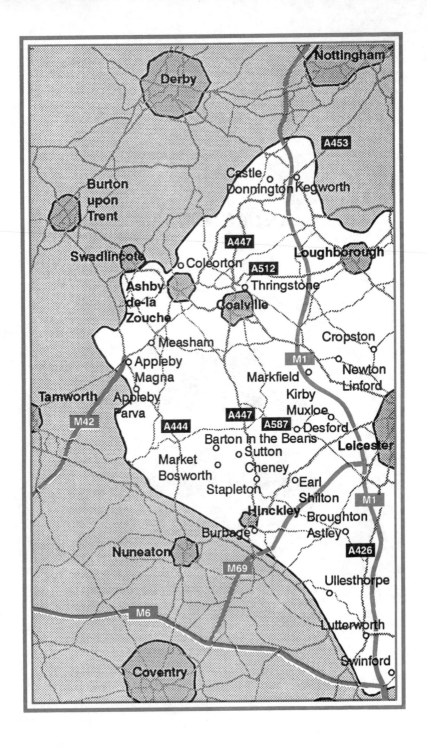

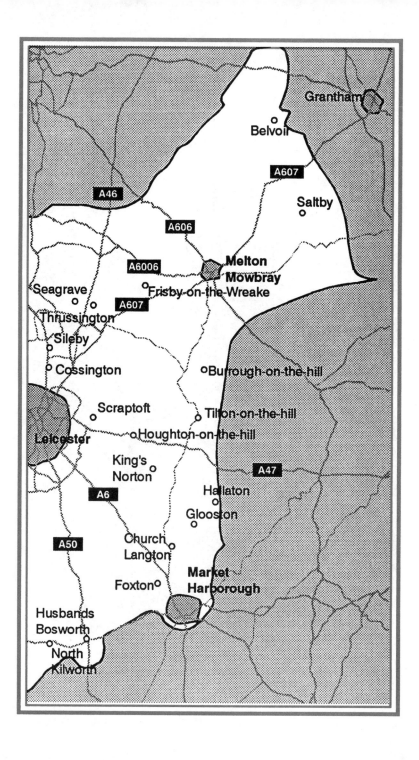

The Campanile, Queens Park. Loughborough.

CHAPTER TEN

Leicestershire.

Leicestershire, in the very heart of England covers eight hundred and twenty square miles of pleasant countryside. Most counties suffer from popular myths and Leicestershire is generally dismissed by those who have merely driven through it as flat, pretty well covered with red brick towns and villages, and somewhere in the background a lot of fox hunting goes on.

Its most attractive features are shy and quiet and have to be sought out but they amply reward the explorer. The county is divided into two almost equal parts by the River Soar which flows northward into the Trent. It separates the east and west by a broad valley, flowing like a silver ribbon through historic **Leicester** in the very heart of the county. This capital town was thriving in Roman days and is one of the oldest towns in England. It has managed to retain outstanding monuments of almost every age of English history.

Nearly half of the county live in Leicester, the rest are in over two hundred villages. Agriculture and industry grew hand in hand; the long hair of the sheep is famous for producing fine woollens, and the end of the 17th century saw the beginning of the now world-wide hosiery trade. **Loughborough** has been famous for making bells for more than one hundred years, their product pealing from many of England's church towers.

At **Melton Mowbray**, wondrous pies have been made on a commercial scale since 1830 and if you have only ever had a factory pork pie you have not lived. Red Leicester cheese was made in the southern part of the county in the 1700's but now the only genuine product is made at Melton Mowbray, which also makes Stilton and of course the superlative pork pies. There can be few towns in Britain that immediately make the mouth water just to think of the food it produces.

Every schoolchild knows the name of **Bosworth Field**, one of the momentous battles which changed the course of English history. Henry Tudor defeated Richard 111 in the battle in 1485 to become Henry V11. Fought on an August morning in the west of the county, the countryside around Bosworth has changed little in five hundred years. For followers of English history it is a necessary part of a pilgrimage and a comprehensive museum reveals the details of this event.

All who know Leicestershire know **Swithland Wood** and the experience of walking through the dense carpet of bluebells in early summer is without parallel. **Charnwood Forest** has an area of sixty square miles, but the little mountain region has lost much of its woodland. Even so it remains an area of outstanding natural beauty, rich in flora and fauna of all kinds.

All in all, there is much to see and so we will arbitrarily embark on our journey around Leicestershire in **Market Harborough.**

One of the most attractive features of the picturesque small town is its wide main square. Its most notable building is the former grammar school, built in 1614. It stands above the street on carved wooden pillars; pedestrians can walk underneath it. The space below the school used to be a butter market but sadly no more.

The parish church of **St Dionysius**, built circa 1200, is topped by a steeple which is a landmark for miles around. The interior of the church has galleries added since 1683 to accommodate an overflow in the congregation. The town was a trading centre as early as 1203, and markets are still held every Tuesday and Saturday. Industrial development has not destroyed the town's wealth of fine Georgian buildings. The inn sign that swings outside **The Three Swans** is a worthy example of 18th century ironwork.

Charles I made his headquarters in the town before the Battle of Naseby, and when he was defeated Cromwell occupied Market Harborough and from here wrote to Parliament telling them of his victory.

North of Market Harborough lies the historic village of **Foxton.** It is such a picturesque place, close to the Grand Union Canal and the famous **Foxton Locks.** Travelling a couple of miles west from Market Harborough we came to **Husbands Bosworth** and could not help but comment on such an intriguing name, indeed Leicestershire is full of places with unusual names. The name was chosen to distinguish it from Market Bosworth, some miles away. It was the 'farmers Bosworth' while the other was a market town. It stands high on the south border and an amble round can make an enjoyable break in a
268

journey with its attractive old brick houses, including a Baptist Chapel of 1807.

There is a chilling story of nine local women who were tried and convicted of witchcraft in 1616. A boy of twelve, was thought to be bewitched as he would suddenly have violent fits, striking himself repeatedly and making animal noises. He accused the women of making the spirits of animals enter his body and they were all burned at the stake. The boy's fits continued, and a few months later six more women were accused. It was only the intervention of King James himself who recognised the boy's epilepsy that saved the women from the same fate as their unfortunate sisters.

Manor Farm is situated in the beautiful village of **Bruntingthorpe**, north of Husbands Bosworth; a working cattle farm of 20 acres, though you wouldn't know it as you arrive. A sweeping driveway leads you past a natural pond where ducks, geese and sundry animals frequent before arriving at the impressive 19th century home of Janet. Set deep in the heart of the countryside, there are many lovely walks and hostelries of excellent quality to quench your thirst or satisfy that appetite. Janet is quite a character and her charm will ensure your stay is one to remember. There are four en suite letting rooms privately located on the top floor of her three story home where the views are impressive. The rooms have central heating and television but retain character and charm with original wooden doors and interesting furniture. Many of Janet's visitors have become friends and return for further visits. Bruntingthorpe is approximately midway between the A50, M1 and the A426.

Manor House Farm, Peatling Parva Road, Bruntingthorpe, Lutterworth. Tel: 0116 2478347

We next travelled to the town of **Lutterworth**. Lutterworth is notable for the fact that Wycliffe was rector here, under the protection of John of Gaunt. His widespread opposition to papal abuses was bad enough but when he instigated the translation of the Bible into

Old Grammar School. Market Harborough.

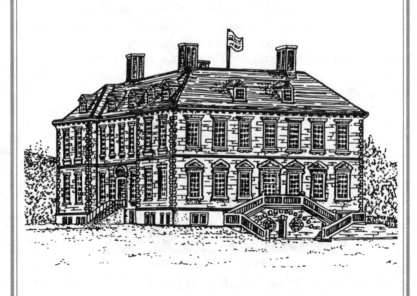

Stanford Hall

English he became totally persona non grata. He died in 1384 and was buried in the Lutterworth church, but when he was excommunicated in 1428 his body was exhumed, burned and his ashes scattered on the River Swift.

Standing in a lovely 18th century courtyard which forms the focal point of the **Greyhound Coaching Inn**, it is easy to imagine how Lutterworth must have been in earlier days. Here, all the old brickwork and features have been carefully renovated, even the old 40 foot well has been kept. The Greyhound was built in 1720 as a coaching and posting inn, and is now a grade 11 listed building refurbished to exacting standards by owner managers Robert and Janet Eggleston. The Georgian hotel caters for the discerning traveller, and as such has thirty individually decorated and designed en suite bedrooms or suites; every possible luxury is provided for your comfort.

Two of the five ground floor bedrooms have been designed for the disabled visitor. The old arched cellars have been renovated to form the Cellar Bar with a Bistro atmosphere. Excellent cuisine to suit every taste can be ordered in the large restaurant where menus change every month, utilising available seasonal produce. The Greyhound is within easy reach of many famous places and is situated only minutes from the M1, A5 and M6.

The Greyhound, Market Street, Lutterworth, Leicestershire.
Tel: 01455 553307 Fax: 01455 554558

Situated in the heart of Lutterworth, on the main street and near The Greyhound, is the excellent **Roseanne's Tea Rooms**. Housed in a listed building this is a family business headed by Diane Lennon with help from daughter Sarah, mother Joyce and not forgetting Margaret and Sue who help with the cooking and daily running of the concern. Roseanne's is full of charm and character with many of the buildings original features, including the floor and ceiling beams, still remaining. The furnishings and decorations are of a very high standard and compliment the age of the place. Open during the day from Monday to Saturday there is a delicious range of home cooked dishes available whether you are after breakfast, lunch, afternoon tea or a light snack at any time of the day. With its lovely, relaxed and friendly atmosphere this is a wonderful place to take a break.

Roseanne's Tea Rooms, 27 Market Street, Lutterworth, Leicestershire Tel: 01455 552212

At a site south of the town of Lutterworth, where their two main roads, Watling Street and Fosseway, met, the Romans founded the settlement which is now known as **Highcross**, but was originally called 'Venonae'. Within the grounds of **Highcross House**, stands the remains of the Earl of Denbigh's monument, built in 1712, to commemorate the end of the 100 Years War between England and France. Highcross House itself is a former 16th century coaching inn, originally called The Sun Inne and many of the original features remain within this beautiful listed building.

Going hand in hand with all this charm and character, Jain Galliford offers wonderful accommodation with excellent up-to-date facilities. You can choose from an original four poster room, a half tester room, even rooms with Jacuzzis! All the letting rooms are individually decorated and furnished with magnificent antique furniture and memorabilia to enjoy. Jain is renowned for her delicious dinners and Highcross House is a very popular venue for weddings and other special celebrations.

Highcross House, Highcross, Lutterworth Tel: 01455 220840

Recently purchased by new owners Mike and Susan Walker, the ivy clad **White Swan**, at the nearby village of **Shawell**, with its pretty hanging baskets and colourful tubs, looks very inviting upon arrival. Step inside where the quality furniture and carpets combined with features such as panelled walls create a very comfortable interior and intimate restaurant area.

Although run as a village inn, the new owners want to cater for local people and visitors from further afield. with its fine home-cooked and freshly prepared dishes, good atmosphere and fine range of real ales, The White Swan is a good place to aim for.

The White Swan, Main Street, Shawell, Leicestershire. Tel: 01788 860357.

For many, a favourite pastime when travelling around the various counties is to visit stately homes. The more interesting ones are almost always those where a family is still in residence. This is so at **Stanford Hall**, just one and a half miles from **Swinford**. Mentioned in the Domesday book, the parish of Stanford is an ancient one. Some years after it was given to the Benedictine Abbey of Selby by a Norman companion of the Conqueror in 1069, another grant of Stanford land was made in 1140 to the Abbey by King Stephen. When the dissolution of the monasteries took place, Sir Thomas Cave purchased the original manor from Henry VIII in 1540.

The present building dates from the reign of William and Mary, around 1690, and has a majestic facade that adds to the its pleasing design. Inside, the rooms contain interesting collections of Stuart and Jacobite paintings, costumes and furniture. The stables house a motor museum and a replica of an 1898 flying machine.

Ullesthorpe, north of Lutterworth is ideally situated for the motorway networks and for many centres and places of interest. **The Chequers Country Inne** at Ullesthorpe is an ideal base for business or pleasure breaks. Set amidst rolling countryside the inn has a peaceful and relaxed atmosphere. Reminiscent of a coaching inn, the Chequers was originally a farmhouse in George 111's reign and has genuine oak beams, slate and granite floors, interesting fireplaces with stone hearth surrounds and numerous antiquities. The owners of this hotel have built a well deserved reputation for their hospitality and fine cuisine. All tastes are catered for from traditional home-cooked bar meals to meticulously created a'la carte dishes, with a selection of over twenty main courses served in the delightful restaurant with full silver service. Fourteen en-suite bedrooms provide very comfortable accommodation with all possible conveniences and for the extra special occasion you can book a bedroom with four-poster bed. The bars have a range of over fifty bar snacks and a minimum of seven traditional cask ales changing daily, with non smoking areas and a family room. There's an excellent wine list with top quality cognacs and a choice of more than twenty five malt whiskies compliment the fine food. Professional presentation with friendly service.

The Chequers Country Inne, Main Street, Ullesthorpe, Lutterworth, Leicestershire. Tel: 01455 209214 Fax: 01455 209144
Situated close by in beautiful countryside is **Ullesthorpe Court Hotel and Golf Club**, an exclusive retreat offering luxury and comfort and an impressive range of leisure facilities. Ullesthorpe Court is a 17th century manor house with an interesting history and fine architectural details. The thirty nine en-suite bedrooms are equipped with every possible convenience including satellite television channels.

Fine cuisine is served in the Court Restaurant and the hotel's traditional country pub is popular for bar snacks and a carvery. The Golf Club provides for social golf, club competitions, family breaks and various tournaments. The course is a 6650 yard par 72. The splendid leisure facilities include floodlit tennis courts, indoor heated pool, fitness room, sauna, jacuzzi and solarium. The hotel offers special golf and leisure breaks and must surely be a superb spot for all the family.

274

Ullesthorpe Court, Frolesworth Road, Ullesthorpe, Leicestershire.
Tel: 01455 209023 Fax: 01455 202537

Hinckley has been done scant justice by many writers on Leicestershire. Shakespeare touched the old market town with immortality when he referred to Hinckley Fair in Henry IV. He may have wandered along Church Walk where the old timbered houses still lean forward under the bent brows of their thatch.

In 1834, Joseph Hansom made the first hansom cab and drove it along Regent Street at full gallop to demonstrate that it could not be overturned. He received only three hundred pounds for his invention, and it did not become popular for another twenty years. In those days the assizes for the whole county were held here having been moved from Leicester in 1610 because an epidemic of the plague was raging there (over one hundred and forty people died in Hinckley alone in 1626).

Situated near to Hinckley in the pleasant Leicestershire village of **Earl Shilton** and just a few miles from Leicester is the **Fernleigh Hotel and Restaurant.** It is a large privately owned hotel with all modern-day comforts. The 27 en-suite bedrooms have television with free video service, telephone, radio alarm and tea making facilities. The executive suites have the further luxury of Jacuzzi baths and four-poster beds.

A nicely presented restaurant with smart tableware offers choices of a'la carte or fixed price menus. The hotel policy is for use of fresh produce whenever possible and there is a good variety of quality dishes to choose from. The cocktail bar remains open late for residents and food is generally on offer during the day. Barry's Bar offers you pub-style entertainment in the lower part of the hotel where good ales are available and, here too, food is available. Children are welcome and assistance given to anyone disabled.

Ashby Castle.

Fernleigh Hotel, Wood Street, Earl Shilton, Nr. Hinckley,
Tel: 01455 847011

The name **Burbage** was originally Burbach and evidently came from the bur thistle which grew abundantly in its fields. It was a stylish and prosperous village at one time and one of its earliest incumbents was the 9th Earl of Kent who was rector here for fifty years. Burbage has a fine large common and a wood which attract people from far and wide. The River Soar rises here to begin its winding journey to the Trent and the church of St Catherine has a spire which can be seen for miles.

From Burbage it is easy to get to **Broughton Astley** along the B581, one of those thriving, expanding villages which has managed to retain a character of its own in spite of incorporating two other villages, **Sutton Elms** and **Princethorpe**. The reason is that the area has become a commuter base for London, Coventry and Rugby.

Moving towards Leicester in the North, pick up the B4114 and include the village of **Narborough** on your route. The village has retained a delightful olde worlde atmosphere as has the **Narborough Arms** located in its centre.

It was originally constructed on the site of an ancient Catholic church and the present building is said to date back to the 14th century. Although the brewery owners have carried out a programme of refurbishment to provide excellent facilities, the style and character remain in keeping with its age.

A mixture of single, double, twin and family rooms are available, all with en-suite facilities and tastefully furnished. Appetites are well catered for with a splendid selection of meals from 'Lite bites' to 'Big bites' listed on a giant blackboard and offering exceptional value for money. All credit to the brewery and the managers Paul and Elizabeth.

Narborough Arms, 6 Coventry Road, Narborough, Leicester.
Tel: 0116 2848212 Fax: 0116 2866401

Ten minutes from the city of Leicester, yet strategically placed for access to key areas of interest, is the **Charnwood Hotel** at Narborough. The hotel enjoys quiet surroundings in an acre of wooded garden with large lawn areas where guests can relax and enjoy their food and drink. A very spacious and comfortable restaurant displays high class table settings with fresh flowers, and through its many picture windows affords a very pleasant view of the garden which is attractively illuminated after dusk. A choice of a'la carte and table d'hôte menus are offered with a comprehensive wine list. The twenty bedrooms with en suite bathrooms/shower are well appointed with the comfort of central heating, television and other facilities. The bar lounge is a comfortable room for pre-dinner aperitif or social gathering.   This excellent hotel has 4-Crown classification by ETB.

The Charnwood Hotel, 48 Leicester Road, Narborough, Leicester.
Tel: 01162 862218 Fax: 01162 750119

To the west, **Sutton Cheney,** is traditionally where Richard III took communion , just before he went to battle a mile away on

278

Bosworth field. This lovely village houses some fine examples of Jacobean architecture. **The Almshouse** is one such example. "Think of all the charm and character that is essentially England and that is the Almshouse". So states the brochure for this most interesting and historic country house accommodation and restaurant. Cherry and Phil became the proprietors in 1984 and have lovingly restored it keeping as near to its original Jacobean character as possible.

The Almshouse was built in 1612 by Sir William Roberts (Knight) who was Lord of the Manor at Sutton Cheney. There are six guest rooms each tastefully furnished in keeping with the surroundings. All rooms have television and other facilities, most are en-suite.

The Almshouse original stable block has been converted into a timbered restaurant and tea can be taken on the terrace overlooking the beautiful gardens. The Almshouse is well known for its fine cuisine and booking is certainly advisable. In the winter, a lovely log fire burns in the guest lounge. Whilst full English breakfast is provided all diets are catered for. A truly unique and fascinating find.

The Almshouse, Sutton Cheney, Nr. Market Bosworth, Leicestershire. Tel: 01455 291050 FAX 01455 290601

Market Bosworth is just a couple of miles north of nearby Sutton Cheney and it is from this small seven hundred year old market town that the Battle of Bosworth took its name. It is a village of no great size but its former grammar school had a high reputation in the Midlands. Originally founded in early Tudor times, in 1601, it was given a new lease of life by Sir Wolstan Dixie. It was to this school that Samuel Johnson came to teach after leaving university. He hated it so much that even Boswell failed to induce him to talk about his time here.

Overlooking the Market Square in Market Bosworth is **Ye Old Black Horse Inn** with its clean painted walls and hanging baskets it offers a welcoming appearance. Step inside and you find an informal

Steam on the Great Central Railway

atmosphere as befits this historic old country inn. After 20 years in London, Charlie and Linda Buxton came to the Black Horse four years ago and are "proud to offer exceptional quality food at sensible prices". Charlie and Linda invite you to enjoy just a single course or a three course meal from a menu of traditional and continental wholesome food accompanied by fine wines from around the world.

There are also Lunchtime Specials listed on the blackboard and traditional ales from the bar. The quality and selection of food here is very impressive. The management thoughtfully provides a brief history of the area and details on some interesting places within walking distance of the inn. There is private car parking to the rear.

Ye Old Black Horse Inn, Market Placce, Market Bosworth,
Tel: 01455 290278 FAX 01455 290082

Also situated in the market place of this historic village is the outstanding **Softleys** hotel and restaurant. Owned and personally run by John and Annie McCallion and Stephen Allton-Evans, this establishment is renowned throughout the area for its excellent food, drink and accommodation; it also features in the major guide books.

The building itself is 260 years old and takes its present name from the Rev Derek Softley, a Methodist minister from the nearby village of Barwell. There have been many visitors to Softleys over the years; during the Second World War soldiers waiting to go to France were billeted here, Dr Samuel Johnson may well have dropped in while he was an usher at Market Bosworth Boys' Grammar School, and local folklore says that George Frederick Handel was a regular when he was staying at nearby Gopsal Hall composing parts of his famous 'Messiah'. Today's visitors can expect a warm welcome in a very characterful and cosy establishment.

Softleys, Market Place, Market Bosworth. Tel: 01455 290464

Across the market place from the school is a fine house with its portico and cornice and handsome Georgian windows. It was built by the Dixies about 1700. The prettiest of streets leads to the church rising among the trees, the pinnacled tower crowned by a spire.

Ye Olde Red Lion Hotel in Park Street dates back, in parts, some four hundred years, so you can expect to find lots of character in this establishment. Character is also present in the bubbly and lively personalities of the owners: Alan, Claudia, Derick and Sonjia who are busy establishing a good name and growing clientele. There are four letting bedrooms, two en-suite, both with four-poster beds. Delicious homemade meals are available at lunchtimes and a suntrap terrace area at the rear is inviting when weather permits. Help will willingly be provided for disabled customers. Colourful hanging baskets add the finishing touches to this nicely presented hotel.

Ye Olde Red Lion Hotel, 1 Park Street, Market Bosworth, Leicestershire. Tel: 01455 291713. FAX 01455 292422

At **Ambion Hill**, near Market Bosworth, is **Bosworth Battlefield Visitor Centre and Country Park.** It was here, on 22nd August 1485 that the Armies of Richard III and Henry Tudor faced each other.

The battle that followed put a new King on the throne and changed the course of history. Here, you have the opportunity to visit one of Britain's best interpreted Battlefields.

At the Visitor Centre there are exciting exhibitions that bring those events of the 15th century to life. a Medieval street has been recreated, and the collections of arms, armour and heraldry of the period are extensive. Also in the Visitor Centre is the Film Theatre which shows clips from the famous film of Shakespeare's Richard III including the battle scene and the death of the King.

Refreshments can be obtained at the Bosworth Buttery Cafeteria. Across the park there is a unique Battle Trail with a series of imaginatively illustrated Trail Boards. In addition to this, there are special events throughout July, August and September where you can see battle re-enactments, falconry displays, jousting and much more. Ring for details. The Visitor Centre is signposted from the A5, A444, A447 and B585 roads.

Bosworth Battlefield Visitor Centre and Country Park, c/o Department of Property, County Hall, Glenfield, Leicester. Tel 01162 656961

Just north of here is the wonderfully named **Barton-in-the-Beans**. Apparently the county used to be called 'bean-belly Leicestershire', on account of the crops of beans which formed part of its staple diet in more poverty-stricken times. The beans grown were supposed to be sweeter and more tender than anywhere and consequently were considered food fit for men, whereas in other counties they were fed only to swine.

A writer in 1720 said they are 'so luxuriant that they appear like a forest towards harvest time'. Barton-in-the-Beans has never had a church but the Baptist Chapel, founded in 1745, was later rebuilt in 1841, and is said to be the earliest of the General Baptists in this part of the Midlands.

Easily found off the A447, **Nailstone** is a quiet and peaceful little village where Barbara and Peter Payne have provided outstanding bed and breakfast accommodation at **Glebe Farm** for the past ten years. Originally a six hundred year old single story thatched property, the present building is a most attractive two storey brick house with slate roof, pretty windows and attractive gardens giving it a picture-postcard appearance and a welcoming look.

Glebe Farm is still a 53 acre working farm which deals primarily with Suckler Cows, but the farmhouse is separate from that side of things. There are three spacious and comfortable letting rooms and two bathrooms. No evening meals are provided but there are plenty of pubs and restaurants nearby. One word of warning - leave room for Barbara's big breakfast. Very homely and friendly atmosphere. Member of the Tourist Board.

Glebe Farm, Rectory Lane, Nailstone, Nr. Market Bosworth,
Tel: 01530 260318

Twycross is the home of an interesting church and an interesting zoo. Amongst the yew trees the church stands on hillock and in its east window glows stained glass seven hundred years old. When the French Revolution threatened the lovely Sainte Chapelle in Paris, much precious glass was taken for safety from the Gothic shrine and bought by a rich Englishman, some of it eventually finding its way to Twycross and is a rich and rare treasure. A term which could be applied to the zoo if you like animals a lot. There are gorillas, lions and elephants, a pets' corner, children's adventure playground, a miniature railway and in the summer you can have a go at riding on a donkey. There is also a shop, a cafe and a bar and the zoo is open daily from February to November.

Appleby Magna further along the A444 has a 14th century church and a moated manor house which unfortunately is not open to the public. In the adjacent village **Appleby Parva** the grammar school building dates from the 17th century.

Measham is a place of brickmaking and coalmining, with the Ashby Canal flowing darkly past and the River Mease meandering nearby. A number of stone hammer-heads have been excavated here and solid wooden wheels and wedges of flint bound in hazel and have survived for thousands of years preserved in peat. Measham Hall lies about a mile east of the village off the road to Swepstone and is a fine example of Georgian architecture.

Sir Walter Scott's romantic novel 'Ivanhoe' sets the scene well for the North West region of Leicestershire whose history, natural beauty and charm combine to offer a warm welcome to visitors and tourists alike. The superbly named **Ashby-de-la-Zouch** was noted for the noble sport of jousting where no doubt many a maiden's honour was won or lost by knights in shining armour. Such tournaments took place near **Ashby Castle,** which was later attacked by Cromwell's Roundheads and consequently ruined.

Much of the region's attraction and beauty dates back still further; to the east is the edge of the Charnwood Forest, whose exposed volcanic rocks and granites are over two thousand million years old.

Although the Leicestershire coalfield is not far away, Ashby remains a pleasant little town and there is much to see.

Market Street takes its name from the weekly market granted in 1219, and there were also no fewer than four annual fairs. Visually the most rewarding part of the town is the west end of Market Street where the Spa quarter is situated. Old, half-timbered buildings blend with modern architecture to make an attractive town with good shopping facilities, a number of impressive churches, parks and an imposing castle ruin. The Bull's Head is thought to be the oldest building. Cromwell reputedly had a drink here when the 15th century castellated manor was taken by Parliament after a years siege in the Civil War.

In the former upper courtyard of the castle stands the 19th century Manor House, now a school. Also of interest is the elegant seventy feet high monument to the Countess of Loudoun erected in 1874 and inscribed with a tribute to her from Disraeli. The castle ruin has a massive keep and many of the rooms are easily identifiable.

Whilst in the centre of Ashby-de-la-Zouch, you could enjoy outstanding cuisine in the **La Zouch Restaurant**. The owners, Geoff and Lynne, have jointly over 30 years experience in catering and opened La Zouch thirteen years ago which is now firmly established as one of Leicestershire's premier places to eat. The restaurant has a very comfortable and cosy feeling with low ceilings, pictures and prints and pleasant lighting.

With such a splendid selection available, you may have difficulty making your choice from the a'la carte or table d'hôte menus which also include vegetarian and vegan dishes. On warm days, you can eat on the terrace in the secret garden. Closed Sunday evening and Monday.

La Zouch Restaurant, 2 Kilwardby Street, Ashby-de-la-Zouch, .
Tel: 01530 412536

Mill Lane, a quiet mews, houses a 'hidden place' not to be missed. **The Mews Wine Bar**, a Queen Anne style listed building, is recommended by a major food guide for its good food and fine wines. Here, in a warm and relaxed atmosphere, fresh and creative culinary ideas from the Continent are combined with years of experience and a broad knowledge and understanding of good old fashioned English home cooking. The result is an imaginative and comprehensive menu which offers something for everyone.

The stylish cuisine is served in 'The Old Room', with original oak beams and bay window seats, and 'The Conservatory', a sunny garden room with an arched glass roof and trailing plants. The helpful, friendly staff keep a keen eye on detail do their utmost to ensure that your visit is an enjoyable one.

The Mews Wine Bar and Restaurant, Mill Lane,
Ashby-de-la-Zouch. Tel: 01530 411002
286

If you are looking for somewhere to stay here, the **Queens Head Hotel** with its striking timber and white painted frontage has all the creature comforts for an enjoyable stay. You'll find a very pleasant ambience here and excellent facilities. Recently refurbished, the 'Queens Lounge' is full of character and interest and makes an ideal meeting place; buffet lunches are also served here every day.

The ten letting bedrooms are comfortably furnished to a high standard and most have en-suite bathrooms; all have television and other facilities. The intimate restaurant offers superb English cuisine from table d'hôte and full a`la carte menus. Residents can enjoy the extra luxury of a Sauna, sunbed or use of the modern gymnasium. A treat in store!

The Queens Head Hotel, 79 Market Street, Ashby-de-la-Zouch, Tel: 01530 412780

The **Cedars Guest house** is quietly situated close to the centre of Ashby-de-la-Zouch on the A50. The large red brick Victorian house and annex is set in its own 3/4 acre of grounds with impressive lawns. Here Pauline and John have offered quality bed and breakfast accommodation for twelve years and have 2 crown classification by the Tourist Board. There are eleven letting bedrooms with a mixture of family, double, twin and single rooms, eight of which have en-suite bathrooms.

Hallaton Village Green.

Nottingham Street. Melton Mowbray.

The rooms are spacious, well decorated and offer a real 'home from home' feeling of comfort. Some rooms are suitable for those requiring wheelchair access. Children are welcome and pets can be accommodated by arrangement. Breakfasts are wonderful and there's no shortage of places to eat in the evening.

The Cedars, 60 Burton Road, Ashby-de-la-Zouch, 01530 412017

Set in the delightful village of **Smisby**, north of Ashby-de-la-Zouch, adjacent to the church and overlooking the ancient 'Ivanhoe' tournament fields, **Smisby Manor** is an impressive building by any standards. This magnificent property, circa 15th century, stands in 65 acres and was formerly a farmhouse which at one time formed part of the Calke Abbey Estate. Tom and Claire are your present-day hosts who provide luxury accommodation and fine cuisine. Six lovely en-suite letting bedrooms are available all with television and tea making facilities and are furnished to a high standard. Following the same luxury theme, the busy a`la carte restaurant accepts reservations on a 'booking only' basis and it is therefore well worth planning ahead to maximise your enjoyment from a visit here.

Smisby Manor, Annwell Lane, Smisby, Ashby-de-la- Zouch, Leicestershire. Tel: 01530 415881

Whilst in the area of Ashby-de-la-Zouch, then an interesting place to visit is The Ferrers Centre at **Staunton Harold**. It is there you will find a number of interesting craft workshops, gift shop, the Ferrers Gallery and **Staunton Stables Tea Room**. Michael and Alison Kemp established the tea room eleven years ago in a converted stable block now known as the Ferrers Centre which surrounds a magnificent Georgian courtyard behind Staunton Harold Hall.

Open throughout the year except Mondays, the tea room offers mouth-watering cakes and pastries, cream teas, light bites and, between 12.00 noon and 2.30pm, 'Staunton' homemade lunches are available. All lunches are freshly prepared to order. Indoor seating allows for about thirty six to forty people and further seating is available in the courtyard. Take time to admire the interesting collection of ornamental tea pots and model cars and take home some special preserves and cakes which you'll find on sale.

Staunton Stables Tea Room, The Ferrers Centre, Staunton Harold,
Ashby-de-la-Zouch, Leicestershire. Tel: 01332 864617

Guests have been relaxing at **Hall Farm, Coleorton**, since the late 18th Century. It is situated in lovely grounds at the end of a quarter-mile drive just off the A512. Now, with its new owner, you can experience a warm and friendly atmosphere.

The farm house has seven spacious bedrooms, most en-suite and all with refreshment facilities and colour television. Cathy, who only recently took ownership of Hall Farm, has already made her mark creating a twenty seat restaurant open to residents every night and to non-residents at weekends.

The splendid menu offers many mouth-watering and varied dishes. With such individual attention, you are hardly likely to be disappointed here. Discover this gem before everyone else does

Hall Farm, Ashby Road, Coleorton, Leics. Tel: 01530 411185

The town of **Coalville** has a less than romantic name, but don't let this put you off visiting, for the town has much to offer. Originally called Long Lane, this town sprang up on a bleak common when Whitwick Colliery was opened in 1824. George Stephenson was responsible for establishing the early railway here in 1832 as well as erecting the churches.

Just a few miles from Coalville, set in lovely countryside and the village of **Griffydam** is the **Waggon and Horses** public house.

A white painted, old coaching inn with roots back in the 17th Century, it has plenty to offer the passing visitors with its old world character. Bev. and Tim are new tenants here and are working hard to create a good atmosphere. There's Marsdens and Ansells good ale to be enjoyed and a neat little beer garden. Try some country air with your refreshment. Large private car park.

Waggon and Horses, Rempstone Road, Griffydam, Coalville, Leicestershire. Tel: 01530 22239

Near the colliery village of **Thringstone** are the remains of **Grace Dieu**, a 13th century Augustinian nunnery. In the centre of the village is an interesting pub which is well worth seeking out. **The Fox Inn** does not at first strike you as a typical English pub. For example, There is no white painted exterior or thatched roof, nor signs advertising bar food. The clean brick exterior looks more like a detached house. Step inside and you have a thriving public house with typical old fashioned ideas.

No food on offer here, just a warm welcome and plenty of chatter in good surroundings, with a fine selection of ales from Shipstones and Bass all kept in fine order. There's room for wheelchairs, a skittle alley and at the rear of the inn is a beer garden where families are encouraged and the thirst can be quenched at leisure. Call in and while away a few hours.

The Fox Inn, Main Street, Thringstone, Coalville,
Tel: 01530 222220

Further north, **Castle Donington,** was originally called just Donington, but adopted the prefix when the Norman castle was built to command the River Trent crossing. It was demolished by King John to punish the owner for supporting Magna Carta and rebuilt in 1278 when no less than four of its subsequent owners were executed. The high-spired 13th/14th century church displays a pleasing blend of Early English, decorated and perpendicular architecture with interesting features. As well as timber-framed houses and shops, sports fields and clubs, there are facilities for angling and boating from the nearby marina on the River Trent.

On the corner of the High Street and Bondgate is a fabulous place to stay - **The Donington Manor Hotel**. Dating back to 1794 when it was built as a posting house and coaching inn, the building was completely restored in 1967. Many of the original 18th century architectural features have been retained and add to the elegance of this graceful Georgian building.

292

The hotel has also been considerably extended and adapted to meet the demands of today's discerning guests.

The Hotel is a popular venue for businessmen in this prosperous commercial area. Over half of the rooms are doubles and are appointed to a most luxurious standard. They include several full suites with sitting rooms, many 4-poster beds and 2 superb brass bedsteads. Several rooms have the most amazing bathrooms; they are of individual designs and deliberately so, to be different. No one stays in these special rooms and forgets where they have been, as in so may chain hotels.

There are three dining areas in which you can sample the excellent products of a highly regarded kitchen. The main, formal Adam Room can seat 40 diners, while the cosier, oak-panelled Gun Room seats 25. The à la carte restaurant is open for lunch and dinner seven days a week and offers a menu with over 30 specialities. Larger parties, dinner dances and other functions are accommodated in the Rawdon Room. Built in 1973, this splendid banqueting suite and ballroom, brilliantly lit by six crystal chandeliers, is ideal for wedding receptions.

This excellent establishment has been recognised with an AA/RAC 3 star rating and is of an English Tourist Board 4 crown standard. The hotel also features in Les Routiers guide.

The Donington Manor Hotel, High Street, Castle Donington, Derby Tel: 01332 810253

Set in 32 acres and formerly a dairy farm, **Willow Farm Motel** is easily located from junction 24 of the M1 or from the A6 at Sawley crossroads. Take the B6540 and turn right when entering Castle Donington. the Motel is a family run concern comprising the 18th century farmhouse and converted English barn which features plenty of old beams and timber. The barn now houses the reception area, dining room (where full English breakfast is served), a very attractive gallery lounge and two elegant character bedrooms adjoining. The additional converted buildings form a courtyard area where eight twin bedded rooms have their individual entrances including a disabled persons bedroom. All the rooms are modern and furnished to a high standard; they have en-suite facilities, full central heating, remote control television and tea /coffee making equipment. David and Ellen opened the Motel in March 1991 though have lived here since 1985. They are delightful people with a warm and a friendly manner. Highly recommended by the English Tourist Board. Pets by arrangement.

Willow Farm Motel, Station Road, Castle Donington. Tel: 01332 850799 Fax: 01332 853077

As you drive through the centre of Castle Donington on the B6540 you will see the pretty cottage style frontage of **Morton House Hotel** with its crisp white exterior and spreading creeper. Ken and Michelle Boddy & family are the new owners of this private hotel which at one time was an old coaching house. They offer bed and breakfast plus

evening meal if required, at very reasonable prices. The rooms are cosy and welcoming with television, tea making equipment and some rooms have en-suite facilities. The licensed bar displays signed photographs from racing drivers who have stayed here in the past together with a collection of paper money from around the world. Awarded Two Crowns by English Tourist Board. Nice village atmosphere.

Morton House Hotel, 78 Bondgate, Castle Donington. Tel: 01332 812415.

Just off the M1 at Junction 23A is the East Midlands Airport. Part of the airport, and clearly signposted after entering the main airport site is the **East Midlands Airport Aeropark and Visitor Centre**. Here the world of aviation and its historical achievements are brought together to be enjoyed by visitors young and old. You can admire at close quarters the many aircraft on display as well as watching plenty of other planes as they land or take off. The visitor centre offers fascinating exhibits on the history of flight as well as demonstrating how a modern-day international airport operates. Open every day of the year from dawn until dusk, except Christmas Day, Boxing Day and New Years Day.

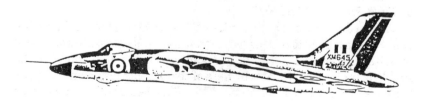

East Midlands Airport Aeropark, Castle Donington, Derby Tel: 01332 810621

Kegworth is a large village with several interesting examples of what is now called 'vernacular architecture', ie. native building including much dating from the days when it was a manufacturing village full of framework-knitters. It possesses an 'almost faultless' late decorated church, which is largely 14th century with some stained glass and a splendid Royal Arms dated 1684.

Situated next to the Market Place in Kegworth is the outstanding **Kegworth Lantern Hotel**. Dating back to 1685, it was the former home of one of the sons of Charles Wells the brewer whose brewery stood adjacent to the house. Dave and Ann Bilson moved here a year ago, with their daughter Lizzie, and immediately set about a complete refurbishment of the premises which is just about finished.

Personally run by the family, with the help of a dedicated staff, this is a wonderful place in which to stay, eat or drink, or all three! The bedrooms are excellent, with all the home comforts. The varied and wide ranging menu in the cosy and intimate restaurant offers a mouthwatering choice of dishes. Dave, who prides himself on the condition of his beers, maintains a list of real ales that constantly changes. However, although the facilities here are of the highest quality, it is the warm and friendly atmosphere that makes this such a super place to stay. You can be assured that your visit or stay at the Lantern will be an enjoyable one, one to savour and one that you can honestly put your hand on your heart and recommend to your family and friends.

Kegworth Lantern Hotel, 1 Market Place, Kegworth .
Tel: 01509 673989

In a delightful setting on the banks of the River Soar, on the edge of Kegworth, is the picture postcard **Anchor Inn**.

The Inn itself dates back to the early 18th century but the present building was constructed in 1927 though it does give the impression of being much older. Barry Bichener and Liz White came here in 1992 and have succeeded in keeping the old village pub values alive.

There is a tremendous atmosphere and a warm welcome is offered to all. Open all day, every day, there is a fine range of traditional real ales and if you are feeling peckish a wonderful selection of tasty snacks can be ordered from the bar.

Well decorated and furnished throughout, the lounge bar features an interesting collection of well over three hundred water jugs all hanging from the beams. The Inn also has three double letting rooms for bed and breakfast available all year round and for the keen angler a day or season licence for fishing the River can be obtained from the Inn.

The Anchor Inn, Station Road, Kegworth Tel: 01509 672722

Also on the banks of the River , **The White House** pub and restaurant overlooks terraced gardens and enjoys views of the boat moorings. This is a fine place to take a break from your journey. The pub is open all day, serves well kept real ales, and in its attractive restaurant delicious food. You would be well advised to book for the restaurant well in advance as it is a very popular place to eat, particularly at weekends. Situated on the A6 at the edge of Kegworth, heading towards Loughborough.

The White House, London Road, Kegworth. Tel:01509 672245

Chris and her daughter came to **The Britannia Inn** on the edge of Kegworth Village a year ago and in that time have created a warm, friendly atmosphere. There is a pop quiz on a Wednesday night, a General Knowledge Quiz on a Sunday night and occasional Live Music. With good ale, good food and plenty going on they have certainly put the Britannia back on its feet. The inn has good off road parking and a secluded beer garden with BBQs in the summer. The Brittania also has an open fire which makes it an ideal place to call on cold winter days.

The Britannia Inn, London Road, Kegworth.   Tel: 01509 672212

And now, as they say, for something completely different! **The Top Railway Inn** - found on the main road off Shepshed Road between Ashby-de-la-Zouch and Loughborough, combines some history with up-to-date facilities and a sense of fun.

Built during the mid 19th century as a 'watering hole' for navvies building the developing and busy railway - alas now no longer in evidence, it is now the H.Q. for the Monster Raving Loony Party.

John and Debra are the licensees; John being a former lead guitarist with Screaming Lord Such's band - 'The Savages'. The inn is different in many ways - as you might imagine! Very often you'll find a free buffet in evidence to accompany the excellent and well kept ales; there is always something happening in this characterful pub. You'll find a really friendly atmosphere, good food and a good time is guaranteed.

Top Railway Inn, 186 Charnwood Road, Shepshed, Loughborough, Leicestershire.   Tel: 01509 503686

On the A6 between Kegworth and Hathern by the A6 is **Whatton Gardens,** twenty five acres of formal and wild gardens, with trees, shrubs, rock pools with fish and plants, and a very nice picnic area.

We travelled south and came to **Loughborough**, known for its bells, which have rung around the world since 1858 when the bell foundry of John Taylor moved to the town from Oxford.

The tower of the parish church of All Saints has a peal of ten bells, and contains a memorial to the bell-founding Taylor family. Much of the building dates from the 14th century despite its 19th century appearance, and the aisles have windows dating from about 1300. The oak roof of the nave is carried on beams which spring from carved musician angels resting one stone supports and the west wall is decorated with 15th century brasses.

Not far from the railway station, is a fascinating place called **The Bell Foundry Museum**. The famous John Taylor Company was started in 1784, and has been at this site on Freehold Street for 180 years. This unique museum relates to all aspects of bell founding from the 13th century and forms part of the largest working bell foundry in the world. Interesting exhibits show the evolution of the makers craft, the techniques of moulding, casting, tuning and the fitting of bells. Visitors of all ages are sure to enjoy a visit here, the admission charge is minimal and the museum is open Tuesday to Saturday, and Bank Holiday Mondays. An organised tour lasts 1 1/2 hours, and party visits can be arranged.

The Bell Foundry Museum, Freehold Street, Loughborough, Leicestershire Tel: 01509 233414

In Queen's Park stands the impressive **Loughborough War Memorial Tower and Carillon**. The tower was "erected in Grateful Memory of the Men of Loughborough who gave their lives for freedom in the Great War". It is an impressive sight, which is enhanced by the rather special carillon contained within. This carillon consists of 47 bells and because the playing of such sets of bells is such an art, it is necessary to appoint a Borough Carilloner. Recitals are performed throughout the summer months, by both the resident carilloner and guest players. Listening to such a recital is a beautiful way to spend a summer evening and a unique experience. To find out more, pick up the fascinating booklet about the memorial from the Tourist Information Centre.

Loughborough War Memorial Tower and Carillon, Charnwood B.C.
Southfield Road, Loughborough.Tel: 01509 842384

In Steeple Row, behind the Parish Church, you will find the **Old Rectory Museum**. This historic building is a rare survival of a 13th century stone built manor house. It was members of the Loughborough and District Archaeological Society who discovered that parts of the original medieval building were hidden behind later alterations. Their work created national interest, and saved the Rectory from being demolished. The museum is only open on Saturdays, from April to October. Free Admission.

The George Hotel is representative of a number of interesting old inns which have their historic roots in the days when the carriage and four   plied the main routes of the country with passengers and mail, stopping off for a change of team and overnight accommodation in such hostelries. It is believed the George was just such a stopping point on the Burton to Nottingham route. Nowadays, it is the Motorway routes which give convenient access to many places of interest and business venues in the area. The hotel retains its 'olde worlde' character and atmosphere in the bar lounge and restaurant, where French and English cuisine features highly on the extensive a` la carte menu. The George has twenty bedrooms, mostly en -suite and all rooms are tastefully furnished and have TV, radio, and other facilities.   Children are welcome, and there are some facilities for disabled guests. ETB - 3 Crown classification.

The George, Belton, Loughborough. Tel: 01530 222426

For those interested in steam trains, go to the Central Station and there you will see Loughborough's links with the steam age preserved. The Main Line Steam Trust runs locomotives from here to Quorn and Birstall, a distance of about ten miles and includes the Swithland Reservoir viaduct.

Just off the A6 and adjacent to the award winning Great Central Steam Railway is the **Great Central Hotel**, a solid, Victorian, family run hotel built in 1901 just two years after the laying of the railway in this area.

The eighteen spacious and comfortable bedrooms are en-suite and have telephone, satellite TV, and refreshment facilities. Downstairs, the bar is a honey pot to railway enthusiasts who can indulge their fantasies while admiring the railway relics and memorabilia which includes three magnificent large model railway engines.

Those more concerned with the type of refreshment on offer will themselves be well satisfied with the twelve or thirteen different ales on offer. The Master Cutler Restaurant is open every lunchtime and evening with plenty of selection and at reasonable prices; either Table d'hôte or a'la carte.

Wilma and Mike are the owners of this hotel and will ensure you have a most enjoyable stay with them. Awarded Three Crowns by the Tourist Board and two star rated with AA and RAC.

The Great Central Hotel, Great Central Road, Loughborough, Leicestershire. Tel: 01509 263405 FAX: 01509 264130

Lying in the outskirts of this historic market town, and opposite the railway station, is the **East Midlands Hotel**. Whilst the hotel is not small, it has 53 tastefully decorated en suite bedrooms, it maintains a friendly and relaxed atmosphere. There are two bars, the Railway Inn bar mirrors a traditional English 19th century pub with hand-pulled ales and a hearty lunchtime snack menu and, by contrast, the Wayfarers Lounge with its lively and up-to-date atmosphere. The Victorian Restaurant oozes olde worlde charm with intimate coves and flickering candles for discreet dining. Created from part of the original tavern which was constructed in 1840 the dining room seats 60 comfortably. After all that eating and drinking, the hotel gives you the opportunity to work off a few pounds in the Falcon Leisure Centre. With a heated indoor swimming pool, fully equipped gymnasium and a Nordic sauna this is a super facility even for the least energetically inclined.

East Midlands Hotel, Nottingham Road, Loughborough, Leicestershire Tel: 01509 233056

The **Quality Friendly Hotel** is one of the best in Loughborough and really does live up to its name. This modern stylish hotel is situated on the A512 only five minutes away from junction 23 of the M1 and makes a good place not only to stop for a night, but to stay for a while to explore the surrounding area. Guests have free use of the hotel's leisure club facilities which includes a superb swimming pool. The 94 bedrooms are very well equipped indeed, some even have their own kitchen area with a microwave oven and fridge. All rooms have en suite bathrooms and colour televisions. The hotel has a fine carvery serving a variety of excellent food.

The Quality Friendly Hotel, New Ashby Road, Loughborough. Tel:01509 211800

Sitting impressively in the attractive village of **Cropston** is the **Bradgate Arms**, a 'Milestone Tavern', owned by the Wolverhampton and Dudley Breweries. The pub was originally a farmhouse, built in the 19th century. Today it is a thriving and popular pub, one of the most popular in the area; with its 'olde worlde' charm and interesting memorabilia contributing to the wonderful atmosphere it isn't difficult to see why. Keith and Karen Horton, the managers, keep a wide range of fine ales, so why not sample one of the interesting 'guest ales' which are always available. You would also be well advised to select a meal from the wide variety of superb food which is on the menu. This is a fine pub, we recommend that you pay it a visit.

The Bradgate Arms, Cropston, Leicester. Tel: 01533 2340336

The Reservoir Inn in this pretty village is well worth a visit. It dates back to the 19th century and sits proudly in over six acres of land. You can be sure of finding a warm and friendly atmosphere in this charming country pub. In addition to an unusual 'guest' beer, a wide variety of well kept ales are always available along with a varied selection of delicious food at reasonable prices. On sunny days the lovely beer garden becomes very popular, particularly with families as there is a play area for children to enjoy in safety. This stylish pub is situated at the junction of the B5328 and the B5330.

The Reservoir Inn, Reservoir Road, Cropston. Tel: 0116 2362165

The village of **Newtown Linford** stands on the borders of **Bradgate Park** and has some attractive old houses and a fine 18th century church which features a painted coat of arms.

In this picturesque village is **Jade Bradgate Tea Rooms & Bistro.** It is one of those places you often wish you could find for a pleasant lunch or afternoon tea in the right surroundings.

There are adequate tables and chairs inside, whilst outside, more seating with sunshades is available to cater for larger parties.

Special consideration has been given for the elderly and disabled customer. This is a new business venture for Richard and Janine but already they are building a reputation for good quality food and a large variety of freshly baked cakes and savouries.

Their Bistro (on the same premises) will be opening on Friday and Saturday evenings towards the end of 1995, when bookings will be essential. The owners have lots of enthusiasm and flair - a place worth finding.

Jade Bradgate Tea Rooms & Bistro, 542, Bradgate Road, Newtown Linford, Leicestershire. Tel: 01530 243664

Lady Jane Grey was born at **Bradgate** in 1537, the eldest granddaughter of Henry V111's sister, Mary. Many will know of her from the history books, and her untimely end after reigning as Queen for only nine days.

It is from this connection, **Gibson's Grey Lady Restaurant** is named. Set in the heart of Charnwood Forest it can be easily accessed from the M1 Motorway, A50 and the many county roads in this beautiful area. The part thatched and Swithland slate building has been carefully and tastefully extended and is set in lovely gardens and grounds. In refurbishing the restaurant, Chef/proprietor Martin and his wife Liz have created elegant surroundings with tasteful decor in restful colours.

The cocktail bar is an excellent starting point in which to relax with a pre dinner drink. In the restaurant, a carefully chosen range of dishes offers several classics as well as more unusual ones, including French, English, Oriental and a variety of vegetarian choices. The restaurant is open for dinner from Tuesday to Saturday and serves traditional Sunday lunch from the carvery. Top quality served with style!

Gibson's Grey Lady Restaurant, Sharpley Hill, Newtown, Linford, Leicestershire. Tel: 01530 243558

Malcolm and Pamela O'Shea established **Bradgate Nurseries & Garden Centre** in 1970 having both had experience in associated fields - Malcolm was a technical representative with Fisons advising commercial growers for nine years, whilst Pamela gained her knowledge in the florist side of the business.

Situated opposite **Bradgate Park** main entrance, the nursery has been developed over the years into a major garden centre. With a lifetime of experience as horticulturists Malcolm and Pamela have built the business over twenty five years to encompass all aspects of the garden and associated leisure goods. In addition to an extensive selection of trees, shrubs, pot and house plants, and a vast array or sundries, they also have garden buildings displayed, an aquatics centre and tents & trailer tents. This is a marvellous centre to visit with the benefit of sound advice and help for your planting and garden requirements.

Bradgate Nurseries & Garden Centre, Bradgate Road, (opp Bradgate Park Main Ent.), Newtown Linford, Leics. Tel: 01530 242985

On the edge of Charnwood forest, on the A50 at Markfield is **Field Head Farm**. The attractive hotel is built of local stone in the style of the original building which dates back to 1672. Warm and cosily furnished, the 28 bedrooms all have an en-suite bathroom, colour TV, direct dial telephone, hair drier, trouser press and drinks-making facilities. For a more romantic stay, why not ask for the room with the four-poster bed and champagne?

The restaurant can be found in the original farmhouse and incorporates four separate dining areas. The charm of the old farmhouse has been retained, with low ceilings, exposed oak beams and open fireplaces featuring throughout. Over one fireplace you can even see the date of building carved into the wood.

The menus offer a wide selection of à la carte dishes and house specialities, with a fine wine list to complement your meal. The bar area is just as delightful, and ideal for relaxing with a drink with friends. For the more business-minded, the hotel can provide full photocopying, fax and conference facilities in each of two function rooms. These rooms are also available for private dinner parties and wedding receptions. This excellent establishment holds both AA and RAC 3 star rating.

Field Head Hotel, Markfield Lane, Markfield, Leicestershire Tel: 01162 245454

A commitment to customer care and the personal supervision of its owner Jeremy Lord, underlines the success of **Quorn Grange** in **Quorn**, an impressive, ivy clad, country house hotel easily accessed from the A6. Originally a country house restaurant, it has been carefully and sympathetically enlarged to offer 15 beautifully appointed en-suite bedrooms, many having lovely views over the gardens and countryside. Guests can relax in the spacious conservatory which is most comfortably furnished or stroll in the gardens at leisure.

The elegant and stylish dining room offers a refreshing approach to good English food and quality service. The superb a' la carte menu is changed every month with the Chef regularly creating innovative new dishes. Many fine wines are available and your hardest decision will be leaving this excellent country house hotel.

Quorn Grange, Wood Lane, Quorn, Leicestershire. Tel: 01509 412167.   FAX: 01509 415621

This little area , bounded by the M1 to the west, the A6, now busy dual carriageway, to the east , and with a new link road seeming to eat away at the countryside in between, has become a quiet haven away from the endless roar of the traffic . Golf courses, woodland, and water are all here to be enjoyed. One place that has seen dramatic change throughout its history is **The Forest Rock** public house ,built in the mid 19th century and set in the picturesque village of **Woodhouse Eaves** where even the village name conjures up a tranquil and peaceful setting.

Run by Simon and Helen Adams for the past three years, they have created a lively and very pleasant atmosphere. The inn is spotlessly clean and nicely decorated and furnished. The ale is kept in tip top condition and bar snacks are available at most times.

Outside is a small well-tended beer garden and easy car parking. Help is available for the disabled and children are welcome.

The Forest Rock, 16 Church Hill, Woodhouse Eaves, Loughborough, Leicestershire. Tel: 01509 890314

One of **Rothley's** two greens - Town Green - incorporates some of the finest timber framed houses in the county. One or two are cruck-built, in which curved tree trunks are joined to form the framework of the house. Slightly more 'modern' are the Tudor box-frame houses also in evidence here. Town Green lies on the edge of **Rothley Park,** site of Rothley Temple which was built in the 13th century by the Knights Templars. The temple was later incorporated into an Elizabethan house which was added to over the succeeding centuries and finally converted in 1960 into the Rothley Court Hotel.

From about 1550 it was the seat of the Babington family. William Wilberforce, a family friend, drafted his bill for the abolition of slavery at the house while on a visit in 1791. A small monument records the occasion. In 1800, the historian Thomas Babington Macaulay, later Lord Macaulay of Rothley, was born here, and the hotel maintains the room as it was on the day he was born.

The original Templar chapel is still used for occasional services and the parish church of St Mary the Virgin has some fine memorials and a carved Norman font. In the churchyard is a Saxon cross of the 8th or 9th century. Rothley Station, which was built for the Central Railway in the 1890's, is restored to its original condition, complete with nostalgic advertising where you can catch the restored steam train from Loughborough.

Cossington Mill, in the village of **Cossington**, is one of the three mills mentioned in The Barrow on Soar records of 1086 and there has been a mill on this site for over one thousand years. First a corn mill and later incorporating a paper mill, the machinery was finally taken out in 1938 after all milling had ceased in 1928. The delightful buildings, on the banks of the rivers Wreake and Soar, have now become an outstanding restaurant with a wide spread reputation owned and run by Rob and Jan King. This is a very popular place and booking is essential. The dining areas are full of character, charm and intimacy, and, with such a scenic position, this a very enjoyable and unusual eating place.

The menu is extensive and offers the best in English cuisine with the help of French and more exotic influences. All the dishes are freshly prepared by a dedicated team of chefs and waiting staff and you can be sure of a delicious meal whatever the season. This is a refreshingly different place in which to enjoy a meal, from a light lunch to an evening banquet!

Cossington Mill, Cossington, Leicestershire Tel: 01509 812205

From here it is only a short distance to the ancient city of **Leicester**. The historic centre still retains much of interest from Roman times to the 20th century. There is a great open air market held in the square near **Gallow Tree Gate.** It has been here on the same site since at least 1200 and probably long before. There is something going on here every weekday; but the most interesting days are Wednesday, Friday and Saturday, and there are many bargains to be had or you can just soak up a wonderful atmosphere.

Leicester was founded just before the Roman conquest and they called it Ratae Coritanorum (capital or Coritani); it is also mentioned in Domesday Book under the name of Ledecestre.

If you enjoy ancient ruins, **The Jewry Wall Museum and Site** in St Nicholas Circle is to be recommended being devoted to Archaeology to 1500 AD. It is a modern building adjacent to the Roman bath site and houses some extremely important exhibits. The Bronze Age Welby Hoard, and the Roman Milestone from Thurmaston are here. There are several important Romano-British mosaics, Roman wall plaster and items from Anglo-Saxon burials. The displays and the information on them in this museum make a visit extremely interesting.

At some time, late Medieval painted glass was removed from Wygston's House and brought to Jewry Wall and the second century Roman wall and bath site are open to the public.

The Jewry Wall Museum and Site.   Leicester.

St Nicholas Church, close to the Jewry Wall, is one of the best known Anglo-Saxon churches in England. It stands on the site of the Roman basilica and was built with materials from the Roman ruins. In the walls we could see stones from four different periods namely Roman, Saxon, Norman and Medieval English.

Courses of herringbone masonry formed by Roman tiles are round the massive central tower built by the Normans and enriched with arcading. There is Saxon masonry in the west wall and two deeply splayed windows, their round heads formed by double rows of Roman tiles.

Our next stop was the **Guildhall** in Guildhall Lane and you can certainly understood why it is described as one of the most remarkable civic buildings in England. The Great Hall was built of timber in 1390 as a meeting place for members of the Corpus Christi Guild and later used by the Mayor and his brethren.

The hall was used as the town hall until the new municipal building 1876 was erected. The Mayor's Parlour, adjoining the Great Hall, was built early in the reign of Henry VII, and has a wonderful oak panelled chimney-piece. Set in the leaded panes of the windows is black and gold painted glass showing the Tudor Rose, the Prince of Wales feathers, a chalice and some of the seasons.

Did You Know...

The Hidden Places Series

Covers most of Britain?

For our full list see back of book

The Guildhall.   Leicester.

We left the Guildhall and entered **Wygston's House**. This important medieval building at 12, Applegate, St Nicholas Circle, houses a fantastic display of 18th-20th century costume.

Wygston's House.   Leicester.

The materials and colours are superb and when you look at some of the fantastic gowns you can almost hear the swish of silk skirts as the ladies moved round a room. In addition to the costumes there is also a reconstruction of a draper's and shoe shop of the 1920's.

From here it is just a short walk to **the Castle**. The 12th century Great Hall is now concealed within 18th century brickwork as it is used as the Crown Court. It has a charming setting, however, with the riverside gardens on one side and the spacious green on the other. The remains of the original Norman motte (or central mound) can still be seen.

In a wonderful setting on the edge of the castle green above the

River Soar is the **Church of St Mary de Castro**. It was founded in 1107 by the first Earl Leicester as a collegiate chapel, and was extended several times during the next three hundred years. Near the altar are five stone sedilia, or seats for the clergy, which date from 1180 and are regarded as the finest of their kind in England. Its spire rebuilt in 1783, makes a dramatic impact and acrobats were once wont to slide down a rope from the top to the castle green below.

If you want to get a clear understanding of the past history of Leicestershire then a visit to **Newarke Houses Museum** will delight you. It is a social history collection from 1500 to the present day. There are displays showing 17th century panelled rooms and a 19th century street scene amongst others. An amazing array of clocks is laid out in one room, musical instruments in another and sports and pastimes have not been forgotten either. Even the garden has been kept in period with the right flowers and a marvellous herb garden.

The Newarke Houses Museum.   Leicester.

The 16th century Chantry House forms part of the Newarke Houses Museum. If you enjoy things military then it is well worth while popping into **The Museum of the Royal Leicestershire Regiment**, its address is The Magazine, Oxford Street just by Newarke. You will get a complete picture of the history of the Royal Leicestershire Regiment (17th Foot) including momentous battle trophies and relics all housed in this early 15th century Newark Gateway.

The city is a good transport centre with seven great roads radiating from it. There are also three railway stations and the Grand Union Canal linking it with the Trent and the Thames. It was from Leicester that Thomas Cook organised his first excursion, to Loughborough of all places, and of course, never looked back.

Leicester only gained city status in 1919 and the **Church of St Martin** became a cathedral in 1926. It stands dignified and quite impressive close to the Guildhall, although it is a little swamped by modern buildings which surround it. The noble tower and spire are fairly distinctive and we enjoyed ambling around this relatively modern but none the less interesting place of worship.

For those demanding top quality accommodation, service and absolute convenience, the place to aim for is **Hotel St. James** in the heart of Leicester City Centre. The hotel sits astride a six storey car park which is free of charge to guests and has direct access into the reception; alternatively, there is a private lift from ground floor level. For such a large hotel, the Saint James has a very 'personal' feel about it; the staff have time for a smile, and clearly, the Manger Mr. Thierry Heinis, has a high regard for the comfort and well being of his guests. The hotel is smartly decorated with an excellent range of facilities. The seventy three well appointed bedrooms have en-suite bathroom/ shower, remote control television, direct dial telephone, trouserpress and hairdryer.

All have recently been refurbished and have individual name plates using ladies names from all over the world. For relaxation, the Library bar with its tasteful decor and a most interesting selection of old and classic books, is the perfect setting to unwind and take a leisurely drink; it remains open late for residents.

The Gallery Restaurant has panoramic views over the Leicester skyline; many of the table positions have window views creating a wonder atmosphere in which to dine. Meals are prepared to a high standard from fresh produce bought from local suppliers and the menu offers an excellent choice of International cuisine complimented by an interesting selection of wines. Additionally, the 'Saint James' has extensive Conference and Banqueting facilities and the management will be delighted to cater for your Special Day.

Hotel Saint James, Abbey Street, Leicester. Tel: 0116 251 0666
Fax: 0116 251 518

Hidden away in a quiet niche yet close to the centre of Leicester stands **The Pump and Tap** public house. Full of character and charm, this is a real, old fashioned drinking pub that was formerly called the West End. With bare wooden floor boards, comfortable seating and an excellent range of top class real ales this is a wonderful place to relax and enjoy a pint. Open every evening, Saturday lunchtime and all day Sunday there is always something going on and, in particular, Jam night is Tuesday evening to if you sing or play an instrument come along and join in the fun.

Opposite the pub is the **Rum Runner Restaurant** which offers excellent and delicious borderlands cuisine from Mexico and South America or, if that sounds too hot, try upstairs where you will find the **Que Pasa Restaurant**, a small type of Cantina. Both restaurants are beautifully decorated and furnished and provide the ideal atmosphere in which to enjoy a pleasant and interesting meal.

The Pump and Tap, 42 Duns Lane, Leicester Tel: 01162 540324

Leicestershire Museum and Art Gallery, in New Walk is considered to be the major regional Art Gallery, which, when you have seen what they have in their collection, you are sure to agree. The European art collection from the 15th century includes German Expressionists and French Impressionists.

The Art Collection is by no means the only treasure in this fine building. There are displays of natural history including the Rutland Dinosaur. There is glass and silver and a particularly impressive collection of English drinking glasses and French art glass. There is English silverware from Elizabethan times to the present day. If you interested in Egyptology, then there is the Ancient Egypt Gallery, full of fascinating items and if you happen to be in the Museum on a Thursday between October and March, you can enjoy one of the super lunchtime concerts.

Leicestershire Museum & Art Gallery.   Leicester.

Several 18th century buildings survive in Leicester, among them is Belgrave Hall in Church Road, built during the Queen Anne period in 1709 and two miles north of the city centre. Very carefully **Belgrave Hall,** has been kept in its original state. Everything about it retains the atmosphere of an 18th and 19th century house. The rooms are all delightfully furnished with items of the era. In the stable block there are well preserved coaches, the harness room has tack still hanging on the walls and there are agricultural implements that would have been in use at that time. The gardens are a sheer pleasure, some period, some botanical including a rock and water garden and green houses with over six and a half thousand species of plants.

Moving out of Leicester and heading west along the A47 takes you over the M1 to the village of Kirby Muxloe.

The chief interest in **Kirby Muxloe** is its castle which is unusually built of brick and not stone. It was the first medieval brick building in Leicestershire and the bricks were all made on site. Dated 1480 but only the great gatehouse and one of the four angle towers remain intact. Surrounded by a moat fitted with gun ports and with its flotillas of moorhens and ducks, it is a very picturesque place to visit.

A most colourful scene awaits you at **Tropical Birdland** reached by following the B582 to **Desford** and taking Main Street and into Lindridge Lane. Created by Richard Hooper in 1982 as a hobby, it opened its doors to the public in 1987. Tropical Birdland is first and foremost a breeding centre for rare and endangered species. You will find here at least seventy different species of tropical and exotic birds discovered in the Walkthrough Aviaries, at the Macaw Lawn, the Hatching and Breeding Room, and where, on your guided walk, you can see the water garden and Koi Carp ponds. Plans are already in

316

progress for further expansion, and by visiting Tropical Birdland you are helping the fight to save "Rare and Endangered Species". Now one of the premier places of interest in Leicestershire.

Tropical Birdland, Lindridge Lane, Desford, Leicestershire. Tel: 01455 824603.

On the other side of the city to the east is **Scraptoft**, much less spoilt than many of the peripheral villages in this part of the country. The church of All Saints is of ironstone fabric with limestone dressings, all built around 1300. Nether Hall is dated 1709 and is built of brick with Swithland slate roof and guarded by noble iron gates. The houses, church and hall seem to peer over a cliff onto the pasture below and although there seems to be little that is spectacular, it is pleasant to amble through these little villages . To the southeast of Leicester for example there are a number of villages to be found between the A6 and A47which are worth a detour.

Glooston, a village in a hollow, was occupied during Roman times. The site of a villa was discovered in 1946 on the east bank of the stream and the Roman Gartree Road runs just south of here.

For the more energetic holidaymaker a walk to **Hallaton** is a very pleasant way to spend an afternoon. Mentioned in the Domesday Book as Alctone, the village lies in rich grazing lands of the Welland Valley. Every Easter Monday the villagers of Hallaton turn out in force to challenge neighbouring Medbourne in a boisterous 'bottle kicking' contest, steeped in pagan ritual. First a huge hare pie is cut into portions and distributed by the rector. Some is left over to be scattered on Hare Pie Bank.

The T-shaped house at the eastern end of the village reveals, behind its 17th century facade, a remarkable 13th century house. The old hall, south east of the church is an H-plan house built in 1650. Near the church is a medieval bridge of three arches and the church itself is surrounded by sycamore, oak and beech trees. It is notable for the great beauty of an aisle in the south transept which has a twenty feet window flooding it with light. In the tower arch the huge clock pendulum can be seen swinging.

All these villages surround the Langtons chief of which is **Church Langton** which is famous for one of the finest churches in the county. It is a lovely place beautified by a famous rector in the 18th century, William Hanbury whose passion in life was music and flowers. His great ambition was to found a music festival here but that was not to be.

We travelled north to **Kings Norton,** on the edge of the east Leicestershire hill country. It has one of the most appealing village churches in the Midlands. We felt it was almost cathedral like, as we first saw it across the fields. Built in 1757 by a Leicester architect called John Wing, the church has been called 'L' perfect expression of 18th century Anglicanism'. Inside all is clear light and serenity and it retains all its original fittings and the beautiful three decker pulpit, box pews and west gallery are a joy. Close to the church is the old manor house and nearby is a brick dove-cote of the late 17th century.

A little further north and you will come to **Houghton on the Hill** which has a matchless situation of the great escarpment of the county, above the Plain of England. Not far from the village of **Tilton-on-the-Hill**, the delectable rolling park of **Launde Abbey** lies close to the Rutland frontier. We felt it was nestling in its own world of lonely lanes and ancient woodlands being so far from the main road. From all directions the drives lead to the house, an H-Shaped Elizabethan and 17th century manor with gabled wings and dormers. Unexpectedly, we came upon the chancel of the Augustinian priory church standing behind the north wing, still in use for worship.

Burrough-on-the-Hill stands nearly six hundred feet above sea level on the marlstone escarpment and the great earthwork of Burrough Hill is the grandest Iron Age hill fort in the county. Some of the ancient mounds are still twenty feet high and the countryside is seen in a vast panorama all around from this eighty two acre site.

Frisby-on-the-Wreake, which is north of the A607 between Leicester and Melton Mowbray became front page news when an 18th century rector here, Rev. William Wragge, suddenly startled the village by announcing that he would marry any couple who came before him without banns or license.

He did a roaring trade until the law caught up with him and he was sentenced to fourteen years transportation. Far too old for the sentence to be carried out, he faded into obscurity and the Leicestershire Gretna Green once more became the quiet farming village we see today.

Further down the river towards Leicester is **The Star Inn** in the village of **Thrussington** in the heart of the Leicestershire countryside. Until twelve months ago, when Lyndsay took over the Inn's lease, she had worked here for twelve years. Now, she has made changes to give a new lease of life to the place. Whilst still offering well kept real ales in the bar area and the old style lounge, Lyndsay has converted two rooms,(one upstairs) into restaurant dining rooms with attractive furnishing and decor; indeed one has a more continental air with its pretty pink table coverings. Traditional home cooked food is available seven days a week and there is plenty of variety at very reasonable prices. Booking is essential at weekends

The Star Inn, Thrussington, Leicestershire. Tel: 01664 424220
Crossing the elegant bridge built in 1832 across the Eye (a tributary of the Wreake) and the canal, we found ourselves in the ancient market town of **Melton Mowbray.** The Tuesday market - there is also one on a Saturday - was recorded as a profitable concern in 1077 and certainly dates from Saxon times. For those of us who enjoy browsing it is a gem. The Old English settled here as early as the 5th century, one of their pagan cemeteries has been discovered on the outskirts of the town. Melton takes the second part of its name from the great Norman family of Mowbray who owned the manor by 1125.

We found this town bright and cheerful with many decent 18th and 19th century houses. There are several notable buildings. The so called **Anne of Cleves house,** though now used as a restaurant, is basically 15th century and was either a Chantry House belonging to the church or perhaps the dwelling house of one of the rich woolmerchants, who must have subscribed to the magnificent enlargement of the once Norman church of St Mary in the late 15th century. Opposite the church is the Masion Dieu founded as an almshouse in 1640 and in the market place the former Swan Inn retains a fine porch over the pavement. Melton became the hunting metropolis of England; the meeting place of the Quorn, Cottesmore and Belvoir hunts and was frequented by the nobility and gentry from all parts of the country. As late as 1939 it was said that, at the beginning of the season, a thousand fine hunters were stabled in the town. Many of the stables have now been converted into flats, but a number of the larger houses belonging to the wealthy, are still to be seen.

The King's Head Hotel in Nottingham Street stands on a plot of land with a long, interesting history. Originally known as 'Spittle End', the first recording of possession was 1322 to the Knights Templars. It is possible that properties were first built on it in 1750. Today an impressive building housing a fine hotel, restaurant and bar occupies the site. The beautifully fitted restaurant seats approximately 40 people with the tables well spaced. The menus offer an excellent choice of food, after dinner you can retire to a private coffee lounge, separate from the public bar area. A superb function room suitable for special occasions is also available. The hotel accomodation is of a high standard, the rooms are spacious, well equipped and make a good base from which to explore this interesting area.

The King's Head Hotel, Nottingham Street, Melton Mowbray. Tel: 01664 62110

Through the centuries, the **George Hotel** has played an important part in the town's life giving the traveller and local people alike a friendly welcome and cheerful hospitality. Today, the resident owners, Brian and Beryl Chaimberlain, continue with those traditions and combine the charm of this hotel with every modern comfort.

The 14 luxury guest bedrooms have individual character, are comfortably furnished and all have private bathroom or shower room. Equipped with all conveniences from remote control television to modern sockets and direct dial telphones. There are a number of delightful rooms with four-poster beds. The Ferneley Restaurant has a warm and friendly atmosphere where you can enjoy a candlelight

320

dinner and haute cuisine. A select a la carte menu offers English and international dishes complemented by an extensive wine list. There is plenty of room to circulate and relax in The George with bars catering for all tastes. Many facilities are within a few minutes walk of the hotel.

The George Hotel, High Street, Melton Mowbray, Leicestershire. Tel: 01664 62112 Fax: 01664 410457

For a good down to earth old English inn and hospitable welcome, call at the **Bricklayers Arms** in Melton Mowbray, where Rick and Yvonne and their friendly staff will serve you up with lots of chat, real ales and a selection of meals and snacks everyday of the week. You will find the Bricklayers at the top of Timber Hill; it's a really friendly pub. Rick and Yvonne also own and run a **Guest House** at 86 Burton Road wherein a lovely Victorian house there are four letting rooms. It is open all year round.

Bricklayers Arms, 16 Timber Hill, Melton Mowbray, Leicestershire. Tel: 01664 65178

Dickinson and Morris is the oldest remaining pie bakery in Melton Mowbray and is the town's sole producer of a truly authentic Melton Mowbray Pie. **Ye Olde Pork Pie Shoppe** is one of the town's oldest landmarks and as a bakehouse boasts a distinguished history which spans more than four centuries. John Dickinson rented the property in 1851 and began making pork pies using a hand-raised crust and in 1854 created the Original Melton Hunt Cake which now attracts customers worldwide. After a ruinous fire devastated the building in 1991 the shoppe's future was threatened but in 1992 work began on restoration of the shoppe and it was again opened to the public in October 1992.

With over 140 years of experience, Dickinson and Morris know a thing or two about making the 'real thing' and offer fun evenings for groups of people who are invited to hand raise a Melton Mowbray Pork Pie for themselves. Join customers from all over the world who visit this famous pie shop.

Dickinson & Morris Ltd. Ye Olde Pork Pie Shoppe, 10 Nottingham Street, Melton Mowbray, Leices. Telephone & Fax: 01664 62341

A very pleasant way to walk off pies or cakes as well as for the enjoyment is to follow the Jubilee Way - a fifteen and a half mile waymarked walk mostly on field and woodland path between Melton Mowbray and Woolsthorpe, just across the Lincolnshire border. It will take you through the Vale of Belvoir, via Scalford, Belvoir Woods and Castle and eventually, if you really have overindulged, you can link up with the Viking Way at Woolsthorpe!

On the outskirts of Melton Mowbray is **Sysonby Knoll Hotel and Restaurant** set in secluded grounds of two acres with a frontage to the River Eye. This Edwardian style Country House has been owned and managed by the same family for thirty years who have tastefully extended it to provide all the facilities of a modern hotel. Stella and Richard with their team of friendly staff are very keen to create a relaxing holiday for their guests who can enjoy the secluded gardens, sit and take in the view across the river and fields from the Gazebo, tone up in the outdoor swimming pool or relax in the new conservatory.

322

The well appointed bedrooms, of which there are twenty four with en suite bathrooms, all have luxury facilities and two of the rooms have a superb four-poster bed with full canopy.

Renowned for its excellent cuisine, the hotel has both a' la carte or table d'hôte menus, or you can simply enjoy something light and tasty from the bar. Riding, Golf and other attractions are nearby. ETB 4-Crown Commended. AA & RAC.

Knoll Hotel, Asfordby Road, Melton Mowbray, Leicestershire. Tel: 01664 63563 Fax: 01664 410364

A gentler meander for us was the **Egerton Park Riverside Walk** in Melton and we then ended up in the **Melton Carnegie Museum** at Thorpe End. It has good coverage of the history and the environment of the Borough of Melton. Here we saw local exhibitions, hunting pictures, and displays on Stilton cheese and pork pies. It frequently has special exhibitions of other prints and paintings as well.

Nottingham Street. Melton Mowbray.

In the edge of the historic town of Melton Mowbray, and close to the Vale of Belvoir, Rutland Water and the market towns of Stamford,

Oakham and Grantham, lies the **Quorn Lodge Hotel**. This magnificent establishment, built in the 19th century as a hunting lodge and gentlemen's hostel, is now owned and personally run by Julie and John Sturt. Since coming here in 1992, the couple have extensively refurbished the building, while retaining many of its original features including the old door to the gun room. All the 19 en suite bedrooms are individually designed and decorated in a variety of styles and really do create a home from home atmosphere.

The hotel's restaurant, open from Monday to Saturday, is extremely popular and bookings are advisable. The extensive menu, of well-known and classic English dishes, is delicious to read and the wine list offers an interesting selection of fine wines to compliment any meal. Whether you are staying here on business or for pleasure the Quorn Lodge Hotel offers the ideal atmosphere in which to relax and recharge your batteries.

Quorn Lodge Hotel, 46 Asfordby Road, Melton Mowbray, Leicestershire Tel: 01664 66660

South of Melton down the B6047, it is worth turning onto the B647 which will enable you to call in at the **Carrington Arms** in the pretty village of **Ashby Folville.** Here, you'll find a clean white building with black timbers, an impressive looking Coat of Arms and tables and chairs with green table shades.

Although built at the turn of the century, a much older inn originally stood here dating back to 1547. Formerly named the Royal Oak, it later took the name of the local estate owner - Carrington. Mick and Wendy have been the Tenants here for eleven years and the good food you can enjoy is all prepared by Wendy. Food is served at lunchtime and in the evening. There's a good selection of ales and other beverages available from the bar and live music and other entertainment is on hand at various times.

The Carrington Arms, 1 Folville Street, Ashby Folville, Melton Mowbray, Leicestershire. Tel: 01664 840228

Heading out of Melton again but this time in a northeasterly direction, **Saltby** was our next port of call, high up towards the Lincolnshire border. It has a little seven hundred year old church, one of its farms has a windmill and under its surface a Roman pavement has been found.

Not far away on Saltby Heath are the mysterious earthworks known as King Lud's Entrenchments, a long mound of earth with a tumulus at each end. Lud was the sky god worshipped by the ancient Britons and tradition has it that King Lud was buried at one end during the Dark Ages. There was certainly a King of Mercia call Ludeca, who was killed in battle in 827, but it is more likely that the mounds were the boundary between two ancient Kingdoms. The Welsh name for London was Caer Ludd (Lud's town) and Ludgate Hill preserves the name, which is nothing to do with Leicestershire, but we thought it was quite interesting anyway.

The area surrounding Melton Mowbray and its cluster of villages is highly populated with racing stables, so it is not unusual to see strings of fine thoroughbred race horses sedately enjoying the road work which prepares them gently for their early morning, nearby local gallops. What better name for a pub in the vicinity that **The Nags Head Inn** in Saltby. Originally housing the village butcher and baker, this traditional pub serves delicious food at reasonable prices. There is also accommodation, one twin with its own bathroom and a double bedroom, both having tea/coffee making facilities. situated in the midst of delightful countryside The Nags Head will provide you with good food and comfortable accommodation.

Five miles away is **Belvoir Castle** which is well worth a visit. It was built in the closing decade of the 11th century by Robert de Todeni, one of William the Conqueror's standard bearers. The name is first recorded in 1130 as Belveder and in 1145 as Bello Videre - beautiful view.

The castle suffered great damage in the Civil War and the 8th Earl built a mansion on the site in 1654, but in 1816 it suffered again in a great fire. The castle was finally completed in 1830 and today is one of the showplaces of the Midlands. There are some wonderful paintings including work by Van Dyck, Reynolds, Hogarth and one of the finest of the Holbein portraits of Henry VIII.

The gardens are particularly beautiful, on the side of the hill, the Duchess' Garden is full of terraces and stone statues; the Duke's Walk is an entire valley filled with flowerbeds and trees and the Water Garden in summer is filled with azaleas and rhododendrons, a marvellous spectacle. A dovecote in the grounds stands on the site of Belvoir Priory founded in 1076 and suppressed in 1539. Only four monks ever lived there.

A fitting end to this part of the book and a good place to spend some time before heading off to the next port of call; the county of Rutland.

Belvoir Castle

Rutland

Normanton Tower, Rutland Water

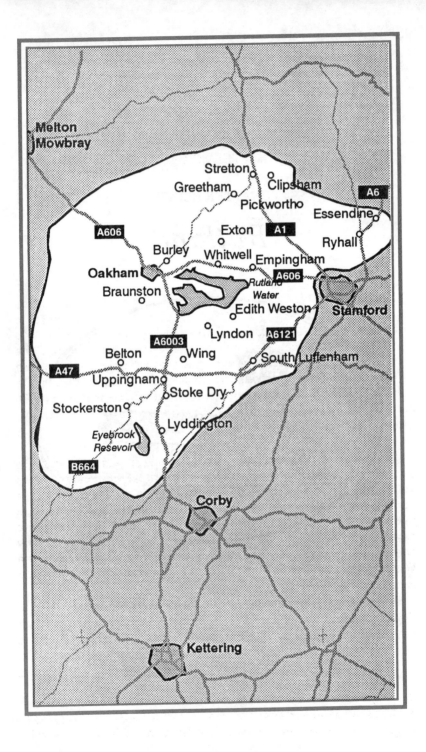

CHAPTER ELEVEN.

Rutland.

For years **Rutland** kept up a vociferous battle to retain its status as the smallest county in England but in 1974 it was forced into marriage with Leicestershire. This decision, after a nationwide campaign by the locals, has now been reversed. Rutland, like the counties that surround it has villages of thatch and ironstone, clustered around their churches and the countryside is rich in pasture where once deer were hunted. Its central feature is **Rutland Water**, its 3100 acres making it one of the largest man made lakes in northern Europe. Started in 1971 to supply water of the East Midlands towns, it was created by damming the valley near Empingham.

The result is an attractively landscaped lake, around five miles long which also serves as a popular recreational and leisure centre where sailing, water skiing and windsurfing are pursued. There are many picnic sites at **Whitwell, Normanton** and an information centre just south west of **Empingham**. At the west end you will find a nature reserve and for information and access a centre at **Lyndon.** By Normanton you'll see a neo classical church which now houses a Water Museum, orginally built in 1764, extended in 1826 and refurbished in 1911.

Entering the county along the busy A47 from Leicester to Peterborough, there is an easy and pleasant detour along quieter roads leading to Oakham. Turning left off the A47 onto the B6047 and heading north brings you to **Tilton on the Hill.**

The village is noted for its early English church which has a collection of rather strange gargoyles.

Set in the midst of beautiful countryside and within its own 100 acres is **Halstead House Farm and Nature Trail** a delightful place to visit set in **Halstead**, a tiny hamlet near Tilton-on-the-Hill.

Normanton Tower. Rutland Water.

Halstead House Farm is a working turkey farm and, alongside the turkeys, in the farmyard you can see and walk amongst pigs, goats, rabbits and various breeds of poultry and ducks. Out in the undulating fields are rare breeds of cattle, sheep, goats and donkeys.

The Nature Trail, around the farm and surrounding pastureland, also takes in the old railway line linking Leicester, Melton and Market Harborough. After a walk around the farm and trail what better than to stop and take a cup of tea at the Tea Room and Garden. In this friendly atmosphere you can enjoy home cooked cakes and light meals and also take a leisurely stroll around the colourful flower beds.

Halstead House Farm and Nature Trail, Tilton-on-the-Hill, Leicestershire Tel: 01162 597239

Oakham, the county town of Rutland, is where you'll see some of the beauty of the place and learning something of the old county's history. The infamous Titus Oates was born here in 1649. His ability to create malignant fantasy in order to set the Catholics and the Protestants against each other became well- known as he invented the idea of a Popish Plot against Charles II.

Oakham was the home of another oddity too, Jeffery Hudson, a three foot six inch midget. He worked for the Duke of Buckingham at nearby Burley-on-the-Hill where the Duchess treated him like a pet poodle, dressing him up and showing him off to visitors.

Once when Charles 1 and his Queen Henrietta Maria came to **Burley** there was a special surprise for them. A huge cold pie was placed on the table before them at dinner and when the pie was opened, out jumped Jeffery Hudson.

The Queen was very taken with this midget and asked the Duchess to give him to her. Off he went back to court where he became a popular toy but also exceedingly vain thus making many enemies, and finally killing one of them in a duel. That was not all his adventures, he was captured twice by pirates whilst crossing the

Channel and was sold as a slave in Barbary. The Duke of Buckingham paid a ransom for him and for a while he returned to Oakham but yearned for London and eventually was thrown into prison, accused of being involved in the Popish Plot conjured up by Titus Oates.

A street market is still held twice weekly in the Market Place which contains an historic Buttercross and a set of stocks. The whole county of Rutland seems to come to these busy markets which are fun.

In the Market Square is **The Whipper-in,** a 17th century hotel furnished with antiques, where fresh flowers are on display and log fires burn in the lounges and bars. There is a warm friendly welcome as you arrive at reception accompanied by professional service. The twenty four bedrooms are designed and furnished to the highest standard of comfort each with private bathroom, and all modern facilities including 24 hour room service.

The award winning restaurant specialises in imaginative English country cooking with special emphasis on game and fish; the a la carte menu offers a superb choice supported by an extensive wine list. The Market and Lounge Bars are popular meeting places for the locals where you can relax with a drink or enjoy one of the 'Bistro' style dishes. The Whipper-In offers special holiday breaks but whenever you stay at this hotel you will be guaranteed the best in hospitality.

The Whipper-In Hotel, The Market Place, Oakham, Rutland.Tel: 01572 756971 Fax: 01572 757759

Just off the market place is **Oakham Castle**. A romantic place with a sense of history epitomised by the 12th century Great Hall of this wonderful Norman castle. The pillars supporting its magnificent arcades have carved capitals so much like the ones in the chancel of Canterbury Cathedral that it must have been the same craftsman who were responsible for both. There is a lot to take in but what is especially memorable is the amazing collection of horseshoes.

It is a long standing tradition apparently that any peer of the realm coming to Oakham for the first time must present the castle with a horseshoe. You can see them hanging all around the walls of the hall. They are all shapes and sizes, large and small, some wooden some rusty and in amongst them you will see one presented by Queen Elizabeth 1 and one by Queen Elizabeth 11.

Oakham Castle.   Oakham.

It was no distance from the castle to **All Saints church** with its 14th century tower, a fine parish church and standing watchfully over the town. With the loss of the county of Rutland came the importance of protecting its history. This, you will find, is done admirably at **The Rutland County Museum**, on Catmos Street. The Museum is dedicated to Rutland life and includes agricultural equipment, implements and wagons. There are local craft tools, 19th and early 20th century domestic items and a whole range of archeological finds. The Museum is housed in a splendid 18th century former riding school of the Rutland Fencibles, a volunteer cavalry regiment.

Did You Know...

The Hidden Places Series
Covers most of Britain?
For our full list see back of book

The Rutland County Museum.   Oakham.

Taking the little road north out of Oakham we were almost immediately in **Burley -on-the-Hill** where the Rutland Agricultural Show is held in August and a 17th centurt mansion stands close by, considered to be the most attractive mansion in the county. Picturesque **Home Farm** at Burley-on-the-hill is reached by the B668 from Oakham; it's a lovely mellow thatched cottage of 'picture postcard' appearance surrounded by one and a half acres and with outstanding gardens created by the owners - William and Victoria Dickenson.

To stay here is a most delightful experience since the cottage is furnished with beautiful antiques which are bought, sold and restored by William in his Antiques business. The three charming bedrooms with tasteful furnishings comprise of two double and a single room. Evening meals are prepared by arrangement and Victoria will provide packed lunches and fill flasks for you. Children are welcome as are well-behaved pets. Home Farm may prove a difficult place to leave.

Home Farm, Burley-on-the-Hill, Oakham, Rutland. Tel: 01572 757333

Situated on the edge of Oakham and within five minutes walk of the County Museum, Oakham Castle and the Town Centre, is the 18 acre **Rutland Farm Park** with the offer of 'something for everyone'. Opened to the public in 1981 the Park has been preserved as part of a family farm aided by the Countryside Commission. The farm buildings constructed about 1830, have many interesting features and reflect the type of farming of a hundred years ago. In the park you will see some of the more unusual animals such as Longhorn Highland cattle, Longwool sheep, various breeds of pigs, poultry and waterfowl. There are Old English Goats, Shetland and Exmoor ponies too.

Old farm vehicles are on show with tools and implements used by the old farm workers, reflecting times prior to modernisation.

The woodland and stream are a special feature of the Farm Park where magnificent mature trees are established and bamboo, rhododendron, Magnolia and ferns flourish. Over 70 species of birds have been recorded at the farm and over 80 different wild flowers can be seen at various times of the year. Surely an interesting and educational day out for all the family.

Rutland Farm Park, Catmose Farm, Uppingham Road, Oakham, Rutland. Tel: 01572 756789

North of here at **Ashwell**, you'll find the **Rutland Railway Museum.**

In a southerly direction from Oakham you'll pass by **Braunston -in- Rutland**, a lovely ironstone village above the River Gwash. The church here has traces of earlier 12th and 13th century buildings. Following the minor roads through attractive country you'll come to **Belton -in- Rutland**, where you'll find a country craft centre.

To the west is **Stoke Dry**, which overlooks the **Eyebrook Reservoir.** Sir Everard Digby who was executed for his role on the Gunpowder Plot was born here in 1578 and there are Digby monuments in the church here. Close by lies **Lyddington,** which has the **Bede House**, overseered by English Heritage, it is a 15th to 17th century building that is the remaining part of a manor house that belonged to the Bishops of Lincoln.

Uppingham, standing by the A6003 is a pleasant town where Uppingham School was founded in 1587 to become one of the leading public schools under the headship of Dr Edward Tring during the 19th century.

The **Lake Isle Hotel** is a small personally run restaurant and town hotel. Fresh ingredients arrive from all over the country to create superb dishes to the highest standard. Special 'wine evenings' are held from time to time to enable guests to fully appreciate the unique wine cellar stocked with over three hundred varieties.

The theme continues to the twelve luxury en suite bedrooms named after wine regions, where guests will find fresh fruit and a decanter of sherry thoughtfully provided. All rooms have been interior designed and are complimented with all facilities.

The Lake Isle Hotel, 16 High Street East, Uppingham. Tel: 01572 822951 Fax: 01572 822951

The historic and magnificent former 16th century coaching inn, **The Falcon Hotel**, stands proudly overlooking the market square. Privately owned for the past three years, it blends the character and style of its age with the modern facilities that visitors look for today. There is a wonderfully inviting wood panelled snug bar and down the centre of the hotel, where the carriages used to pass to getting to the stables, is the Brasserie which serves informal meals throughout the day. The Garden Terrace Restaurant offers a wonderful range of essentially English dishes which are carefully prepared from fresh seasonal produce.

Each of the 25 bedrooms are different but all are stylishly decorated and furnished to a high standard. Charming in every way, it comes as no surprise to find that the Falcon Hotel comes highly recommended by Ashley Courtenay.

The Falcon Hotel, High Street East, Uppingham, Rutland
Tel: 01572 823535

338

Also in the market square stands **The Vaults.** This 17th century inn is full of character and charm and its owner has been in residence for the past twenty eight years. There are three twin rooms and one family room, all en suite. Rooms have colour television and hot drink making facilities. Lunch and Dinner is served daily and can be taken in the upstairs restaurant, seating 30 people, or in the bar.

There is an inventive and varied menu, and other 'daily specials' are offered. The Vaults is well situated for Corby, Leicester, Melton Mowbray and Peterborough.

The Vaults, Market Square, Uppingham, Rutland. Tel: 01572 823259

Just a couple of miles south of Uppingham, in the centre of the quiet village of **Lyddington**, is the **Marquess of Exeter** hotel, a 16th century coaching inn.

A warm, friendly welcome awaits all visitors to the hotel which is a rare combination of historical inn, high class restaurant and modern accommodation facilities.

The main restaurant itself is comfortable and spacious offering a choice of a la carte or gourmet fixed price menus with an extensive wine list all served in a relaxing atmosphere. The well stocked Earl of Exeter bar, with its inglenook fireplaces and low oak beams, is an ideal place to meet and enjoy a quiet drink before or after your meal. Finally, all the ensuite bedrooms are furnished to a high standard and provide excellent modern comforts; there are also two executive suites, with separate lounges, available.

This excellent establishment, with the same owner as the Charnwood Hotel, Narborough, has been recognised by Egon Ronay and Les Routiers for its cuisine, overall comfort and professional service. A wonderful place to stay in the heart of the ancient county of Rutland.

The Marquess of Exeter Hotel, Lyddington, Near Uppingham Tel: 01572 822477

Situated on the Rutland Northampton border on the A6003 in **Caldecott,** and near to the river Welland is **The Plough Inn.** A free house owned and personally run by Alan and Gill, offering everything you would expect from a good English pub.

The building dates back to 1868 and until just afterthe second world war remained a private dwelling. The Plough Inn has a good and varied menu of home cooked food offering 3 course meals,special childrens dishes, and a further choice from the blackboard and bar snacks. Alan keeps a good cellar and a fine range of real ales including Mansfield Bitter, Riding Dark Mild, Old Baily, and Adnams Broadside. There is a small but useful beer garden to the rear of the inn.

The Plough Inn, 16 Main St., Caldecott, Rutland. Tel: 01536 770284

Skirting the border and heading northeast along the course of the Welland the B672 brings you to **South Luffenham** where, hidden away by the church steeple is the **Boot and Shoe Inn**, personally run by Rosemary and Mick Bunker with thirty years of experience behind them. In the 17th century the buildings were originally a small inn, three cottages and a bakery. Villagers still remember taking their Sunday joint to the Bakery to be cooked whilst they slipped into the pub for a drink. This is a traditional pub offering accommodation, first- class ales and fresh home-cooked food.

The excellent menu offers plenty of variety including such dishes as Dressed Crab, Rainbow Trout, Liver & bacon casserole, Vegetarian food and 'Grown-up' Ice Cream and desserts. In the dining room there is a Inglenook fireplace for winter warmth, and outside, there are patio areas to take in the pleasant days of sunshine.

The Boot and Shoe Inn, The Street, South Luffenham, Rutland. Tel: 01780 720111

North east of here we came to the village of **Wing**, one of the most attractive villages in Rutland boasting its own maze.

The Kings Arms at Wing offers instant appeal with its old stone walls, multi-pane widows and old slate roofing. It more closely resembles lovely old cottages on either side of a village street, yet it is private, set in the heart of the country and offers quality in all respects. The building dates from 1649 and has many original features to admire.

There are three luxury en-suite bedrooms with tea and coffee making facilities, colour television and radio alarms. The Kings Arms has a first class restaurant and offers traditional English food with the emphasis on freshness. A well stocked bar offer best ales, selected wines and of course non alcoholic beverages. With open fires to warm you in the winter and a lovely garden for enjoyment in the summer months, the Kings Arms will welcome you the year round.

The Kings Arms, Top Street, Wing, Rutland. Tel: 01572 737634

We continued via **Edith Weston**, which gets its name from Edith, widow of Edward the Confessor .This tranquil village is in the heart of the most wonderful countryside on the south shore of Rutland Water.

Here, nestled around the beautiful 11th century church and village square you will find **Rutland Cottage Holidays**. After their first visit to the area in the mid 1980's, Brian and Jennifer Wallis made many returns to Rutland before buying their first home in the village.

Their superb holiday cottages have been carefully and fully refurbished to a very high standard and include full central heating and open fires; kitchens with every modern appliance; bathrooms with baths and powerful electric showers and lovely bedrooms with pine furniture and attractive soft furnishings.

Brian and Jennifer will greet you on arrival and, having already placed a complimentary basket of fresh food and a bottle of wine in your cottage, will be on hand to advise and help in any way.

Children are welcome and well behaved dogs by arrangement. The cottages are available throughout the year even for weekend breaks. East Midlands Tourist Board awarded both cottages the 5-Key Highly Commended rating and there can be no doubt of a wonderful holiday in store in this location and luxurious accommodation.

Rutland Cottage Holidays, Stone Cottage, 34 Weston Road, Edith Weston, Rutland.   Telephone and Fax: 01780 720087

Normanton, is a little further along on the south shore of Rutland Water where you'll find something very special at the **Normanton Park Hotel**. This sixteen bedroom hotel has been transformed from its former function as a coach house and stable block of the now demolished Normanton Hall.

The building is of the Georgian period and inside the refurbishment defers to this period with its elegant furnishings and decorations. The hotel offers luxury accommodation with its ensuite letting rooms which include TV, direct dial telephones and coffee making facilities. Two of the rooms have been designed with the disabled in mind, with wider doors, handrails, and specially constructed bathrooms and toilets. The Orangery Dining Room offers a full range of home cooked a la carte dishes and a traditional Sunday lunch menu as well as a glorious view of Rutland Water.

More informal dining can be found in the stylish two-tier Sailing Bar or on the Courtyard Patio. The residents' Cocktail Lounge has a blazing log fire throughout the winter and, during the summer, doors lead out onto the patio overlooking the lake.

Across this famous lake lies **Barnsdale Lodge**, a 17th century farmhouse, where the country-lover is welcomed with all luxury and warmth of an English country house from a bygone era.

Normanton Park Hotel, Normanton Park Road, Rutland Water South Shore, Rutland Tel: 01780 720315

Barnsdale Lodge Hotel, The Avenue, Rutland Water North Shore, Rutland Tel: 01572 724678

Following the south shore of Rutland Water you'll come to **Empingham**, which is dominated by the attractive tower and spire of St Peter's Church. It is a well proportioned building with an eye catching west front. Its interior features include fragments of ancient glass.

Following our circular route around Rutland Water and on the A606 is **Whitwell** where you will find on the main street

The Noel Arms. Situated close to the North shore of Rutland Water this is very much a family run hotel and restaurant.

Now in its 17th year with the Healey family, Son Nicholas is head chef trained in Paris at the George V; There is a lovely atmosphere in the Noel Arms which is run to very professional standards whilst maintaining a warm friendly ambience.

The hotel has nine bedrooms tastefully decorated, some with private bathroom and shower and all equipped with colour television, radio, telephone and drink making facilities.

The elegant A La Carte restaurant and Cocktail bar is ideal for those wishing to dine in style. The hotel has fresh seawater tanks housing Lobsters and other seafood to ensure maximum freshness. There is also a dining area in the bar which is well known for its comfort and relaxed atmosphere.

Children will be welcomed, and with many activities so close to hand, the Noel Arms makes an ideal holiday location.

The Noel Arms Inn, Main Street, Whitwell, Rutland. Tel: 01780 460334/352.

North of here , and turning off the A606 (Oakham to Stamford Road)is **Exton**, situated in one of the largest ironstone extractions ares in the country. It is a charming village and the Old Hall, now ruined, is thought to have been built during the reign of Elizabeth I. It was burned down in 1810 and was replaced by a New Hall in the middle of that century, Overlooking the village green is the **Fox and Hounds**, a 17th century coaching inn in picturesque surroundings and looking more like the local manor house. Originally it was a gentleman's hunting lodge which became an inn in the late 18th century. David and Jennifer Hillier provide quality food cooked to order every day of the week, served in a stone built dining room or in a pleasant lounge overlooking the lovely gardens. On Sundays, a traditional three course lunch is served. There are three letting bedrooms should you decide on a longer stay in this lovely area.

The Fox and Hounds, The Green, Exton, Rutland, LE15 8AP Tel: 01572 812403

On the B668 the other side of Exton Park you'll come to the village of **Greetham** where if you are looking for a local hostelry for refreshment or accommodation, try the **Black Horse Inn**. This small unspoilt country pub is situated between the A1 and Oakham and is where Mike and Audrey Hall will greet you with a warm welcome. Although they have been at the Black Horse for only a short time, they have twenty-five years of experience in the licensed trade, so making customers feel at home in this 250 year old traditional English inn comes naturally to them. Three excellent letting bedrooms have recently been refurbished and are in keeping with the charm and style of the inn. Home cooked food is served in the cosy dining area and daily 'specials' are featured on the customary blackboard. The inn has a good selection of Mansfield traditional beers. No smoking in the dining area and bedrooms please.

Black Horse Inn, Greetham, Rutland. Tel: 01572 812305

On the outskirts of the village of Greetham lies the magnificent and recently built **Greetham Valley Golf Club**.

Set in 250 acres of grounds, including 10 acres of existing mature woodland to which a further 15,000 trees and shrubs have been added, Greetham Valley comprises an impressive 27-hole championship course, 9-hole par 3 pay and play course, and a floodlit golf range. The modern purpose built club house has a delightful lounge and bar area with panoramic views of the valley and golf course.

The 120 seater restaurant is tastefully decorated and comfortably furnished and is a lovely place to enjoy first class cuisine and wine to match.

Built and personally run by the Hinch family, who still farm the surrounding land, this is an excellent golfing centre that also offers charming and professional hospitality.

346

Greetham Valley Golf Club, Wood Lane, Greetham, Oakham, Rutland Tel: 01780 460444

The most precious possession of the little hamlet of **Clipsham** which lies across the A1 is the heraldic glass in the north chapel. As you look at it remember that it was shattered in the Wars of the Roses and brought here; when you see the sun glisten on it, it gives one an eerie feeling to think that the same sun was lighting the glass in the war that drove the Plantagenets off the throne and put the Tudors in their place.

It was from the ancient church at **Pickworth** by the Lincolnshire border that this glass came and where you can still see some 14th century wall paintings.

Further south stands **Little Casterton** which was a Roman station and beyond is **Tolethorpe Hall.** One of the most beautiful things in the county has to be the 13th century tower and spire of the church at **Ryhall** which stands just beyond the manor. There is a nice little legend about the village which bestrides a little river.In the church St Tibba, niece of King Penda of Mercia, is held up by two flying horses and surmounted by a helmet and eagle crest, the whole being supported by cherubs. Inside the house there are panelled rooms.

The road leads through the pretty countryside to **Essendine** where the church forms a wonderful background, and a fitting place to conclude this journey through the heart of England. We hope that you have enjoyed reading the book and that it will encorage you to seek out some of the "Hidden Places" which are there waiting to be discovered. Safe Journey.

TOURIST INFORMATION CENTRES

ASHBY-de-la-ZOUCH, North Street 01530-411767

BIRMINGHAM, Convention & Bureau Centre, 2 City Arcade 0121 643-2514

BOSWORTH BATTLEFIELD, Visitors Centre, Sutton Cheney, Nr Market Bosworth.

BRACKLEY, 2 Bridge Street 01280-700111

BROMSGROVE, Bromsgrove Museum, 26 Birmingham Road 01527-31809

BURTON UPON TRENT, Octagon Centre, New Street 01283-516609

CORBY, Civic Centre, George Street 01536-407507

COVENTRY, Bayley Lane 01203-832303

DAVENTRY, Moot Hall, Market Sq 01327-300277

DUDLEY, 39 Churchill Precinct 01384-250333

HINCKLEY, Library, Lancaster Road 01455-635106

KENILWORTH, Library, 11 Smalley Place 01926-52595

KETTERING, The Coach House, Sheep Street 01536-410266

LEAMINGTON SPA, Jephson Lodge, Jephson Gardens, The Parade 01926-311470

LEEK, Market Place 01538-381000

LEICESTER, 2-6 St Martin's Walk, St Martin's Square 01162 511300

LICHFIELD, Donegal House, Bore Street 01543-252109

LOUGHBOROUGH, John Storer House, Wards End 01509-230131

MARKET HARBOROUGH, Pen Lloyd Library, Adam And Eve Street 01858-462649

MELTON MOWBRAY, Melton Carnegie Museum, Thorpe End 01664-69946

NEWARK, The Gilstrap Centre, Castlegate 01636-78962

NORTHAMPTON, Visitors Centre, 10 St Giles Square 01604-604180

NUNEATON, Library, Church Street 01203-384027

OAKHAM, Library, Catmos Street 01572-724329

OUNDLE, 14 West Street 01832-274333

RUGBY, Library, St Matthews Street 0788-535348

RUTLAND WATER, Sykes Lane, Empingham, Oakham 01780-86321

STAMFORD, Stamford Arts Centre, 27 St Mary's Street 0780-55611

STOKE-ON-TRENT, Potteries Shopping Centre, Quadrant Road, Hanley 01782-284600

STRATFORD-ON-AVON, Bridgefoot 01789-293127

TAMWORTH, Town Hall, Market Street 01827-59134

TROWELL (M1), Northbound Granada Services 01602-442411

WARWICK, The Court House, Jury Street 01926-492212

WELLINGBOROUGH, Library, Pebble Lane 01933-228101

Index

Y

THE HIDDEN PLACES

If you would like to have any of the titles currently available in this series, please complete this coupon and send to:

M & M Publishing Ltd
Tryfan House, Warwick Drive,
Hale, Altrincham, Cheshire, WA15 9EA

	Each	Qty
Ireland	£ 5.90	......
Scotland	£ 5.90	......
Northumberland & Durham	£ 5.90	......
The Lake District & Cumbria	£ 5.90	......
Yorkshire and Humberside	£ 5.90	......
Lancashire & Cheshire	£ 5.90	......
North Wales	£ 5.90	......
South Wales	£ 5.90	......
The Welsh Borders	£ 5.90	......
The Cotswolds (Gloucestershire & Wiltshire)	£ 5.90	......
Thames and Chilterns	£ 5.90	......
East Anglia (Norfolk & Suffolk, Cambs & Essex)	£ 5.90	......
The South East (Surrey, Sussex and Kent)	£ 5.90	......
Dorset, Hampshire and the Isle of Wight	£ 5.90	......
Somerset, Avon and Dorset	£ 5.90	......
Heart of England	£ 5.90	......
Devon and Cornwall	£ 5.90	......
Set of any Five	£20.00	

Total £

Price includes Postage and Packing

NAME..

ADDRESS...

....

...............................POST CODE......................................

Please make cheques payable to: M & M Publishing Ltd